All Things Chaucer

All Things Chaucer

An Encyclopedia of Chaucer's World

VOLUME 2

K–Z

Shannon L. Rogers

GREENWOOD PRESS

Westport, Connecticut • *London*

Library of Congress Cataloging-in-Publication Data

Rogers, Shannon L.
  All things Chaucer : an encyclopedia of Chaucer's world / Shannon L. Rogers.
    p. cm.
  Includes bibliographical references and index.
  ISBN 0–313–33253–3 (v. 1 : alk. paper)—ISBN 0–313–33254–1 (v. 2 : alk. paper)—
ISBN 0–313–33252–5 (set : alk. paper)
  1. Chaucer, Geoffrey, d. 1400—Encyclopedias.   2. Poets, English—Middle English,
1100–1500—Biography—Encyclopedias.   3. Civilization, Medieval, in literature—
Encyclopedias.   I. Title.
  PR1903.R55 2007
  821′.1—dc22   2006027206

British Library Cataloguing in Publication Data is available.

Library of Congress Catalog Card Number: 2006027206

ISBN: 0–313–33252–5 (set)
        0–313–33253–3 (vol. 1)
        0–313–33254–1 (vol. 2)

First published in 2007

Greenwood Press, 88 Post Road West, Westport, CT 06881
An imprint of Greenwood Publishing Group, Inc.
www.greenwood.com

Printed in the United States of America

∞™

The paper used in this book complies with the
Permanent Paper Standard issued by the National
Information Standards Organization (Z39.48–1984).

10 9 8 7 6 5 4 3 2 1

The publisher has done its best to make sure the instructions and/or recipes in this book
are correct. However, users should apply judgment and experience when preparing recipes,
especially parents and teachers working with young people. The publisher accepts no
responsibility for the outcome of any recipe included in these volumes.

For Ben,
still my muse

Contents

Preface   *ix*

Acknowledgments   *xi*

Alphabetical List of Entries   *xiii*

Guide to Related Topics   *xvii*

Introduction   *xxiii*

Chronology of Important Events in Chaucer's Time   *xxxv*

All Things Chaucer   *1*

Appendices   *469*

    Genealogy of Edward III   471

    Map of Route to Canterbury   475

Bibliography   *479*

Index   *491*

Preface

While much of the appeal of *The Canterbury Tales* lies in its universal assessment of human nature and character, there remain many elements within this and other of Chaucer's works that can make his world seem to be an alien landscape. Issues of time and place, unfamiliar language or word usage, and differences in moral, religious, and other social and cultural attitudes can all baffle the modern reader. These volumes are intended to demystify Chaucer's world: to explain the background to his works, to place him contextually, and to add historical resonance to any reading of his poetry.

These two volumes will survey the texts of Chaucer's writing, provide historical background and information on items mentioned in all of his works, and serve as a portal to medieval culture, identifying for readers the individual items that make up the physical culture of Chaucer's time. These items include weapons, clothing, housing, food, money, and tools and will be discussed in detail, going beyond mere definitions to explain form and function of everyday and obscure items. The book will hopefully broaden any reader's understanding of Chaucer and contribute to her ability to interpret and analyze his writings. In addition to physical things, this book also explores the customs, rituals, and belief systems that comprise medieval culture. Although this work is intended for a wide readership, I have utilized primary source materials and analyzed the impact of rituals, superstitions, politics, and other aspects of daily life in a way to be useful to multiple levels of expertise, including professional scholars.

As such, the book is intended to be a companion to Chaucer. It is meant, above all, to be a resource to which one can refer while reading Chaucer. The individual entries are arranged alphabetically, in encyclopedic form.

There is some overlap between the content of related articles, which is intentional. If one were, for instance, to refer to the entry on the Knight, one would also find similar material covered in the entries on Weapons and Chivalry. Likewise, the suggestions for "Further Reading" that are included at the end of each entry sometimes refer to similar or identical sources. However, each individual entry is a focused assessment of the subject in question and includes its relevance to Chaucer's works. Most are introduced by a related quotation from Chaucer, in both Middle English and modern translation. Throughout the text are specific references to Chaucer's works as they relate to the entry in question, either in quotation form or simply by line references.

In addition to individual suggestions for further reading, there is also a full bibliography referencing all of the works used in this compilation. This might be of most interest to readers who are interested in more broadly conceived subjects, along with the "Guide to Related Topics." For those readers who seek specific subjects—to learn a more narrow topic in depth or to consult a specific question raised by a close reading of a Chaucerian text—the individual entries themselves, introduced by the "Alphabetical List of Entries," will provide information on a specific subject. At the close of each entry, in order to serve the needs of all readers, are "See Also" directives to seek information in related topics.

In order to set Chaucer's life and work into its proper historical context, I have tried to provide ample biographical details about him in the introduction. The interaction between his professional career and his poetic are discussed at length, accompanied by details about his family. I have also included a broad discussion of the intellectual trends of his time and where he fits into them. For those who would like a simple reference guide to what was going on during Chaucer's life, there is a chronology, listing both important historical events and personal Chaucerian moments.

In addition to the many illustrations that accompany the text, the entries are followed by two appendices that help place Chaucer both historically and geographically. The first is a genealogical chart of the lineage of Edward III, showing Chaucer's close marital relationship to the royal family. The second is a map of the route of the Canterbury pilgrims, which illustrates for the modern reader the amount of distance covered by the group of 29, who made the trip on horseback and on foot.

Finally, all references are to Larry Benson's magisterial *The Riverside Chaucer,* and thus all Middle English passages are from this work as well. Any errors in transcription are my own, as are the translations. They are certainly not the sort of masterful and poetic translations I read in the course of this work, but they are functional and should be of service to anyone unfamiliar with Middle English. I do, however, encourage even the most novice reader to give the Middle English originals a try. Read them out loud, pronouncing every letter. It is surprising how the language flows and begins to make sense.

Acknowledgments

The task of categorizing Chaucer's world is an especially daunting one, and I could not have done it without the help of a number of people. In the broader sense, I am in debt to all of those who have come before me to write the scholarship on Chaucer and fourteenth-century England that made this work possible. I would also like to thank the staff of a number of libraries, including the interlibrary loan folks at the Kingston Public Library and the staffs of Juniata College and Penn State Wilkes-Barre. Their prompt response to my numerous requests for increasingly arcane books is admirable and most appreciated.

I would also like to thank Professor Benjamin Hudson of the History Department at the Pennsylvania State University. I would never have been introduced to Greenwood without him, nor would I have probably ever finished my doctorate without his fine mentoring and constant enthusiastic support. Thanks to my patient and long-suffering Greenwood editor, George Butler, for all of his guidance and understanding. I'll bet he thought we'd never get to this stage. I would like to thank my mother for always being excited about this project, even if she still doesn't quite know who Chaucer is.

And finally, any acknowledgements page would be empty without thanking Benjamin Moores. You've been a part of this through every stage. Thank you for the distractions, which helped me keep my sanity, even if I lost a little in focus. Thank you for always being proud of me, even if you pretend you aren't. And thank you for being who you are, because you always inspire me to be more than I am. Rwy'n dy garu di.

Alphabetical List of Entries

Abigail
Abraham
Absalom
Achates
Achilles
Actaeon
Adam
Adonis
Aeneas
Agriculture
Alchemy
Alcyone
Aldgate
Alexandria
Algeciras
Allegory and Dream Visions
Allusions, Biblical
Allusions, Classical
Amphion
Animals
Apollo
Architecture
Ariadne
Armor

Astrolabe
Astrology and Astronomy

Bacchus
Baptism
Bath
Birds
Birth
Black Death
Blanche, Duchess of Lancaster
Boar
Boccaccio
Boethius
Bruges
Burgundy
Business and Commerce

Calendar
Caliope
Cambridge
Canterbury
Cassandra
Castles
Catalonia
Cathedrals

Childhood
Chivalry
Cities, Towns, and Villages
Clerk
Courtly Love
Crow
Cuckoo

Daedalus
Daily Life
Daniel
Daphne
Deianira
Demophon
Dog
Dove
Dreams

Eagle
Echo
Education
Edward III
Edward, the Black Prince
Entertainment
Estates
Esther
Eve

Falcon
Fame
Fashion
Feudalism
Food
Fortune
Four Humors
Fox
Franklin
Friar
Froissart
Furniture

Games
Gentilesse
Goose
Great Schism
Grenada

Hare
Helen of Troy
Heraldry
Heresy
Holidays and Holy Days
Horse
Humanism
Hundred Years War
Hunting
Hygiene
Hypsipyle

Indulgences

Jerusalem
Jews
Job
John of Gaunt
Joseph
Judas

Knight

Lamech
Law
Leather
Lithuania
Lollardy
London
Lucrece

Macedonia
Manciple
Marriage
Medea
Medicine
Merchant
Miller
Monarchy
Money
Monk
Morocco
Music

Names
Narcissus
Nun

Pardoner
Parson
Peasant Revolt
Philosophy
Physician
Pilgrimage
Priapus
Prioress
Private Houses
Prussia

Reeve
Religion
Richard II
Rooster and Hen
Russia

Science
Scrope-Grosvenor Trial
Sex
Sheep
Shipman
Sittingbourne
Southwark
Squire
St. Augustine
St. Benedict
St. Bernard
St. Cecilia
St. Christopher
St. Cuthbert

St. Denis
St. Dunstan
St. Edward
St. Eligius
St. Frideswide
St. Giles
St. Jerome
St. Julian
St. Neot
St. Ronan
St. Valentine
Stratford-at-Bow
Summoner
Syria

Tapestry
Taverns
Teutonic Knights
Thessaly
Thomas à Becket
Tournaments
Travel
Trojan War

Weapons
Westminster Abbey
Wolf
Wood
Wool

Yeoman
Ypres

Guide to Related Topics

Art and Architecture

Architecture

Castles
Cathedrals

Private Houses

Tapestry

Business and Industry

Business and Commerce

Leather

Merchant
Money

Shipman

Wood
Wool

Daily Life

Baptism
Birth
Black Death
Business and Commerce

Calendar
Castles
Cathedrals

Childhood

Daily Life
Dreams

Education
Entertainment
Estates

Fashion
Feudalism
Food
Furniture

Games

Holidays and Holy Days
Hunting
Hygiene

Leather

Marriage
Medicine
Monarchy
Money
Music

Names

Pilgrimage
Private Houses

Sex

Taverns
Travel

Wood
Wool

Literature

Abigail
Abraham
Absalom
Achates
Achilles
Actaeon
Adam
Adonis
Aeneas
Alcyone
Allegory and Dream Visions
Allusions, Biblical
Allusions, Classical
Amphion
Apollo
Ariadne

Bacchus
Boccaccio
Boethius

Caliope
Cassandra

Daedalus
Daniel
Daphne
Deianira
Demophon

Echo
Esther
Eve

Helen of Troy
Hypsipyle

Jews
Job

Joseph
Judas

Lamech
Lucrece

Medea

Narcissus

Priapus

Nature

Animals

Birds
Boar

Crow
Cuckoo

Dog
Dove

Eagle

Falcon
Fox

Goose

Hare
Horse

Rooster and Hen

Sheep

Wolf

People

Abigail
Abraham
Absalom
Achates
Achilles
Actaeon
Adam
Adonis
Aeneas
Alcyone

Amphion
Apollo
Ariadne

Bacchus
Blanche, Duchess of Lancaster
Boccaccio
Boethius

Caliope
Cassandra
Clerk

Daedalus
Daniel
Daphne
Deianira
Demophon

Echo
Edward III
Edward, the Black Prince
Esther
Eve

Fame
Fortune
Franklin
Friar
Froissart

Helen of Troy
Hypsipyle

Jews
Job
John of Gaunt
Joseph
Judas

Knight

Lamech
Lucrece

Manciple
Medea
Merchant
Miller

Monk

Narcissus
Nun

Pardoner
Parson
Physician
Priapus
Prioress

Reeve
Richard II

Shipman
Squire
St. Augustine
St. Benedict
St. Bernard
St. Cecilia
St. Christopher
St. Cuthbert
St. Denis
St. Dunstan
St. Edward
St. Eligius
St. Frideswide
St. Giles
St. Jerome
St. Julian
St. Neot
St. Ronan
St. Valentine
Summoner

Thomas à Becket

Yeoman

Places

Alexandria
Algeciras
Alisaundre

Bath
Bruges
Burgundy

Cambridge

Canterbury
Catalonia

Grenada

Jerusalem

Lithuania
London

Macedonia
Morocco

Prussia

Russia

Sittingbourne
Southwark
Stratford-at-Bow
Syria

Thessaly

Westminster Abbey

Ypres

Religion
Calendar
Canterbury
Clerk

Great Schism

Heresy
Holidays and Holy Days

Indulgences

Jerusalem
Jews

Lollardy

Monk
Music

Nun

Pardoner
Parson
Pilgrimage
Prioress

St. Augustine
St. Benedict
St. Bernard
St. Cecilia
St. Christopher
St. Cuthbert
St. Denis
St. Dunstan
St. Edward
St. Eligius
St. Frideswide
St. Giles
St. Jerome
St. Julian
St. Neot
St. Ronan
St. Valentine
Summoner

Thomas à Becket

Rituals and Myths
Allusions, Biblical
Allusions, Classical

Baptism
Birth

Dreams

Fame
Fortune

Religion

Science
Alchemy
Astrolabe
Astrology and Astronomy

Black Death

Four Humors

Hygiene

Medicine

Physician

Science

Town and Country

Agriculture
Aldgate

Castles
Cathedrals
Cities, Towns, and Villages

War and the Knightly Ethos

Armor

Chivalry
Courtly Love

Gentilesse

Heraldry
Hundred Years War

Knight

Squire

Teutonic Knights
Tournaments
Trojan War

Weapons

Introduction

Whan that Aprill with his shourse soote
The droghte of March hath perced to the roote,
And bathed every veyne in swich licour
Of which vertu engendred is the flour;
Whan Zephirus eek with his sweete breeth
Inspired hath in every holt and heeth
The tendre croppes, and the yonge sonne
Hath in the Ram his half cours yronne,
And smale foweles maken melodye,
That slepen al the nyght with open ye
(So Priketh hem Nature in hir corages),
Thanne longen folk to goon on pilgrimages,
And palmeres for to seken straunge strondes,
To ferne halwes, kowthe in sundry londes;
And specially from every shires ende
Of Engelond to Caunterbury they wende,
The hooly blisful martir for to seke,
That hem hath holpen whan that they were seeke.

When April with its sweet showers
Has pierced to the root the drought of March,
And bathed every plant in such moisture
That every flower is engendered with life;
When the west wind with his sweet breath
Has inspired in every wood and heath
The tender shoots to spring, and the young sun
Has traveled halfway through the sign of Aries,
And little birds make sweet melodies,
Which sleep all night with open eyes
(As Nature prompts them to do, and encourages),

> *Then folks long to go on pilgrimages,*
> *And pilgrims seek strange lands,*
> *To foreign halls, renowned in many distant lands;*
> *And especially from every shire's end*
> *In England they all find their way to Canterbury,*
> *To seek the holy blissful martyr,*
> *Who will give them help when they are sick.*

(*Canterbury Tales,* General Prologue, I A, 1–18)

Thus run the opening lines of one of the most famous and influential pieces of English literature, Geoffrey Chaucer's *Canterbury Tales*. Begun most likely in the year of the poet's wife's death, the *Canterbury Tales* represent a lifetime of experience and learning, as well as a keen eye for understanding and describing human behavior. The structure of the *Tales* was most probably modeled upon Boccaccio's *Decameron*, which also uses the device of group entertainment through the telling of tales. For Boccaccio the framing scenario was the passing of time by a group of young nobles who have fled the Black Death. For Chaucer, the tales are told by a socioeconomically mixed group who are on a pilgrimage to visit the shrine of Thomas à Becket in Canterbury Cathedral. They meet at the Tabard Inn in Southwark, not far from where Chaucer spent most of his married life, and proceed from there, providing readers with a compelling glimpse into the personalities and social structure of fourteenth-century England as they make their way from London to Canterbury.

Geoffrey Chaucer was born sometime between 1340 and 1344. The precise date of his birth is uncertain; however, we know a great deal more about his life than we do about other literary figures, including Shakespeare. This is thanks, in part, to his years of service within the households of royalty and within the government. England's most famous poet was, at the end of the day, a civil servant, and as such his history is reasonably well documented. Because he lived through interesting times, Chaucer's placement within the inner circle of England's government would make him historically important even if he had never written a single line of poetry.

Given the highly stratified class system of the Middle Ages, at first consideration it would seem unlikely that Geoffrey Chaucer would ever have risen to serve a king or befriend the king's brother. Chaucer's father, John, was a vintner or wine merchant originally from Ipswich who had settled in London on Thames Street, a wealthy mercantile area. This area would have brought Geoffrey into contact with Italian merchants, which would account for his later command of the language that made him useful in royal diplomatic missions. Chaucer's mother, Agnes de Copton, was a wealthy middle-class heiress. Agnes had previously been married to the Baron of the Exchequer and Keeper of the King's Purse. Her marriage to John Chaucer was her second, and it was perhaps her connections from the first marriage that enabled young Geoffrey to move easily in aristocratic circles.

However his placement there was achieved, it is certain that Geoffrey became a page in the household of Elizabeth, Countess of Ulster, in 1357. Elizabeth was married to Edward III's brother Lionel, Duke of Clarence. This was quite a step upward socially for the son of middle-class mercantilists. It was in this position that he most likely met both his later patron, John of Gaunt, another of Edward's brothers, and his future wife, Phillippa de Roet, who was also in the countess's household. Philippa was the daughter of Sir Paon de Roet, a Flemish knight in the retinue of Philippa of Hainault, Edward III's queen.

Although his parents were able to afford to educate him prior to this time, it is uncertain to what degree, if at all, they did so. It is, however, far more probable that he received a reasonably thorough course of training while in the countess's household (see Education). This education would encompass some modification of the liberal arts program of the trivium (grammar, dialectic, and rhetoric) and the quadrivium (arithmetic, music, astronomy, and geometry). Given his adult command of so many areas of learning—including French, classical literature, and astronomy—it is clear that he learned several languages, including Latin, and received some education in arithmetic, theology, music, and philosophy.

It is also a possibility that Chaucer attended the law schools of the Inns of Court sometime in the early 1360s, because there exists a mention in the record books of the Inner Temple of a "Geffrye Chaucer" who was "fined two shillings for beatinge a Franciscan Fryer in fletestreate" (*fined two shillings for beating a Franciscan friar in Fleet Street*). In order to be fined by the society, he would have had to have been a student there. It unclear whether this was the same Geoffrey Chaucer as the poet; however, his thorough knowledge of legal matters and his characterization of the Man of Law seem to indicate some familiarity with the profession (see Law).

All speculation on his completed education aside, the next official mention of Chaucer is as a soldier in the king's forces under the Duke of Clarence. This would have involved Chaucer in the action of the major martial conflict of his time, the Hundred Years War (see Hundred Years War). While besieging Rheims in 1359, Chaucer was captured by the French and held for ransom. This ransom—£16—was eventually paid by the Keeper of the King's Wardrobe. That perhaps Chaucer was not considered to be a vital part of the army is revealed by the fact that this figure is slightly less than the ransom paid for Sir Robert de Clynton's horse. This experience among soldiers, however, may have provided Chaucer with his rather cynical attitude toward the knighthood that is reflected so many times throughout the *Canterbury Tales,* not only in his portrayal of the Knight and the Squire, but in details from several tales, including the "Tale of Sir Thopas" (see Chivalry, Knight, and Squire).

Not long after he was ransomed, Chaucer was employed by Prince Lionel in October 1360 to carry letters from Calais to England. After that mission, the next six years of Chaucer's life are a complete mystery to us today. It is possible that he accompanied Lionel to Ireland when the Duke became Viceroy there. Or, more probably, Chaucer moved into some form of service with the king. Whatever the case may be, we next find him in the record books in February 1366, when he was granted safe transport by Charles II of Navarre. The precise nature of his business and why he required such safe passage, however, remains unknown.

That same year was accompanied by personal changes on both ends of the emotional spectrum. Sadly, Chaucer's father died (the year of his mother's death remains unknown). On a happier note, however, Chaucer married Philippa, who had by now become an attendant to Philippa of Hainault, Edward III's queen. The queen awarded Philippa Chaucer an annual annuity of 10 marks or roughly £7. The first recorded mention of Chaucer himself within the royal household is from June 1367, when he was awarded an annual salary of 20 marks (£13). The nature of his service is uncertain—he is described in the records as both a squire and a valet.

It is clear that Chaucer's career at the heart of the royal court was on the rise. He rapidly advanced within the ranks of being one of forty or so men in the king's service whose duties ranged from anything including serving meals to traveling on official business. Chaucer traveled to Spain in 1368 with the Black Prince, and may have carried messages to Prince Lionel who was in Milan. Later that same year, Chaucer officially became an Esquire to the King's Household. When John of Gaunt's first wife, Blanche, died in September, Gaunt awarded Chaucer a lifetime annuity of £10, perhaps as a reward for writing the *Book of Duchess* (see Blanche, Duchess of Lancaster and John of Gaunt). Although the figures behind the characters of the Black Knight and Duchess White have been debated, it is generally accepted that the grief-stricken Knight is John of Gaunt who has lost his Blanche (meaning "white") to an untimely demise. His dangerous heartbreak is chronicled in the *Book of the Duchess* along with an admonition to try to get beyond it for his own physical and mental safety. Chaucer's exploration of grief and its physical toll on the human body is remarkably modern here and has been born out by medical evidence. His closeness to the personages involved, in a capacity apparently beyond that of trusted and paid servant, is alluded to in the deeply personal understanding of the Knight's grief as well as by the assumption that Gaunt asked Chaucer to write something in Blanche's honor.

It is clear that Chaucer had already been widely recognized as a poet of considerable talent. While the dating of some of the shorter poems is uncertain, his first probable work would have been his translation of the *Roman de la Rose*. The first definite original poetic work would then be the *Book of the Duchess*. However, the fact that Gaunt asked Chaucer to write this work in honor of Blanche is a strong indication that he was already known as a poet, and that reputation would have to have been based upon some real poetic evidence. Earlier poems may have been lost or were merely presented orally at court. Unfortunately, the lack of any prior poetic output is another frustrating hole in the historical record.

Chaucer's career continued to advance throughout the 1360s and 1370s, with perhaps his most important assignment occurring in 1372 when he was sent to Italy to negotiate the use of English ports by Genoese merchants. While there, he discussed with the Duke of Genoa which ports might be used by these merchants as permanent headquarters, a crucial financial arrangement for both Genoa and England. From there, he traveled to Florence to negotiate some government loans. While staying in Florence, it is quite probable that Chaucer not only obtained a copy of Dante's *Divina Commedia* (*Divine Comedy*) but met Petrarch and Boccaccio. Any one of these three events would have made a deep impact on the English poet. The possibility that he was exposed to the three most important Italian poets of his time is an event of potentially monumental import to his development as a wordsmith.

Upon his return to England in May 1374, Chaucer was given the dubious reward of the position of Controller of the Customs of Wools, Skins, and Hides for the port of London. Because wool was England's chief export, this position carried a great deal of importance and demonstrated the high degree of confidence on the part of the crown in Chaucer's abilities. However, it was a position that was also fraught with an equal amount of burdensome responsibility. The taxes collected on wool and leather funded the costs of war and the running of the government and thus were a chief source of the king's annual revenue. The position carried a salary of £10 per annum, which was added to his annuity of £13. Chaucer was also given the use of a house over Aldgate rent free, an award that was made to him by the mayor and aldermen of the city. His only costs for the use of the house would be for upkeep and repairs. Chaucer was also required to allow its use in times of war if it was needed defensively.

Geoffrey and Philippa must have been quite comfortably well off at this time, with their combined incomes and lack of living expenses. He had also been awarded a gift from Edward III of a gallon of wine each day for life—probably in reward for writing a poem for the king. This he collected until 1378, when he had it commuted to an annuity of 20 marks. Keeping up with court life and fashion was no doubt of some expense. However, the Chaucers had a modestly sized family of two or three children—two sons, Thomas and Lewis, and a possible daughter, Elizabeth—which meant that their household upkeep was minimized while the combined income of him and his wife totaled somewhere near £99. It is therefore rather sad that he felt a financial pinch in his final years, as is evidenced by the poem "The Complaint of Chaucer to His Purse." His expenditures on an impressive library of more than sixty books make it clear that Chaucer spent what he earned.

In 1376 and 1377 he traveled again to the Continent on royal business. It is known that he was in France, potentially to conduct truce negotiations. Later, he appears to have traveled there again to conduct betrothal negotiations for the young Richard II and a French princess—negotiations that eventually fell through, as Richard would ultimately marry Anne of Bohemia in 1382. In 1378, Chaucer again traveled to the Continent on business connected with the war with France, this time going to Lombardy. The following year, it is probable that he began working on the *House of Fame*.

The 1380s brought a variety of events for the Chaucers. In 1380, Geoffrey would face serious charges of *raptu,* a legal term that could indicate either rape or abduction. The details of the case are completely unknown, except that the woman in question, Cecily Chaumpaigne, eventually released Chaucer from all charges. However, during the course of the proceedings, he must have faced many moments of anxiety about the outcome and the potential effects on his family and career.

1381 brought the Peasant Revolt, or Wat Tyler's Rebellion (see Peasant Revolt and Richard II), a defining moment in English history in which the peasants of Kent and Essex rose in rebellion in response to the substantial poll tax levied by Richard II. It is again unknown how much of the revolt Chaucer witnessed personally (see Aldgate). However, his connection with court life would have given him an enviable position to learn inside details of the event. Many of the peasants who were eventually killed came from the area of the city where Chaucer grew up and still owned a house. Four days after the revolt, Chaucer sold his father's house to a merchant by the name of Henry Herbury. His reasoning for doing so is unclear and forever hidden by the intervening time. It would be farfetched, however, to speculate that the area's connection with the revolt made his house unpleasant to him. More likely, it had become a burden to maintain or he had better uses for the money it was worth. It is around this time that Chaucer wrote the *Parliament of Fowls,* in honor of Richard II's engagement to Anne of Bohemia.

In 1382, Chaucer's official duties expanded when he was awarded the controllership of Petty Customs, which included collecting import and export duties on wine and other miscellaneous merchandise. Even with these additional duties, Chaucer continued to travel on official business. He was appointed a deputy to cover his responsibilities when he was traveling, demonstrating that his service was highly valued in both positions to the degree that the king was willing to incur extra expense to allow Chaucer to continue to act in all capacities.

As the 1380s progressed, however, Chaucer appears to have increasingly withdrawn from London life. He employed a permanent deputy in 1385 to handle his controller duties. In October of that same year, he was elected as Justice of the Peace in Kent, a very important position because the French were threatening to invade there. In 1386, he would be elected to the House of Commons as a Knight of the Shire in Kent and gave up his lease on the Aldgate house in order to relocate outside the city. During this same period, Chaucer's poetic output was immense, demonstrating a reduction in time necessary to be devoted to his official capacities. He wrote *Troilus and Criseyde* in 1385 and began his translation of Boethius. In 1386, he also probably wrote the *Legend of Good Women* and started the ambitiously conceived *Canterbury Tales,* which would occupy the next decade of his life. It would remain unfinished upon his death.

In June 1387, Philippa Chaucer disappears from the official records, an indication that she had died. It is unknown how she died or how Chaucer took the news. Despite the many sarcastic jibes he makes about the institution of marriage in his works, most evidence indicates that his marriage was a happy one, so it is fairly safe to assume that her loss was a blow to him emotionally. We do know that later that same year he traveled to Calais on undisclosed business. This would be his last official journey, which can be interpreted as either a loss of court support (although not necessarily royal support) or a certain withdrawal from public affairs after his wife's death in order to pursue other interests. The prior interpretation is supported by the fact that three of the men he worked with at the Customs House were executed in 1388. This was at the insistence of the Merciless Parliament, which was dominated by enemies of the king who later would be executed by Richard II when he had regained the reigns of power that had rested shakily in his hands for many years (see Richard II).

That Chaucer retained the king's support is clear from his appointment in 1389 as Clerk of the King's Works. In this capacity, he oversaw the building and repair of 10 royal residences in and around London— including the Tower, Sheen Manor, and Westminster Palace—as well as care and maintenance of all of the hunting lodges in the royal forests (see Wood). Chaucer's salary was two shillings per day, which was three times his salary at the Custom's House. However, when he left this position in 1391, he was owed the entire amount of his three-year tenure there. Clearly, the king was having trouble in managing all aspects of his government at this time, a state of affairs that no doubt contributed greatly to his downfall and eventual overthrow and murder.

The king made good on some of the money owed when he awarded Chaucer a gift of £10 in 1393 and granted him an annual annuity of £20. During the preceding two years, Chaucer had worked for him as Deputy Forester in the Royal Forest of North Petherton in Somerset. It is unknown what his salary was there and whether he was ever paid his overdue wages from being Clerk of the King's Works. He seems to have continued in this position until 1399, living at Park House, when he decided to return to London and leased a house in the gardens of Westminster Abbey. The last recorded payment to him is for June 5, 1400. He died October 25 of that year and was buried in the abbey. This placement of his grave was most likely because he was a tenant there and not for any reasons of honor or position. It is therefore ironic that his tomb would become the focus for the later Poet's Corner.

Through all of his career's movement and his personal developments, Chaucer the civil servant was accompanied by Chaucer the poet. Certainly his work and life experiences must have colored his writing, but nowhere is it blatantly obvious. Or, rather, it is very rarely obvious. As mentioned, he wrote a complaint about the emptiness of his purse and he seems to have used his experiences as a soldier as a background to his portrayals of knights. His mercantile roots more than likely are reflected in his characterizations of the Merchant and the Wife of Bath, among others. The Peasant Revolt is mentioned briefly in the "Nun's Priest's Tale":

Certes, he Jakke Straw and his meynee
Ne made nevere shoutes half so shrille
Whan that they wolden any Flemyng kille,
As thilke day was maad upon the fox.

For certain, Jack Straw and his men
Never made a noise quite so shrill
When they were killing Flemings
As was made this day upon the fox.

(*Canterbury Tales*, "The Nun's Priest's Tale,"
VIII, 3394–97)

The Book of the Duchess and the *Parliament of Fowls* were written in response to specific court events: the death of Blanche of Lancaster and the engagement of Richard II, respectively. However, there are few specific references or allusions to contemporary events in Chaucer's works as a whole.

His strengths in providing historical significance instead lie in his characterization of the people and attitudes of his times. Chaucer's works reveal a great deal about the changing shape of society, both in class perceptions and socioeconomic realities. They reveal a good deal about the decline of the feudal system. And, most famously perhaps, they reveal even more about the changing role of the Church.

While all times can be characterized as times of change, fourteenth-century Europe—and England in particular—are especially good examples of this statement. This century was poised at the cusp of change from medieval attitudes to something that can be described as closer to modern. Although any generalizations about a particular time are fraught with potential for misspeaking, it is clear that the fourteenth century can honestly be characterized as a period of great transition. Many belief systems and social structures that had been in place for centuries were beginning to show signs of wear and decline and new ones were rising to take their place. A very homogeneous society with hierarchies rather statically defined would emerge at the end of the century much more fragmented and fluid. Change was ultimately gradual, but it was punctuated by a number of cataclysmic moments that hastened these inevitable changes.

The first of these moments would be the coming of the Black Death in 1348 (see Black Death). While the causes and origins of the disease remain hotly debated, it is clear that the effects of the disease were to change the shape of European society drastically. After the plague had swept north-ward from Italy through Scandinavia, roughly one-quarter to one-third of the population was gone. The economy, because of the lost population, was in dire straits along with the Church and the feudal structure. Villages were depleted, agricultural production was in shambles, and those who were left to pick up the pieces of the society were facing what must have seemed insurmountable odds.

However, as the cliché goes, when one door closes, another opens, and the survivors of the Black Death soon discovered myriad opportunities for change. These were changes that no doubt would have occurred in due time as European society was moving in that direction anyway. However, the catastrophic losses caused by the Black Death accentuated and hastened these changes. Peasants suddenly found themselves in a position of power that they had never known before. There was much work to be done and few to do it. No longer would it be enough to simply provide a cottage and a strip of land in return for full-time labor. Now, peasants began to demand, and receive, real wages as well as rights. They would be willing to die to protect these advances, as is proven by Wat Tyler's Rebellion in 1381 as well as several other revolts across Europe.

Nobles, in order to protect their assumed position in society, retaliated first by seeking wage caps and later by switching the focus of their land from agriculture to the rearing of livestock—in particular, sheep. This develop-ment is crucial to the ascension of England as a major economic power in the coming decades and lasting for the next 600 years. With the domina-tion of the woolen trade, England came to dominate in nearly every other aspect of the economy and politics.

The fact that the nobility was physically susceptible to the disease eroded the faith that they were somehow inherently superior to those who were not of aristocratic birth and, therefore, qualified to rule unquestioned. The changing face of warfare compounded this effect as well. Common foot soldiers and pikemen were the driving force behind a number of English victories in the Hundred Years War. The place of the knight as sole protec-tor of society was slowly slipping away, and both of these factors combined to wear away the golden façade of aristocratic privilege that had existed for so many centuries.

The belief in the ability of the Church to protect its faithful also wavered in the face of high mortality rates among its clergy and the unwillingness of many priests to administer last rites for fear of contamination. The resulting questioning of the Church's role and suitability to be responsible for the salvation of all the world's souls is reflected in the hostility toward the clergy and other religious figures that is apparent in Chaucer's works (see Friar, Monk, Nun, Parson, Prioress, and Religion). It would also lead directly into the Reformation, as various heretical groups gained traction among the faithful.

From this point forward, individuality rather than community and homogeneity began to assert itself as a value. Individuals sought their own salvation through means that did not involve priestly intercession, in methods such as the pilgrimage that forms the framework of the *Canterbury Tales*. Peasants sought to better their financial position through cash wages and the selling of surplus goods at markets. Cash could be accumulated in order to buy land, or it could be used to travel to a city where one could pursue a nonagricultural trade or take up a mercantile pursuit. The options for those of common birth, in other words, were becoming much more complex.

For the nobility, the interdependence of the agricultural life-style was replaced by the lower maintenance and less communal one of raising sheep. For the knightly class, their position as the primary fighting force and protectors of society was being undermined by new developments in weaponry—in particular, the use of gunpowder—that rendered them obsolete as well as a new reliance on common foot soldiers to wield pikes (see Armor, Estates, Knight, and Weapons). For many centuries the nobles had dominated through their insistence upon their inborn superiority. Too many arguments were rising to refute that idea, weakening their control of the social structure.

The effects of this change are apparent in Chaucer's works. Current in his society were attitudes that reflected a certain degree of uncertainty about the future and an air of the excitement of possibilities, and Chaucer's work reflects these ideas. One of the more pervasive ideas of his time was the image of Dame Fortune and her wheel. The wheel turns indiscriminately, taking people to the heights of achievement and back down into despair and failure, often with no more reasonable explanation than the whims of the goddess (see Fortune). Chaucer uses the image of Fortune and her wheel throughout all of his works, even devoting a short poem to her.

There was also a notion current in Chaucer's day that life itself is like a pilgrimage, with a goal in mind that should essentially bring, if not salvation, some sort of positive outcome. The adventures along the way are what guide us to our end goal and shape the way that we arrive there. Chaucer must have intended his tales to end with the arrival at the tomb of St. Thomas or, as Harry Bailly plans, with the return to the Tabard Inn. The fact that he never achieved either of these potential goals can be viewed as a sort of existential commentary on the uncertainty of our individual journeys through life. However, along the way, he allows us to experience the rich panorama of teeming London life that he was exposed to every day.

This very richness is what has made Chaucer such a beloved and enduring part of our literary culture. He teaches us plenty about his own time through his characters, especially in the *Canterbury Tales,* but he also provides a window into the very essence of human nature. His relevance is timeless for the very reason that the issues and situations he explores are still with us today. He is as much a product of his own time as outside of it, in much the way that Shakespeare would be. Both writers had a keen grasp of human motivations and emotions, the inner worlds that inspire and drive us all. For that reason, his place is assured both as the focal point of the Poet's Corner in Westminster Abbey and as the father of English poetry.

Chronology of Important Events in Chaucer's Time

1327   Edward II is overthrown by his queen Isabella and her lover, Roger de Mortimer. Edward III takes the throne but is controlled by his mother.

1330   Edward III seizes power in his own name, banishing Isabella and executing Mortimer.

1339   Edward III invades France, claiming the French crown as his own and starting the Hundred Years War.

1340   England naval victory at Sluys.

1343   Probable birth year of Chaucer.

1346   Battle of Crécy, resulting in a French defeat by the English. The English also defeat the Scots at the Battle of Neville's Cross.

1347   Truce between England and France. Black Death begins in Italy.

1348   Black Death arrives in England.

1353   Publication of Boccaccio's *Decameron*.

1356   Battle of Poitiers.

1357   Chaucer enters the household of Elizabeth, Countess of Ulster, wife of Lionel, Duke of Clarence and son of Edward III.

1359   Chaucer goes to France with Edward III's army and is captured at the siege of Rheims.

1360   The Treaty of Bretigny ends first phase of Hundred Years War. Chaucer is ransomed for £16.

1361   The publication of Langland's *Piers Plowman*.

1366   Chaucer marries Philippa de Roet, a lady-in-waiting to Queen Philippa of Hainault.

1367	Edward the Black Prince leads expedition to Spain to aid Pedro the Cruel, deposed King of Castile.
1369	Hostilities resume in the Hundred Years War.
1374	Chaucer moves to house above Aldgate and is appointed Controller of Customs.
1376	Death of the Black Prince.
1377	Death of Edward III. Crown passes to his grandson, Richard II.
1378	Pope Gregory XI elected. Start of Great Schism.
1379	Chaucer writes the *House of Fame*.
1380	John Wycliffe is dismissed from the Oxford faculty for teaching religious reform. The Lollards would form heretical pre-Lutheran sect around his teachings.
1381	Wat Tyler's Rebellion.
1382	Richard II marries Anne of Bohemia. Wycliffe translates Bible into English. Chaucer is appointed Controller of Petty Customs on Wines.
1383	Death of John Wycliffe.
1385	Probable date of composition of *Troilus and Criseyde*.
1386	John of Gaunt leads unsuccessful expedition to Spain to claim crown of Castile in the name of his second wife. Chaucer writes first sections of the *Canterbury Tales*. Also moves to Greenwich and is appointed Justice of the Peace and Knight of the Shire.
1387	Probable year of death of Philippa Chaucer.
1399	Death of John of Gaunt. Richard II is deposed by Henry of Bolingbroke (John of Gaunt's son), who takes the crown as Henry IV.
1400	Death of Richard II and of Geoffrey Chaucer.
1478	William Caxton publishes first printed edition of the *Canterbury Tales*.

K

Knight

And certes, if it nere to long to heer,
I wolde have toold yow fully the manere
How wonnen was the regne of Femenye
By Theseus and by his chivalrye;
And of the grete bataille for the nones
Bitwixen Atthenes and Amazones;
And how asseged was Ypolita,
The faire, hardy queene of Scithia;
And of the feste that was at hir weddynge,
And of the tempest at her hoom-comynge;
But al that thyng I moot as now forbere.
I have, God woot, a large feeld to ere,
And wayke been the oxen in my plough
The remenant of the tale is long ynough.
I wol nat letten eek noon of this route;
Lat every felawe telle his tale aboute.

And certainly, if it weren't too long to tell here,
I would have told you in great detail about the way
The kingdom of Femeny
Was conquered by Theseus and his knights;

Knight

And of the other great battles
Between the Athenians and the Amazons;
And how Hippolyta was besieged,
The fair queen of Scythia
And of the feasting at the wedding and the
Storm that accompanied her homecoming.
But all those things I must leave for now
As I have, God knows, a large enough field to cover.
The oxen that pull my plow are weak,
And the rest of the tale I have to tell is plenty long.
I will not let myself get in the way of others either;
Let everyone have time to tell his tale.

(*Canterbury Tales,*
"The Knight's Tale," I (A), 875–90)

The medieval knight has been the object of as much romanticizing as scholarly debate. Even during the Middle Ages, the term was so fluid and so inextricably tied to socioeconomic fluctuations that definitions of exactly what a knight represented were slippery and far from immune to romantic

Godfrey de Bouillon is depicted in this fifteenth-century tapestry. Courtesy of Corbis.

connotations. The term dates back to the Anglo-Saxon *cniht* (or in German or Danish *knecht* and *knegt*, respectively), meaning a servant or follower. The Old Norwegian *knekt* interestingly carried the derogatory definition of rogue or rascal.

No matter the language, early knights were far from noble. It is around the time of the Norman Conquest that the term began to indicate socio-economic rank. By the thirteenth century it had become an intrinsic role for aristocratic men, who either fought or prayed. This elevation was tied to the economy. Poor knights of the eleventh century for the most part were happy to accept their position as those who fought for Christian good (as in the Crusades). However, rising inflation in the late twelfth century that raised rents drastically combined with the rising cost of equipment—war-horse, armor, weapons—and increasingly made knighthood a very expensive career.

Faced with declining numbers of fighting men, in 1292 Edward I made knighthood compulsory for any man who owned land worth at least £40 per year. Because the poorer knights tried to dodge the fiscally crippling service, the wealthy saw an opportunity to distinguish themselves by inventing prestige. They wanted to be known as rich and powerful enough to be able to afford knighthood.

Kings promoted this ideal by founding special orders and by passing sumptuary laws to limit the wearing of silks, furs, and gold to knights. A

Detail of stained glass window at Sainte-Chapelle showing knights and a horse. Courtesy of Corbis.

Effigy of a knight, possibly of the Warenne family, benefactors of the priory at Southwark 1280–1300. Courtesy of Lisa Kirchner.

complex chivalric code—the source of many romanticized notions of knighthood then and now—developed to govern proper knightly behavior.

Furthermore, distinctions were drawn between a knight and a simple man at arms. The minimum annual income for knighthood was raised to £200 per year, and those who sought a military career but fell below that line were forced to become the equivalent of common soldiers. As larger armies were becoming a necessary part of medieval warfare, a system developed whereby these men at arms entered into compulsory service for a set amount of time and pay.

Mercenaries also sold their services to the highest bidder, and, as the feudal system increasingly fragmented power, some men took the title of knight for themselves, without benefit of a lordly dubbing, in order to garner counterfeit honor and prestige. There was simply nobody to gainsay them in many situations. Consequently, by the fourteenth century with its many assaults on long-held notions of privilege and nobility, the mercenary knight was a troubling figure on the social landscape.

In this context, Chaucer's presentation of the Knight is correspondingly complex. On the surface, Chaucer gives his audience the chivalric ideal: "he loved chivalrie, / Trouthe and honour, fredom and curteisie…. / He was a verray, parfit gentil knyght" (*He loved chivalry / and truth and honor, freedom and courtesy…. / He was a very perfect, gentle knight*) (*Canterbury Tales,*

General Prologue, I (A), 45–56, 72). Yet everything about the Knight sets him against the romantic chivalric ideal of his time. His dress is shabby and lacking in the trappings usually associated with a knight in shining armor, trappings that provided an important social clue to a person's rank.

He is also lacking a coat of arms and familial estates. Chaucer appears to attribute this to the Knight's extreme humility, but the martial portion of the Knight's description underlines his position as both obsolescent and out of step with his supposed social class. Chaucer does not mention the main European conflict of his time, the Hundred Years War with France. Instead, the Knight has fought against only non-Christians around the world, maintaining a decrepit version of the Crusades.

The places he has fought in particular brand him as a mercenary. Russia and Prussia, for instance, were prime grounds for military opportunists seeking rank and recognition. Initially, the Knight longs to tell a tale of conquest, but there is not time to go into all of that as well as the narrative (*Canterbury Tales,* "The Knight's Tale," I (A), 875–90). His garrulousness and his excitement about frivolous details of fancy parties and the activities of the rich and powerful undercut the emphasis on his humility. Like Jean Froissart, he delights in the superficial and flashy.

A woodcut of the Knight from a fifteenth-century edition of *The Canterbury Tales.* Courtesy of the Glasgow University Library.

In short, Chaucer's Knight, the supposedly highest-ranking member of the party, is a satirical portrayal.

See also Armor; Chivalry; Estates; Hundred Years War; Weapons

FURTHER READING

Ainsworth, Peter F. *Jean Froissart and the Fabric of History: Truth, Myth, and Fiction in the* "*Chroniques.*" New York: Oxford University Press, 1990.

Alexander, Jonathan, and Paul Binski, eds. *Age of Chivalry: Art in Plantagenet England, 1200–1400.* London: Royal Academy of Arts in association with Weidenfeld and Nicholson, 1987.

Barber, Richard. *The Reign of Chivalry.* Rochester, NY: Boydell Press, 2005.

Barker, Juliet R. V. *The Tournament in England, 1100–1400.* Wolfeboro, NH: Boydell Press, 1986.

Broughton, Bradford B. *Dictionary of Medieval Knighthood and Chivalry. Concepts and Terms.* Westport, CT: Greenwood Press, 1986.

Bumke, Joachim. *Courtly Culture.* New York: Overlook Press, 2000.

Chickering, Howell, and Thomas H. Seiler, eds. *The Study of Chivalry: Resources and Approaches.* Kalamazoo: Medieval Institute Publications, Western Michigan University, 1988.

De Pisan, Christine. *The Book of Deeds of Arms and of Chivalry.* Translated by Sumner Willard. Edited by Charity Cannon Willard. University Park: Pennsylvania State University Press, 1999.

Jones, Terry. *Chaucer's Knight: The Portrait of a Medieval Mercenary.* Baton Rouge: Louisiana State University Press, 1980.

Kaeuper, Richard W. *Chivalry and Violence in Medieval Europe.* New York: Oxford University Press, 1999.

Laing, Lloyd Robert. *Medieval Britain: The Age of Chivalry.* New York: St. Martin's Press, 1996.

Trim, D.J.B., ed. *The Chivalric Ethos and the Development of Military Professionalism.* Boston: Brill, 2003.

L

Lamech

The son of Methuselah, Lamech (Old Testament) was the first man in the Bible who is mentioned as having more than one wife. The Wife of Bath mentions him as one of the justifications of her multiple marriages (*Canterbury Tales,* "The Wife of Bath's Tale," III (D), 53–54). His inability or unwillingness to commit to one woman is referenced in both "The Squire's Tale" and *Anelida and Arcite,* where Canacee and Anelida lament their mates' infidelity:

Certes, ne noon oother man
Syn Lameth was, that alderfirst bigan
To loven two, as writen folk biforn.

For certain, there has been no other man
Since Lameth, that very first one to
Love two women, as is written by folk long ago.

(*Canterbury Tales,*
"The Squire's Tale," V (F), 549–51)

But neverthelesse, gret wonder was hit noon
Thogh he were fals, for hit is kynde of man

Sith Lamek was, that is so longe agoon,
To ben in love as fals as evere he can;
He was the firste fader that began
To loven two, and was in bigamye,
And he found tentes first, but yf men lye.

But nonetheless, it is no great wonder
That he is false, for he is the kind of man
That Lameth was, who lived so long ago,
To be in love as false as anyone can possibly be.
He was the first man to begin
Loving two women, and was the first bigamist,
And he was the first to prove that men are liars in love.

(*Anelida & Arcite,* 148–54)

Further Reading

Brown, Peter, ed. *A Companion to Chaucer.* Malden, MA: Blackwell, 2002.

Frye, Northrop. *Biblical and Classical Myths: The Mythological Framework of Western Culture.* Buffalo, NY: University of Toronto Press, 2004.

Manser, Martin H. *The Facts On File Dictionary of Classical and Biblical Allusions.* New York: Facts On File, 2003.

Law

A SERGEANT OF THE LAWE, war an wys,
That often hadde been at the Parvys,
Ther was also, ful riche of excellence.
Discreet he was and of greet reverence—
He semed swich, his wordes weren so wise.
Justice he was ful often in assise,
By patente and by pleyn commissioun.
For his science and for his heigh renoun,
Of fees and robes hadde he many oon.
So greet a purchasour was nowher noon;
Al was fee symple to hym in effect;
His purchasyng myghte nat been infect.
Nowher so bisy a man as he ther nas,
And yet he semed bisier than he was.
In termes hadde he caas and doomes alle
That from the tyme of kyng William were falle.
Thereto he koude endite and make a thyng,
Ther koude no wight pynche at his writyng;
And every statut koude he pleyn by rote.

There was a Sergeant at Law, wary and wise,
Who had often been at the porch of St. Paul's cathedral,

He was an excellent man.
Very discreet and worthy of all reverence—
Or so he seemed to be, his words were so wise.
He was often a justice at the assizes,
By patent letters, he was authorized to hear all cases.
And his great renown and skills had
Earned him great fees and fancy robes.
There was no one to match him as a property buyer;
Everything he bought was fee-simple;
His purchasing power was beyond reproach.
Nowhere was there such a busy man as him
And yet he seemed busier than he really was.
He could quote from all the books and cases,
Chapter and verse from the time of William I
To that end he could draw up a deed,
And no man could find a thing wrong with his writing
And every statute he could quote from memory.

(*Canterbury Tales,*
General Prologue, I (A), 309–27)

The law codes of the Middle Ages provide the basis for most of the modern Western legal system. In an increasingly complex social system, it is only natural that legal matters would follow suit, expanding in both the realm of canon law as well as secular. By the thirteenth century, schools were firmly established that enabled scholars to specialize in the study of law. They provided lectures on the interpretation of the legal code, which was in constant flux under varying influences, as well as practical advice on the legal practice.

In the west, the first real lawyers emerged from Italy and Bologna in particular. The university at Bologna was the first to offer a formal legal course of study, focusing both on Byzantine and Roman law texts. Scholars at Bologna studied canon law for roughly four years, although the bulk of their study focused on secular law. Students from all over Europe traveled to study there, becoming the first of a respected professional class.

A jury of 12 meet with court officials in fifteenth-century Normandy, ca. 1450. Courtesy of the Library of Congress.

Fourteenth-century illustrations of the Crucifixion and an enthroned king. Courtesy of the Glasgow University Library.

In 1300, lawyers in England established the Inns of Court to enable English students to study law in their native land. The Inns, comprised of four former residences, enabled students to live and study in the same place, a forerunner of the residential university. The professors at the Inns compiled legal cases and briefs every year and used them as textbooks.

In the Sergeant at Law, Chaucer provides a thumbnail sketch of a common lawyer of his time. It is unclear what the Sergeant's rank is, and that appears to be indicative of the changing shape of a profession in its infancy. We know that he practiced common, not canon, law. Yet the title of sergeant implies more prestige; however, because the profession was still evolving, pinning down the precise meaning of any title is difficult.

The rank of King's Sergeant at Law was the highest obtainable rank, short of justice, in the English legal profession. However, it is not precisely clear that Chaucer's Sergeant is a King's Sergeant. He has been a judge at assizes, and we know that he is successful financially. However, Chaucer also tells us that he seems busier than he really was, a sly hint that perhaps he is attempting to make himself appear more important than he really was.

See also Education

FURTHER READING

Arnold, Morris, et al. *On the Laws and Customs of England: Essays in Honor of Samuel E. Thorne.* Chapel Hill: University of North Carolina Press, 1981.

Bellamy, John G. *Bastard Feudalism and the Law.* Portland, OR: Areopagitica Press, 1989.

Hornsby, Joseph Allen. *Chaucer and the Law.* Norman, OK: Pilgrim Books, 1988.

Leather

Leather was a very important resource of the Middle Ages. It was vital to clothing, footwear, armor, a variety of practical needs such as containers and saddlery, and had decorative uses. Tanneries, the producers of leather, were not only an important industry, but, along with the lumber industry, had perhaps the greatest negative impact on the environment.

Although there are a number of acids that will remove the hair from a skin and add suppleness to the finished product, the most common method of medieval tanning was vegetable tanning, a process that involved soaking a skin in a series of solutions of natural tannins, usually extracted from oak leaves and bark. The process, which produced beautiful leather, was lengthy, sometimes taking more than six months to complete.

The hide was first scraped free of hair, then rubbed with manure to soften the skin. The final step was to soak the hides in tannin baths for several months until the skin was cured. The desired end product was strong, durable, and soft, with a subtle sheen. The very finest leather came from goats and was known as Morocco leather for its country of origin.

While the tanning process was completely natural and, strictly speaking, organic, the sheer volume of acidic liquid that was a by-product of the tanning process had serious consequences to the immediate environment. Tanneries were generally concentrated in areas where raw materials, including a source of running water, were plentiful. Because of the smell and waste involved, they were often confined outside of town limits, preferably downstream. It was not unusual for tanneries to severely impact the native fish supply along the rivers they populated.

The uses of leather were myriad and encompassed nearly every facet of daily life. Besides providing connective pieces for armor, leather was used for shoes and boots, belts, buckles, and vests or jerkins. Leather was also used for pouches, purses, and water containers, as well as for saddles and bridles. It was also the primary material used to make sheaths for swords and daggers; thus, the ringing metal on metal sound in films when a sword is drawn is a Hollywood fabrication.

Finally, leather was used for decorative purposes. Books were covered in tooled leather, and wall coverings and screens between rooms were often made of embossed leather. Burnished by a talented craftsman, a leather wall treatment could mimic wood.

See also Armor; Fashion

FURTHER READING

Burns, E. Jane, ed. *Medieval Fabrications: Dress, Textiles, Clothwork, and Other Cultural Imaginings.* New York: Palgrave Macmillan, 2004.

Hodges, Laura F. *Chaucer and Clothing: Clerical and Academic Costume in the Prologue to the "Canterbury Tales."* Rochester, NY: D. S. Brewer, 2005.

———. *Chaucer and Costume.* Cambridge, England: D. S. Brewer, 2005.

Koslin, Désirée G., and Janet E. Snyder. *Encountering Medieval Textiles and Dress: Objects, Texts, Images.* New York: Palgrave Macmillan, 2002.

Netherton, Robin, and Gale R. Owen-Crocker, eds. *Medieval Clothing and Textiles.* Woodbridge, Suffolk, England: Boydell Press, 2005.

Richardson, Catherine, ed. *Clothing Culture, 1350–1650.* Burlington, VT: Ashgate, 2004.

Scott, Margaret. *Medieval Clothing and Costumes: Displaying Wealth and Class in Medieval Times.* New York: Rosen, 2004.

Lithuania

In Lettow hadde he reysed and in Ruse,
No Cristen man so ofte of his degree.

In Lithuania he had raised and in Russia
There was no Christian man who had fought there so often.

(*Canterbury Tales,*
General Prologue, I (A), 54–55)

Lithuania, located northwest of Poland, first became a separate state in 1183 and had developed a fairly influential empire by the fourteenth century. Settled by easterners known as the Balts, Lithuania's history is punctuated by nearly constant conflict with the Teutonic Knights, Muscovite Russia, and the Tartars.

Under the control of the warlord Mindaugas, Lithuania united in the late twelfth century and went on to form alliances with its neighbors that allowed it to both fend off its enemies and to eventually gain control of the Slavic states. In 1260, Lithuania defeated the encroachments of the Teutonic Knights, and, in the next 100 years, expanded to establish an empire that stretched from the Black Sea to the Baltic, Belarus, western Ukraine, and Poland.

The conversion of King Jogailo to Christianity in 1386, a decision influenced by his marriage to Polish heiress Jadwiga (a marriage that made him king of Poland), effected a temporary truce with the Teutonic Knights, although the order was soon back encroaching upon Lithuania's borders.

The Knights would finally be decisively defeated in 1410 at the battle of Grunwald under a combined Lithuanian-Polish force, but not before Chaucer's Knight could assist in sacking a few of Lithuania's cities (*Canterbury Tales*, General Prologue, I (A), 54–55).

See also Knight

FURTHER READING

Cantor, Norman. *The Civilization of the Middle Ages*. Rev. ed. New York: Harper Collins, 1993.

Jones, Terry. *Chaucer's Knight: The Portrait of a Medieval Mercenary*. Baton Rouge: Louisiana State University Press, 1980.

Kaeuper, Richard W. *Chivalry and Violence in Medieval Europe*. New York: Oxford University Press, 1999.

Labarge, Margaret Wade. *Medieval Travellers*. New York: Norton, 1983.

Le Beau, Bryan F., and Menachem Mor, eds. *Pilgrims and Travelers to the Holy Land*. Omaha, NE: Creighton University Press, 1996.

Tyerman, Christopher. *England and the Crusades, 1095–1588*. Chicago: University of Chicago Press, 1988.

Verdon, Jean. *Travel in the Middle Ages*. Notre Dame, IN: University of Notre Dame Press, 2003.

Lollardy

The Parson him answerde, "Benedicite!
What eyleth the man, so synfully to swere?"
Oure Host answerde, "O Jankin, be ye there?
I smelle a Lollere in the wynd," quod he.
"Now! goode men," quod our Hoste, "herkeneth me;
Abydeth, for Goddes digne passioun,
For we schal han a predicacioun;
This Lollere heer wil prechen us somwhat."

The Parson answered him, "Benedicite!
What ails this man to make him swear so sinfully?"
Our host answered, "O Holy Joe, are you there?
I smell a Lollard in the wind, I tell you."
"Now! Good men," said our Host, "listen to me;
By God's name, prepare yourselves
Because I'm making a strong prediction
That this Lollard here is preparing a sermon for us."

(*Canterbury Tales*,
"The Man of Law's Tale," II, 1170–77)

The Lollards were one of the more important heretical groups to precede Lutheranism and the Protestant Reformation. Their founder, John Wycliffe (ca. 1330–1384), was an Oxford-educated theologian, receiving the Doctor of Divinity degree in 1372. He served as Master of Balliol College (Oxford) and Warden of Canterbury Hall (Oxford). As a biblical scholar, he was highly respected and from 1374 was employed as a mediator between the Church and the English crown over issues of authority. Wycliffe pressed for secular authority in several areas, which brought him under negative Church scrutiny for heresy that he was able to survive thanks both to his powerful supporters, Edward III and John of Gaunt, and the confusion that resulted from the Great Schism.

In 1381, Wycliffe began his translation of the Bible into English, a work that was undertaken in secrecy and with the aid of university colleagues who helped him in his preparation of the work. He published it in 1388. A revised and more readable edition was published in 1390 and became known as the Lollard Bible.

The Lollards were begun by a group of itinerant lay preachers who based their teachings on Wyclif's theological writings. His personal connection to them is unclear. The Lollard doctrine was characterized by a particularly anticlerical and anti-Church authority message. Lollards were opposed to the Church's great wealth and maintained that priests should be poor in order to follow in the path of Jesus and the apostles. They claimed no basis existed in the Bible for the pope's authority. Because the pope and his priests were merely fallible men, Lollards encouraged reading the Bible in the vernacular. They also condemned most of the sacraments and rituals such as saint veneration, pilgrimage, holy water, and transubstantiation as superstition and magic. Finally, they interestingly believed in the equality of the sexes, going as far as to approve of female preachers, an idea that did not win them much support among the general public, most of whom considered them to be a mildly fanatical schismatic faction. The Parson's priggish objection to the Man of Law's swearing earns him an accusation of Lollardy from Harry Bailly (*Canterbury Tales,* "The Man of Law's Tale," II, 1170–77).

The Lollards enjoyed initial support from wealthy courtiers who approved of the political implications of shifting power from Rome to the king. However, with the death of Richard II, their influence began to wane and they were put down by statute in 1401, when *De Haeretico Comburendo* introduced burning as a punishment for hereticism in England.

Chaucer's involvement with the Lollards is unclear. As a close associate of Gaunt's, it is likely that Chaucer would have met Wycliffe at court. There are also a number of parallels between the religious attitudes of the two men, which might reflect some influence or the general tone of pre-Reformation heresy that tended to focus on the Church's corruption and wealth.

See also Heresy; John of Gaunt; Religion

FURTHER READING

Aston, Margaret, and Colin Richmond, eds. *Lollardy and the Gentry in the Later Middle Ages.* New York: St. Martin's Press, 1997.

Biller, Peter, and Barrie Dobson, eds. *The Medieval Church: Universities, Heresy, and the Religious Life: Essays in Honour of Gordon Leff.* Rochester, NY: Boydell Press, 1999.

Copeland, Rita. *Pedagogy, Intellectuals, and Dissent in the Later Middle Ages: Lollardy and Ideas of Learning.* New York: Cambridge University Press, 2001.

London

It was during the Middle Ages that London—Chaucer's home city—became one of Europe's leading urban centers. As England became increasingly involved in trade and commerce, it became the country's pre-eminent port city. London lies at the first point at which the Thames can be bridged, which, historically, made it a key location for commerce, communication, and defense. It was under Roman rule that it was first spanned and the city of Londinium was established.

After the Roman withdrawal in the fifth century, invading tribes of Saxons, Angles, and other Germans drove the mixed Celtic and Roman populations westward to Wales and northward to Scotland. The Anglo-Saxons used

City of London's Guildhall. Courtesy of Lisa Kirchner.

The church at the City of London's Guildhall. Courtesy of Lisa Kirchner.

The Tower of London. Courtesy of Lisa Kirchner.

London as an important trading port, although, being agriculturally based, they preferred to live and farm outside of the port city. London began to grow in importance when Christian missionaries entered England in the sixth century and used the city as a base of operations.

From that point forward, London became an important center for trade as well as a source of tax revenue from the trade that thrived, an importance that survived the Viking invasions of the ninth century. In the tenth century, under the reign of Edward the Confessor, the building of Westminster Abbey established the western part of the city as an important administrative center. The Abbey served as both his favorite residence as well as the center of his government.

The Tower of London chapel. Courtesy of Lisa Kirchner.

The city gained ecclesiastical prestige with the coronation of William I at Westminster in 1066. While Canterbury had been and would remain the pre-eminent cathedral city of England, the importance of Westminster Abbey was now undeniable and was bolstered by its political clout. The mayor of London was able to gain the trust of the new Norman invaders and gained for London a royal charter allowing the city to keep its laws and customs under the new rule.

This allowed London to expand and prosper in the following generations, during which many important buildings were constructed, including the Tower of London and its famous stone bridge. The city's increasing wealth gained it a certain degree of power to gain concessions from rulers, and under each successive king more rights were granted to London. Henry I allowed the city to choose its own sheriffs and administer its own courts, an important dilution of royal power in such a heavily populated area. John allowed London the right to annual mayoral elections, free passage on the Thames, and protection for the city's merchants.

By Chaucer's day, the population of London had reached 50,000, the highest in the country. It had suffered losses of roughly one-third to the

A section of the London Wall. Courtesy of Lisa Kirchner.

Black Death, but rebounded quickly. By the close of the medieval period, London had attained a total population of 150,000, swelling outside the original walls and into the suburbs in ever increasing circles. It was the main exporter of wool and wine, making it five times richer than its next closest urban competitor, Bristol.

See also Aldgate; Peasant Revolt

FURTHER READING

Archer, Lucy. *Architecture in Britain and Ireland, 600–1500.* London: Harvill Press, 1999.

Brewer, Derek. *Chaucer and His World.* Cambridge, England: D. S. Brewer, 1978; reprinted 1992.

Carlin, Martha. *Medieval Southwark.* Rio Grande, OH: Hambledon Press, 1996.

Hanawalt, Barbara A., ed. *Chaucer's England: Literature in Historical Context.* Minneapolis: University of Minnesota Press, 1992.

———. *Growing Up in Medieval London: The Experience of Childhood in History.* New York: Oxford University Press, 1993.

Lucrece

The daughter of a Roman consul of the late sixth-century B.C., Lucrece was also the wife of army officer Tarquinus Collatinus. Her great beauty and even greater virtue drew the attention of the local Etruscan prince, who desired to have her for his own. His rape of her and her subsequent suicide have long been attributed to the uprising that threw out the Etruscans and instituted the Roman Republic.

The complete story of her rape is recounted in *The Legend of Good Women* (*Legend of Good Women*, 1680–1885). Chaucer also mentions her frequently as an example of the epitome of virtuous women. In "The Franklin's Tale," she is one of the women whom Dorigen would like to imitate: "Hath nat Lucresse yslayn hirself, allas, / At Rome, whan that she oppressed was / Of Tarquyn, for hire thoughte it was a shame / To lyven whan she hadde lost hir name?" (*Didn't Lucrece kill herself, sadly / In Rome, when she was shamed / By Tarquin's actions, because she could not bear to live / When she had lost her virtuous name?*) (*Canterbury Tales,* "The Franklin's Tale," V (F), 1405–08). Lucrece is mentioned in the introduction to "The Man of Law's Tale" and *The Book of the Duchess* as a virtuous wife (*Canter-*

bury Tales, "The Man of Law's Tale," II (B¹), 63; *Book of the Duchess,* 1082).

FURTHER READING

Brown, Peter, ed. *A Companion to Chaucer.* Malden, MA: Blackwell, 2002.

Frye, Northrop. *Biblical and Classical Myths: The Mythological Framework of Western Culture.* Buffalo, NY: University of Toronto Press, 2004.

Hansen, William F. *Classical Mythology: A Guide to the Mythical World of the Greeks and Romans.* New York: Oxford University Press, 2005.

Manser, Martin H. *The Facts On File Dictionary of Classical and Biblical Allusions.* New York: Facts On File, 2003.

Morford, Mark P. O. *Classical Mythology.* 7th ed. New York: Oxford University Press, 2003.

Nolan, Barbara. *Chaucer and the Tradition of the Roman Antique.* New York: Cambridge University Press, 1992.

Powell, Barry B. *Classical Myth.* Translated by Herbert M. Howe. 4th ed. Upper Saddle River, NJ: Pearson/Prentice Hall, 2004.

Price, Simon, and Emily Kearns, eds. *The Oxford Dictionary of Classical Myth and Religion.* New York: Oxford University Press, 2003.

M

Macedonia

O worthy, gentil Alisandre, allas,
That evere sholde fallen swich a cas!
Empoysoned of thyn owene folk thou weere;
Thy sys Fortune hath turned into aas,
And for thee ne weep she never a teere.

Who shal me yeven teeris to compleyne
The deeth of gentillesse and of franchise,
That al the world weelded in his demeyne,
And yet hym thoughte it myghte nat suffise?
So ful was his corage of heigh emprise,
Allas, who shal me helpe to endite
False Fortune, and poyson to despise,
The whiche two of al this wo I wyte?

Oh worthy, noble Alexander, alas
That ever you had suffered such a fate!
Poisoned by your own men you were;
In the dice game of life, Fortune turned your six into an ace
And for you she never will weep a single tear.

Who will give me tears to lament
The death of such nobility and ability

*Who ruled the entire world as his own kingdom
And yet he still thought it might not be enough?
So full was his courageousness in battle.
Alas, who will help me to accuse
False Fortune, and all poisoners to despise,
As of these two evils I here write?*

(*Canterbury Tales,*
"The Monk's Tale," VII, 2658–70)

Macedonia, located in the Balkans north of Greece, first became a kingdom in the eighth century B.C., but it would be the reign of Philip II in the fourth century B.C. that would unify Macedonia, making it the most powerful state in all of Europe. In 338 B.C., Philip penetrated and conquered the united Greek states and was making plans to attack the Persian Empire when he was assassinated.

His successor, Alexander the Great, accomplished his father's ambition, invading and defeating Persia and creating a Macedonian Empire that stretched across most of the known world, as far as Egypt and India. A portion of "The Monk's Tale" is devoted to Alexander, where he is lamented as another of Fortune's unfortunate victims (*Canterbury Tales,* "The Monk's Tale," VII, 2658–70).

After Alexander's death in 323 B.C., his empire eventually was split into quarters and, ultimately, swallowed by the Roman Empire. The last of the Macedonian descendants of these kingdoms, Cleopatra VII of Egypt's Ptolemy dynasty, was defeated and brought into the Roman Empire in 30 B.C. Following the collapse of Rome, Macedonia passed into the hands of the Byzantines, the Serbians, the Bulgarians, and finally the Ottoman Turks, who held it from 1389 until the nineteenth century.

See also Alexandria; Knight

FURTHER READING

Cantor, Norman. *The Civilization of the Middle Ages.* Rev. ed. New York: Harper Collins, 1993.

Jones, Terry. *Chaucer's Knight: The Portrait of a Medieval Mercenary.* Baton Rouge: Louisiana State University Press, 1980.

Kaeuper, Richard W. *Chivalry and Violence in Medieval Europe.* New York: Oxford University Press, 1999.

Labarge, Margaret Wade. *Medieval Travellers.* New York: Norton, 1983.

Le Beau, Bryan F., and Menachem Mor, eds. *Pilgrims and Travelers to the Holy Land.* Omaha, NE: Creighton University Press, 1996.

Tyerman, Christopher. *England and the Crusades, 1095–1588.* Chicago: University of Chicago Press, 1988.

Verdon, Jean. *Travel in the Middle Ages.* Notre Dame, IN: University of Notre Dame Press, 2003.

Man of Law. *See* Law

Manciple

For wheither that he payde or took by taille,
Algate he wayted so in his achaat
That he was ay biforn and in good staat.
Now is nat that of God a ful fair grace
That swich a lewed mannes wit shal pace
The wisdom of a heep of lerned men?
Of maistres hadde he mo than thries ten,
That weren of lawe expert and curious,
Of which ther were a duszeyne in that hous
Worthy to been stywardes of rente and lond
Of any lord that is in Engelond.

For whether he paid cash or on credit
He always looked for the best prices.
He was always the first on the job and did his very best
Now is that not an example of God's grace
That such an uneducated man should outpace
The wisdom of a heap of learned men?
Of masters he had more than thirty,
Who were experts in the law
And more than a dozen of them
Who were worthy to be steward of rent and land
For any lord in the whole of England.

(*Canterbury Tales,*
General Prologue, I (A), 570–86)

A manciple (or, in Middle English, *maunciple*) was a purchaser of provisions for an institution such as a university or monastery. One part caterer, one part steward, a manciple decided where to buy food and supplies, negotiated with the merchants, and handled the funds to pay. Chaucer's Manciple has been hired to provision the lawyers at the Inns of Court. He is uneducated, but savvy, and embezzles from his employers.

This gives him a sense of superiority out of proportion with his social status. His tale references a ludicrous amount of classical lore, demonstrating his desire to look educated and, thus, above his station. Yet his success in swindling the 30 lawyers who have hired him to feed them is proof of Chaucer's belief that intelligence and ability are not qualities confined to the elite. The Manciple might, in the final analysis, appear to be a rather shady character, but he is canny and talented. His tale underlines these points of his character as it ironically demonstrates the benefits of knowing when to keep one's mouth shut.

See also Estates; Law

FURTHER READING

Bean, J.M.W. *From Lord to Patron: Lordship in Late Medieval England*. Manchester, England: Manchester University Press, 1989.

Cantor, Norman. *The Civilization of the Middle Ages*. Rev. ed. New York: Harper Collins, 1993.

DeWindt, Edwin Brezette, ed. *The Salt of Common Life: Individuality and Choice in the Medieval Town, Countryside, and Church: Essays Presented to J. Ambrose Raftis*. Kalamazoo: Medieval Institute Publications, Western Michigan University, 1995.

Duby, Georges. *The Three Orders: Feudal Society Imagined*. Translated by Arthur Goldhammer. Chicago: University of Chicago Press, 1980; reprinted 1982.

Dyer, Christopher. *Making a Living in the Middle Ages: The People of Britain 850–1520*. New Haven, CT: Yale University Press, 2002.

Hindley, Geoffrey. *The Medieval Establishment, 1200–1500*. New York: Putnam, 1970.

Knapp, Peggy. *Chaucer and the Social Contest*. New York: Routledge, 1990.

Lambdin, Laura C., and Robert T. Lambdin, eds. *Chaucer's Pilgrims*. Westport, CT: Praeger, 1999.

Manors. *See* Feudalism

Marriage

―――――――――――

"Wommen desiren to have sovereynetee
As wel over hir housbond as hir love,
And for to been in maistrie hym above.
This is youre mooste desir, thogh ye me kille."

…

And thus they lyve unto hir lyves ende
In parfit joye; and Jhesu Crist us sende
Housbounds meeke, yonge, and fresshe abedde,
And grace t'overbyde hem that we wedde;
And eek I praye Jhesu shorte hir lyves
That noght wol be governed by hir wyves;
And olde and angry nygardes of dispence,
God sende hem soone verray pestilence!

"Women desire to have sovereignty
Over their husbands as well as over their lovers
They want to have mastery over them.
That is what you desire most I believe, even if it means I will die."

…

And thus they lived until the end of their lives
In perfect joy; and many Jesus Christ send us

Husbands who are meek, young, and fresh in bed
And by God's grace that we outlive those whom we wed;
And thus I pray to Jesus to shorten the lives
Of men who will not be governed by their wives;
And those who are old and angry skinflints who deny their wives
I pray to God to shower upon them disease and pestilence!

(*Canterbury Tales,*
"The Wife of Bath's Tale," III (D), 1038–41,
1257–64)

Marriage, as a Christian institution, developed during the Middle Ages from a simple financial contract into a sacrament. Because marriage was the primary means of providing economic stability—in the sense that land and property were provided for, lineages were protected, and dynasties were assured—the Church found it necessary and desirable to invest the once simple ceremony with a certain degree of religious significance to add weight to the promises being made. Easy dissolution of marriages meant costly threats to the general stability of society. Additionally, the openly accepted practice of noble men keeping concubines had long disturbed the Church.

During Anglo-Saxon times, a marriage was simple. A couple's parents usually decided for them whom each would marry and negotiated the dowry and any additional considerations. The ceremony consisted in sitting down on a bench together publicly and drinking from the same cup. Divorce was essentially just as easy. One party only had to declare three times, again in front of witnesses, "I divorce you" and the marriage was dissolved. Both parties were completely free to wed again, and the wife retained her dowry.

This loose approach presented serious economic and moral consequences, and so the Church stepped in to codify the process, making it officially a sacrament in the twelfth century. Despite the romantic notions of courtly love and courtship—which were encouraged because any degree of affection between the two parties was believed to aid in the potential success of a union—the ultimate decision still remained with the parents, who often chose partners for their children based on property considerations alone.

Thus, the process still began with a meeting between the two families to arrange the

A marriage chest decorated with scenes from Pyramus and Thisbe. © Bibliothèque nationale de France.

settlement of property and dowry money. When both sides were satisfied, a betrothal would become official. Prior to the wedding, banns were read on three Sundays in church. This enabled anyone who had information that might prevent the marriage to come forward.

Unlike today, the marriage was formally conducted at the door of the church, in full view of the public, although a mass might be said within the church for a smaller number of guests. The groom typically gave his bride a ring, signifying her wedded state, and she no longer wore her hair loose and unbound. A feast, the ancestor of the modern wedding reception, followed the ceremony.

Although life expectancies were shorter in the Middle Ages and there is a general belief today that it was fairly common for children to marry, this is largely a misconception. Among the nobility, betrothals in the cradle were not unusual. However, it was forbidden by the Church for girls under the age of 12 and boys under the age of 14 to wed. Long betrothals were, thus, the norm rather than child marriages. For the lower classes, weddings took place much later than one might expect. Most couples waited to marry until they had a home of their own, moving the peasant marital age bracket into the 20s.

Especially among the peasant classes in which rules were slightly looser, betrothal might be followed by consummation, because a betrothal promise was just as legally binding as an actual marriage ceremony. This could lead to serious legal repercussions, however, so it was always important to make sure there were witnesses to any legal contract, whether it be a wedding ceremony or simply the promise to marry.

Pledging one's troth was as serious a promise as any feudal contract. Thus, if the intended bride became pregnant, for instance, and the groom denied the betrothal, witnesses could testify that he was legally obliged to make the wedding official. Once married, it was permanent. Only in very selective circumstances could a marriage be annulled once it had gained sacramental status. If a woman was barren or a man impotent, either party could seek an annulment. A marriage also could be deemed invalid if one of the parties had been coerced (as in *Romeo and Juliet*) or there were issues of consanguinity.

While courtly love tales demonstrate that the woman has the upper hand during courtship, until Chaucer's day it was generally accepted that she would be the subordinate party once married. Any other arrangement would threaten to turn the world "upso doun." However, Chaucer's works all seem to challenge accepted notions of proper marital arrangements, and a number of *The Canterbury Tales* address the marital balance of power.

"The Wife of Bath's Tale" boldly asserts that a woman wants to be the dominant party and nothing less will make her happy. However, she demonstrates at the end of the tale that giving this to a woman will always benefit the man in the end (*Canterbury Tales*, "The Wife of Bath's Tale," III (D), 1038–41, 1257–64).

"The Franklin's Tale" portrays a marriage in which both parties swear to be equals. Although Dorigen and Arveragus do not make this public, and they face terrible tribulations because of their decision, in the end they are rewarded and live happily, even managing to quell the overweening lust of Aurelius for Dorigen:

Of his free wyl he swoor hire as a knyght
That nevere in al his lyf he, day ne nyght,
Ne sholde upon hym take no maistrie
Agayn hir wyl, ne kithe hire jalousie,
But hire obeye, and folwe hir wyl in al
As any lovere to his lady shal,
Save that the name of soveraynetee,
That wolde he have for shame of his degree.

...

"Madame, seyth to youre lord Arveragus
That sith I se his grete gentillesse
To yow, and eek I se wel youre distresse,
That him were levere han shame (and that were routhe)
Than ye to me sholde breke thus youre trouthe,
I have wel levere evere to suffre wo
Than I departe the love bitwix yow two."

Of his free will he swore to her as would a knight
That never in all of his life would he, by day or night,
Take upon himself no mastery
Against her will, nor show any jealousy,
But instead he would obey her and follow her will in all
As any lover should to his lady love,
Except that in the name of sovereignty, he would appear to be master
So that he would not shame his name as a husband.
...

"Madame, I say to your lord Arveragus
That since I see his great nobility and fairness
To you, and I also see your equally great distress,
That to him you would ever act shamefully (and that under duress)
Then to me you should break your promise
For I would never ever seek to cause you both suffering
And I will leave before I come between the love of you two."

(*Canterbury Tales,*
"The Franklin's Tale," V (F), 745–52, 1526–32)

By contrast, both "The Merchant's Tale" and "The Miller's Tale" show very young women who are in subordinate positions to their old husbands and, because of the disparity of their situations, both in terms of power and sex, they eventually cheat on their husbands. Finally, "The Clerk's Tale" demonstrates the destructive nature of too much dominance in a marriage, this time on the part of the husband, who repeatedly and unnecessarily tests his wife's loyalty and endurance:

Griselde is deed, and eek hire pacience,
And bothe atones buryed in Ytaille;
For which I crie in open audience
No wedded man so hardy be t'assaille
His wyves pacience in trust to fynde
Grisildis, for in certein he shal faille.

O noble wyves, ful of heigh prudence,
Lat noon humylitee youre tonge naille,
Ne lat no clerk have cause or diligence
To write of yow a storie of swich mervaille
As of Grisldis pacient and kynde,
Lest Chichevache yow swelwe in hire entraille!

Folweth Ekko, that holdeth no silence,
But ever answereth at the countretaille,
Beth nat bidaffed for youre innocence,
But sharply taak on yow the governaille.
Emprenteth wel this lessoun in youre mynde,
For commune profit sith it may availle.

Grisilde dead as well as her patience,
And both are buried in Italy;
And so I pray all the husbands in this audience
Not to be so quick to assail
Their wives' patience in hopes of finding
Grisildes, for they shall certainly fail in the quest.

O noble wives, full of high prudence,
Never let humility silence your tongue,
Nor let a clerk like me to have cause or evidence
To write about you such a marvelous story
As of Grisilde's patience and kindness,
Lest Chichevache eat you right up!

Be like Echo, and never keep silent,
Forever counter his every statement,
And never keep quiet and innocent,
But instead sharply rebuff him and take the upper hand.
Imprint this lesson well on your mind
Because it will very likely profit you some day.

(*Canterbury Tales,*
"The Clerk's Tale," IV (E), 1177–94)

See also Courtly Love; Sex

FURTHER READING

Duby, Georges. *Love and Marriage in the Middle* Ages. Translated by Jane Dunnett. Chicago: University of Chicago Press, 1988; reprinted in translation 1994.

Jacobs, Kathryn Elisabeth. *Marriage Contracts from Chaucer to the Renaissance Stage.* Gainesville: University Press of Florida, 2001.

McCarthy, Conor. *Marriage in Medieval England: Law, Literature, and Practice.* Woodbridge, VT: Boydell Press, 2004.

Mitchell, Linda Elizabeth. *Portraits of Medieval Women: Family, Marriage, and Politics in England, 1255–1350.* New York: Palgrave Macmillan, 2003.

Smith, Warren S., ed. *Satiric Advice on Women and Marriage: From Plautus to Chaucer.* Ann Arbor: University of Michigan Press, 2005.

Wilson, Katharina M., and Elizabeth M. Makowski. *Wykked Wyves and the Woes of Marriage: Misogamous Literature from Juvenal to Chaucer.* Albany: State University of New York Press, 1990.

Medea

The daughter of Aeëtes, king of Colchis, Medea's career was punctuated by what might be called poor personal and relationship choices. First, she fell in love with Jason and used magic to assist him in completing a series of difficult tasks imposed by her father in order to gain the Golden Fleece. Fleece in hand, the two fled on Jason's ship. Medea was able to delay her father's pursuit by strewing the sea behind them with the limbs of her slain brother. Aeëtes kept stopping to gather them, slowing his progress.

Jason and Medea later married, but he eventually tired of her and tried to set her aside so he could marry Glaucus. Medea responded by murdering the bride with a poisoned robe she had sent with a bridal gift. Mad with grief, she then proceeded to murder her two children by Jason. In a panic, she escaped to Athens.

There, she married King Aegeus and had a son with him. However, because she plotted against the life of Theseus, Aegeus's son by former marriage, Medea was forced to flee again. She returned to Colchis, where she heroically killed her father's usurper and restored Aeëtes to the throne.

Chaucer interestingly takes a wholly sympathetic position in regard to Medea. She is one of the more complicated figures in classical literature because some of her more shocking behaviors were not merely the result of her madness after Jason's betrayal. He devotes a chapter to her in *The Legend of Good Women,* but fails to mention the murder of her children (*Legend of Good Women,* 1580–1679). In *The House of Fame,* he calls her a betrayed woman (*House of Fame,* 401). Her enchantments are displayed on the wall of Venus's temple in "The Knight's Tale," and her image appears in a stained glass window in *The Book of the Duchess* (*Canterbury Tales,* "The

Knight's Tale," I (A), 1944; *Book of the Duchess,* 321–30). Later in the poem, the narrator says that she has been damned for killing her children (*Book of the Duchess,* 725–26).

FURTHER READING

Brown, Peter, ed. *A Companion to Chaucer.* Malden, MA: Blackwell, 2002.

Frye, Northrop. *Biblical and Classical Myths: The Mythological Framework of Western Culture.* Buffalo, NY: University of Toronto Press, 2004.

Hansen, William F. *Classical Mythology: A Guide to the Mythical World of the Greeks and Romans.* New York: Oxford University Press, 2005.

Manser, Martin H. *The Facts On File Dictionary of Classical and Biblical Allusions.* New York: Facts On File, 2003.

Morford, Mark P. O. *Classical Mythology.* 7th ed. New York: Oxford University Press, 2003.

Nolan, Barbara. *Chaucer and the Tradition of the Roman Antique.* New York: Cambridge University Press, 1992.

Powell, Barry B. *Classical Myth.* Translated by Herbert M. Howe. 4th ed. Upper Saddle River, NJ: Pearson/Prentice Hall, 2004.

Price, Simon, and Emily Kearns, eds. *The Oxford Dictionary of Classical Myth and Religion.* New York: Oxford University Press, 2003.

Medicine

Whan he had mad thus his complaynte,
Hys sorwful hert gan faste faynte
And hs spirites waxen dede;
The blood was fled for pure drede
Doun to hys herte, to make hym warm—
For wel hyt feled the herte had harm—
To wite eke why hyt was adrad
By kynde, and for to make hyt glad,
For hit ys membre principal
Of the body; and that made al
Hys hewe chaunge and wexe grene
And pale, for ther noo blood ys sene
In no maner lym of hys.

When he had thus made his complaint
His sorrowing heart began to quickly give out on him
And his spirits weakened near to death;
The blood fled from his body
Down into his heart to make him warm—
For it was clear that his heart was severely harmed—
To which I asked him why it was so
And what it would take to make it glad again,
For the heart is the chief organ

Of the body; and the suffering in his
Made his complexion change color, all green
And pale, for there was no blood to be found
In all the rest of his body.

(*Book of the Duchess*, 487–99)

Medieval medicine was a strange hybrid, in many ways a field in its infancy, yet steeped in the deep and learned tradition of the classical Greeks. It was a time when physicians were just beginning to rely on empirical evidence rather than theory and philosophy, when surgeons were still held below barbers in the hierarchy, when Aristotelian theories governed most diagnoses, and herbs comprised the primary pharmaceuticals.

Scholastic Medicine

For much of the Middle Ages, scholastic medicine dominated the field. Based on the universal belief in the superiority of philosophy as a means of comprehending the world, scholasticism depended on the Socratic method of inquiry. Issues were debated based on theory and ancient experts were cited, but very little in the way of practical medicine was accomplished. For

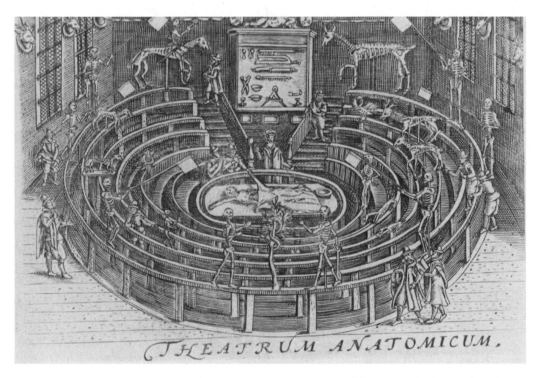

An anatomy class at the University of Leiden, ca. 1625. Courtesy of the National Library of Medicine.

An illumination of a medical lecture from a thirteenth-century manuscript. Note the text being taught is "Tegni of Galen." Courtesy of the National Library of Medicine.

scholastic doctors, using one's hands in the way of barbers and surgeons was degrading manual labor.

Instead, scholastic physicians based their knowledge on the old masters, Hippocrates, Aristotle, and Galen, with a bit of Pliny thrown in for good measure. It was Aristotle who provided what was the most basic of medical doctrines, the one by which nearly every ailment could be explained, diagnosed, and treated: the four humors. Galen provided a great many specifics about the human body, such as his hypothesis on blood flow: "Ne Dedalus with his playes slye; / Ne hele me may no phisicien, / Noght Ypocras ne Galyen" (*Neither Daedalus with his playing sly; / nor the help of any physician, / Such as Hippocrates or Galen*) (*Book of the Duchess*, 570–72).

According to Galen, blood is a by-product of digestion and begins in the stomach, where food is converted to *chyle*. While part of the chyle goes to the spleen, becomes bile, and returns to the stomach, the rest travels to the liver, where it is converted to blood and moves through the vessels to the right ventricle. From the right side of the heart, the blood divides, with half going to the left ventricle and the other half to the lungs where it mixed with *pneuma* or "vital spirit." From there it was distributed to the organs and provided warmth and energy to the body. Any residue was excreted as sweat. This would be the prevalent theory until William Harvey's discoveries in 1628.

Because of his very practical advice and hallowed place as one of the fathers of medicine, Galen was frequently cited as justification for diagnoses. And yet scholastic medicine's resistance to testing Galen's conclusions through ongoing practical exploration doomed scholasticism to failure. Perhaps its most famous adherent was Gentile da Foligno (1290–1348), the fourteenth century's most respected physician and an "arch scholastic." Da Foligno's faith in the ancients made him incapable of dealing with the Black Death when it struck Italy in 1348.

Divorced from actual patients and their symptoms, he prescribed powdered emeralds as a cure, because they were "proven" to crack the eye of a toad. Consequently, he was powerless to cure even himself and died of the Black Death. Indeed, the Black Death may have sounded the death knell for scholasticism in general. Autopsies, in spite of the Church's restrictions on desecration of corpses, were becoming more common, and, although the shift was slow, increasingly, medical experts began to believe that there was no substitute for hands-on practice.

Medical Texts

Because of the dominance of scholastic medicine, medieval doctors relied heavily on texts both ancient and modern to provide the answers to questions of diagnosis and treatment. And yet, by any standards, these texts were woefully inadequate. Many were merely glosses on the works of Aristotle and Galen, and, while these early thinkers certainly were learned, 1,000 years and more should have revealed enough new directions in medical treatment that their works would be rendered quaint reference works to the most basic concepts.

Illustration of a sufferer of leprosy from a fifteenth-century French manuscript. © Bibliothèque nationale de France.

Yet they persisted. Newer and more original works were impractical—heavy, poorly organized, badly indexed. Few recommended personal contact with a patient—most diagnosis was conducted through a combination of astrology, Galenic and Aristotelian theory, and uroscopy (or some other equally theoretical and often nonsensical practice). A surgeon, barber, or apothecary, all of whom were looked down upon by physicians as lowly tradesmen, generally carried out treatments, which relied heavily on folklore, herbalism, and the need to balance the four humors.

The study of texts was conducted in universities, and it was the status conferred by a degree that set physicians apart and above other medical professionals. The ownership of texts in a time before the invention of the printing press, when books were still prohibitively expensive and produced by hand, was a tangible status symbol, conveying the aura of wealth and success.

Some of the more popular medical texts during Chaucer's time were the works of Gilbertus Anglicus and John Gaddesden. Gaddesden (1280–1349/61?), was court physician to Edward II and author of the *Rosa medicinae anglicae* (1314), a compendium of Greek, Christian, and folk medical traditions. He was the most famous physician in England during the late Middle Ages. Chaucer refers to him in glowing terms in *The Canterbury*

Hôtel-Dieu de Paris Hospital, built in 651 but current architecture dates to 1870s. Courtesy of Lisa Kirchner.

Tales, and it is probable that the Doctour of Phisik is based in part on him. The Doctour is also most likely based on Gilbertus Anglicus, whose *Compendium medicinae* (1240) is a trove of medical recipes and descriptions of specific diseases such as smallpox and leprosy.

The Medical Hierarchy

The medieval medical hierarchy was radically different from today. While modern doctors are generally well respected and surgeons are the elite, medieval society thought quite the opposite. Physicians, university trained and philosophically inclined, were at the highest level of the medical professions. They diagnosed patients based not on the degrading process of physical examination but on centuries-old knowledge, theoretical hypotheses based on logic, charts of the body, and the rational balance of the four humors.

Surgeons, on the other hand, practiced physical medicine. They were considered to be the tradesmen of the profession. Along with their medical brothers, the barbers, surgeons were responsible for carrying out treatments, for bloodletting, and, ultimately, for real medical milestones that would improve the field in long-term ways.

The medical hierarchy was rather complex. Physicians were at the top of the totem pole and surgeons placed a distant second. Surgeons handled bloodletting, amputations, and such rudimentary surgeries as were performed: trepanning, stitching wounds, and removing cysts and tumors. Next in line were the barber-surgeons who, along with barber-tonsors, handled bloodletting (under the supervision of a physician) and certain dental procedures such as pulling teeth and filling cavities.

Beneath all of the above were the unlicensed practitioners—midwives and herbalists, mainly—who undertook the bulk of medical needs in rural areas. They were sneered at by the higher-ranking professionals who were all required to be licensed and, in theory at least, to uphold strict standards of conduct and performance.

Apothecaries occupied an unusual place within this structure. They were skilled tradesmen on a level with surgeons (but in the hierarchy ranked below barbers). However, because they sold a product, urban apothecaries especially tended to belong to grocers' companies.

The medieval pharmacy centered on herbs and spices, and the spice trade was a lucrative one. For many, medicine became a distant sideline, as apothecaries gained wealth and political clout. Thus, while

An Illustration of a "zodiac man" from John of Arderne's *Mirror of Phlebotomy & Practice of Surgery,* ca.1425–1550. Courtesy of the Glasgow University Library.

physicians may have looked down upon them as both second-class professionals and lowly merchants, they were forced to recognize the apothecary's socioeconomic equality.

The other skilled tradesmen of medicine-surgeons were looked down upon not only because they worked with their hands, but also for a more mystical reason: they worked with blood, which made their occupation somewhat illicit. The "blood taboo" marked butchers, executioners, barbers, and surgeons. These dual stigmas for most of the Middle Ages held surgeons in a lowly position, one that was compounded by their exclusion—or at best discouragement—from attending universities. During the thirteenth and fourteenth centuries, however, they began to gain more respect and prestige.

This gain was due in part to the Hundred Years War; quite simply, practical medicine was imperative to keeping soldiers on their feet. The Black Death also improved the status of surgeons for similar reasons. Gentile da Foligno, with his belief in the efficacy of powdered emeralds, could not save himself. Through hands-on practice, surgeons at the very least appeared to be men of action:

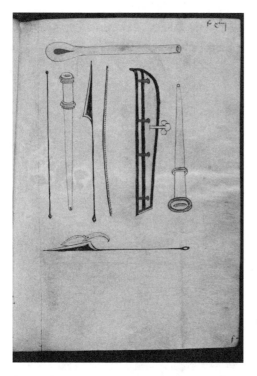

Surgical instruments as pictured in John of Arderne's *Mirror of Phlebotomy & Practice of Surgery,* ca.1425–1550. Courtesy of the Glasgow University Library.

"Sire," quod he, "as to us surgiens aperteneth that we do to every wight the beste that we kan, where as we been withh olde, and to oure pacientz that we do no damage / wherfore it happeth many tyme and ofte that whan twey men han everich wounded oother, oon same surgien heeleth hem bothe; / wherfore unto oure art it is nat pertinent to norice werre ne parties to supporte. / But certes, as to the war-isshynge of youre doghter, al be it so that she perilously be wounded, we shullen do so enten-tif bisynesse fro day to nyght that with the grace of God she shal be hool and sound as soone as is possible."

"Sir," he said, "as for us surgeons we do everything in our repertoire the best that we can, as we have been told that we should do no damage to our patients / and thus there are many times when two men have wounded each other, and the same surgeon heals them both; / because for our art it is not fitting to choose sides of whom to heal. / But for certain, as to the case of your daughter, you know that she has been perilously wounded, however we will do everything day and night to help her and by the grace of God she will be whole and sound again as soon as possible."

(*Canterbury Tales,* "The Tale of Melibee," VII, 1011–15)

The gravity with which their role was taken is evident in this oath of a London Master Surgeon from 1369. Surgeons would swear,

> That they would well and faithfully serve the people, in undertaking their cures, would take reasonably from them, etc., would faithfully follow their calling, and would present to the said mayor and aldermen the defaults of others undertaking cures, so often as should be necessary; and that they would be ready, at all times when they should be warned, to attend the maimed or wounded, and other persons, etc., and would give truthful information to the officers of the city aforesaid as to such maimed, wounded, and others, whether they be in peril of death or not, etc. And also, faithfully to do all other things touching their calling. (Rickert, 173)

Barber-surgeons were a very necessary, but denigrated, part of medieval medicine. Like barber-tonsors, they usually had to focus their business mainly on grooming in order to make an income. There was, however, strength in numbers, and, because they outnumbered surgeons in London by ten to one, the London Barbers Company was over time able to gain some respect for the profession. It was a bumpy road, and many of their problems were self-inflicted. In 1307, the Lord Mayor complained about the barbers' advertising methods of hanging bloody rags outside their shops and placing buckets of blood in their windows.

Given the blood taboo, this was provocative behavior, not to mention that barbers were not allowed to open a vein without a physician present. Not long after, a group of enterprising barber-surgeons ran afoul of the law, accused of operating brothels—called stews—out of the city's municipal baths. The London Barbers Company was able to overcome these hurdles, however, and gained some political clout and medical independence by the second half of the fourteenth century.

Not only did the Black Death help the position of barbers in much the way that it had surgeons, but the vernacularization of science, with the concomitant democratization of most levels of society leveled the playing field somewhat. Over time, practitioners of medicine improved their status, and, by the late fifteenth century, physicians all but abandoned scholastic medicine for more practical approaches. By the nineteenth century, surgeons overtook physicians in terms of respect.

Diagnosis and the Body

By Chaucer's time, medieval medicine had at least started to grasp some of the realities of the human body's structure and functioning. This was due in great part to the justice system. Charts and drawings, influenced by Aristotle and Galen, went only so far in aiding comprehension, and the study of cadavers for purely educational purposes was still frowned upon by the Church. But autopsies were allowed for very practical legal purposes: not only were questions of wrongful or natural death at stake, but questions about childbirth, paternity, and inheritance were believed to be answerable through postmortem examination.

Medieval understanding of the body's operations was still rudimentary at best, particularly in the field (if we may call it that) of obstetrics. Conception was a mystery, and the woman's role in the process was the subject of much debate. Basing their conclusions on Aristotle—and the visible reality of semen—medieval doctors credited men with contributing the "active principle" or the life, and women with contributing "matter." Inexperience with female organs led to amusing suppositions about the uterus: that it was segmented, that women had two, and that it roved throughout the body by the aid of little claws. Menstruation was even more mysterious, and thinkers from Aristotle to Galen to Albertus Magnus posited its purpose and expulsion.

It was generally believed that grief could physically hurt the heart, a notion that has been borne out by modern medicine (*Book of the Duchess*, 487–99). Gilbertus Anglicus attempted to classify the workings of the rest of the organs of the body. Dividing the trunk into two sections at the diaphragm, Gilbertus hypothesized fairly correctly that those above were chiefly intended for respiration. He interestingly devoted a great deal of thought to the functions of the brain. Again, he managed to reach some conclusions that are correct at least in the broad sense. For instance, he connected injuries or diseases to specific parts of the brain to particular responses: the front part caused frenzy, the back lethargy, and the brain in general controls emotions, thoughts, and senses.

On the other hand, some of his conclusions are as absurd as the misapprehensions on the female organs. Gilbertus, having seen the folds of the brain, hypothesized that the hollow spaces were there so that fumes could "fly around" and, like the roving uterus, that the brain could turn itself around inside the skull.

Diagnoses were reached by a variety of methods, few of which would pass muster by today's standards. Astrology, of course, was used to prognosticate about a patient's symptoms and to suggest proper treatment. Symptoms that evidenced an imbalance in the four humors contained tailor-made remedies to restore balance (usually involving bloodletting).

Uroscopy was perhaps the most widely employed method of diagnosis and it, too, could reveal an imbalance in the humors. So dependable was it believed to be that physicians often did not need to hear about any symptoms or have any contact at all with the patient. All that was required was a flask of the patient's urine and the physician could make a diagnosis based on the color, odor, texture, and, in some cases, taste. So central was uroscopy to English medical practice that by 1400 the symbol of English physicians was no longer the Hippocratic staff, but the urine flask.

A folkloric method of diagnosis that curiously remained popular with the nobility was the Goldfinch Diagnosis. The goldfinch had long been a symbol of the resurrection and as a protector against plague and was thus entrusted (much like the weather-predicting groundhog of Punxsutawney, Pennsylvania) with determining ailments by its actions. The goldfinch was placed facing the patient and a turn to the left, right, or away, combined with astrological conditions, indicated a proper course of treatment and diagnosis.

Treatment, whatever the illness, usually involved some combination of bloodletting, cupping (a form of acupuncture in which heated cups are placed on the skin to draw blood through the vacuum that forms beneath the cups), and pharmacological concoctions of varying efficacy:

Ther nas quyk-silver, lytarge, ne brymstoon,
Boras, ceruce, ne oille of tartre noon,
Ne oynement that wolde clense and byte,
That hym myghte helpen of his whelks white,
Nor of the knobbes sittynge on his chekes.
...

Swelleth the brest of Arcite, and the soore
Encreesseth at his herte moore and moore.
The clothered blood, for any lechecraft,
Corrupteth, and is in his bouk ylaft,
That neither veyne-blood, ne ventusynge,
Ne drynke of herbes may ben his helpynge.
The vertu expulsif, or animal,
Fro thilke vertu cleped natural
Ne may the venym voyden ne expelle
The pipes of his longes gonne to swelle,
And every lacerte in his brest adoun·
Is shent with venym and corrupcioun.
Hym gayneth neither, for to gete his lif,
Vomyt upward, ne dounward laxatif.
Al is tobrosten thilke regioun;
Nature hath now no dominacioun.

There was no mercury, sulphur, or white lead,
Borax, ceruse, or cream of tarter,
No ointment that would clean and cure
To help him clear up neither his white head pimples,
Nor the bumps that covered his cheeks.
...
The breast of Arcite swelled, and the wound
Strained at his heart more and more.
The clotted blood, in spite of all the doctor's skill,
Poisoned his belly,
So that neither bleeding or cupping
Nor the drinking of herbal potions was of any help to him.
No expelling or animal power
Could help him to void the venom from his system.
Every muscle in his chest, and the pipes in his lungs
Were corrupted with the poison
And he could not vomit upward or expel downward
Not even to save his life.
All one can say is that
Nature now has domination.

(*Canterbury Tales,*
General Prologue, I (A), 629–33;
Canterbury Tales,
"The Knight's Tale," I (A), 2743–58)

To ease childbirth, medieval medicine recommended rubbing the woman's thighs with oil of roses, providing her with a magnet to hold, or feeding her powdered ivory, vinegar and sugar, or eagle's dung. Headaches could be cured by drinking a potion of vinegar, honey, and southernwood or by grinding 10 peppercorns with vinegar and then drinking or placing against the cheek inside a cloth. For more persistent pain, headache could be cured by following this recipe:

> To take vinegar, wild thyme, royal,
> And chamomile and see the withal;
> And with the juice anoint the nostrils well
> And make a plaster of the other part
> And put it in a good great clout
> And wind your head therewith about. (Rickert, 82–83)

Finally, while medieval surgery was a generally painful and risky procedure, lacking modern surgical instruments and anesthesia, apothecaries could prepare,

> A sleeping ointment, with which if any man be anointed, he shall be able to bear cutting any part of the body without sensation or pain. Take juice of henbane, mandragora, water hemlock lettuce, poppy, both white and black, and the seeds of all the aforesaid herbs if they can be had in equal parts; Thebian opium and Meconium, 1 or 2 drams each; fresh swine's grease as needed. Crush all these well and strongly together in a mortar, and afterward boil them hard and then cool them. And if it be not thick enough, put in a little bee-bread, that is, white wax; and keep it for thy use.
>
> And when thou wilt use thereof, anoint his pulses, his temples, his armpits, and the palms of his hands and the soles of his feet, and very soon he shall sleep so that he shall feel no cutting. (Rickert, 178)

Herbal Medicine

For the most part, the late medieval pharmacy came from the garden. Not only was there little else to use, chemistry being not far advanced beyond alchemy, but there was a general acceptance that everything in nature held some sort of power. The most widely recognized theory governing the use of natural cures (as they comprised more than just herbs) was the Doctrine of Signatures. The theory behind the doctrine was *similia similibus curantor,* or "like cures like."

Medical professionals held that God or nature had imbued each potential curative with certain qualities that gave outward clues to what ailment it affected. Thus, yellow plants, like celandine or saffron, tended to be good for jaundice. Lilies were good for leprosy because their white petals referenced white skin. Similarly, mandrake when pulled was believed to cry like a baby. Therefore it was believed to be good for labor pains, menstrual cramps, and as an abortifacient. Additionally, certain cures were believed effective because of word sympathy. For instance, saxifrages were believed to break up bladder stones because the name means "stone breaking."

Plant lore, like so much of medieval medicine, was based on the writings and drawings of ancient authors, in particular Pliny's *Natural History.* For the most part, medieval authors simply copied ancient texts and integrated Christian overtones, and no interest was shown in empirically testing the claims made so many centuries before.

For instance, violets were used for a wide variety of ailments including headache, coughs, skin eruptions, hangover, and the expulsion of a stillbirth. Dill, besides being important culinarily, was used to cure indigestion, nausea, and flatulence, as well as for swellings and tumors. Quince was believed to cure throat infections, hoarseness, and eye inflammations, as well to stimulate the appetite and provide pregnant women with "diligent and quick-witted children." The herb rue was considered to be something of a miracle plant. It cured snakebites, nightmares, bad breath, and cats that kill chickens. It reduced fever, counteracted poison, and soothed eyes. In addition, it could be used to prevent plague and sexual urges. St. John's wort was good for dysentery, consumption, and depression, while hyssop was a useful expectorant as well as a cure for a weak stomach. In short, there was not a malady that could not be helped by something growing in the ground.

See also Black Death; Four Humors; Physician

FURTHER READING

French, Roger. *Canonical Medicine: Gentile da Foligno and Scholasticism.* Boston: Brill, 2001.

French, Roger, Jon Arrizabalaga, Andrew Cunningham, and Luis García-Ballester, eds. *Medicine from the Black Death to the French Disease.* Aldershot, England: Ashgate, 1998.

Gottfried, Robert S. *Doctors and Medicine in Medieval England, 1340–1530.* Princeton, NJ: Princeton University Press, 1986.

Hildegard of Bingen. *On Natural Philosophy and Medicine: Selections from "Case et Cure."* Translation and introduction by Margret Berger. Cambridge, England: D. S. Brewer, 1999.

Kibre, Pearl. *Studies in Medieval Science: Alchemy, Astrology, Mathematics, and Medicine.* London: Hambledon Press, 1984.

Rickert, Edith. *Chaucer's World,* ed. Clair C. Olson and Martin M. Crow. New York: Columbia University Press, 1948; reprint 1968.

Merchant

A MARCHANT was ther with a forked berd,
In mottelee, and hye on horse he sat.
Upon his heed a Flaundryssh bever hat,
His bootes clasped faire and fetisly.
His resons he spak ful solempnely,

Sownynge alwey th'encrees of hys wynnyng.

…

This worthy man ful wel his wit bisette;
Ther wiste no wight that he was in dette,
So estatly was he of his governaunce
With his bargaynes and with his chevyssaunce.
For sothe he was a worthy man with alle,
But, sooth to seyn, I noot how men hym calle.

There was a Merchant with a forked beard,
Dressed in motley, and sitting high on a fine horse.
He wore on his head a beaver hat made in Flanders,
And his boots were of the highest fashion.
He spoke about his opinions quite pompously,
Always concentrating on the profits he won through his work.
…

This worthy man was quite smart, always using his head;
There was nobody to whom he was in debt,
So careful was he and so noble in his appearance
And he went about talking about bargains and loans,
But, to be honest, I never did learn his name.

(*Canterbury Tales,*
General Prologue, I (A), 270–84)

Chaucer came from a mercantile background; his father was a London wine merchant. And young Geoffrey was, by virtue of education and talent, able to rise to an important position in the royal court. Thus, he was from the merchant class, but essentially outside of it.

This mixed background gave him a unique perspective on the position of merchants in fourteenth-century London. It enabled him to provide his audience in *The Canterbury Tales* with perhaps the first examples of middle-class merchants in English literature. There is not only the character of the Merchant, but a merchant is one of the main characters in "The Shipman's Tale." Even the Wife of Bath exists in a mercantile world, using her inheritances from past husbands as well as her body in trade for new marital connections.

London's merchant class was comprised of a very diverse population. There were many Italians, many of which lived near Chaucer's childhood home. It most likely was his exposure to them that enabled him to learn the fluent Italian that would benefit him in his career at court. While the foreign tradesmen were organized into associations according to their trades and nationality, the English merchants joined guilds. These were, like the associations of the foreigners, organized according to particular area of trade and carried dress requirements—livery—that created visual distinctions among merchants.

Chaucer describes the Merchant in terms that leave his character in question (*Canterbury Tales,* General Prologue, I (A), 270–84). He is dressed well and is apparently quite successful. We know that he does not put himself into debt. However, there is an ambivalence to the description—the fact that the only thing that seems to matter to him is profit—that makes him not seem like the most positive character.

Furthermore, his tale—in which a wealthy old man essentially purchases a young bride for himself—on initial response seems to support this negative point of view. However, the resolution of the tale, in which the man is made to look silly by his bride, who not only cuckolds him but outwits him as well, provides a more balanced view and a surprisingly modern attitude to marriage.

See also Business and Commerce; Money

FURTHER READING

Backman, Clifford R. *The Worlds of Medieval Europe.* New York: Oxford University Press, 2003.

Bisson, Lillian M. *Chaucer and the Late Medieval World.* New York: St. Martin's Press, 1998.

Boitani, Piero, and Jill Mann. *The Cambridge Chaucer Companion.* New York: Cambridge University Press, 1986.

Britnell, R. H. *The Commercialisation of English Society, 1000–1500.* 2nd ed. New York: Manchester University Press, 1996.

Brown, Peter, ed. *A Companion to Chaucer.* Malden, MA: Blackwell, 2002.

Dyer, Christopher. *Making a Living in the Middle Ages: The People of Britain 850–1520.* New Haven, CT: Yale University Press, 2002.

Frugoni, Chiara. *A Day in a Medieval City.* Introduction by Arsenio Frugoni. Translated by William McCuaig. Chicago: University of Chicago Press, 2005.

Le Goff, Jacques. *Medieval Callings.* Translated by Lydia G. Cochrane. Chicago: University of Chicago Press, 1980.

———. *Time, Work, and Culture in the Middle Ages.* Translated by Arthur Goldhammer. Chicago: University of Chicago Press, 1980.

Lerer, Seth, ed. *The Yale Companion to Chaucer.* New Haven, CT: Yale University Press, 2006.

Liddy, Christian D. *War, Politics and Finance in Late Medieval English Towns: Bristol, York and the Crown, 1350–1400.* Woodbridge, VT: Boydell Press, 2005.

Lilley, Keith D. *Urban Life in the Middle Ages, 1000–1450.* New York: Palgrave, 2002.

Masschaele, James. *Peasants, Merchants, and Markets: Inland Trade in Medieval England, 1150–1350.* New York: St. Martin's Press, 1997.

Nicholas, David. *The Growth of the Medieval City: From Late Antiquity to the Early Fourteenth Century.* New York: Longman, 1997.

———. *The Later Medieval City, 1300–1500.* New York: Longman, 1997.

———. *Urban Europe, 1100–1700.* New York: Palgrave Macmillan, 2003.

Miller

The MILLERE was a stout carl for the nones;
Ful byg he was of brawn, and eek of bones.
That proved wel, for over al ther he cam,
At wrastlynge he wolde have alwey the ram.
He was short-sholdred, brood, a thikke knarre;
Ther was no dore that he nolde heve of harre,
Or breke it at a rennyng with his heed.
His berd as any sowe or fox was reed,
And therto brood, as though it were a spade.
Upon the cop right of his nose he hade
A werte, and theron stood a toft of herys,
Reed as the brustles of a sowes erys;
His nosethirles blake were and wyde.

...

Wel koude he stelen corn and tollen thries;
And yet he hadde a thombe of gold, pardee.

The Miller was a husky man
All brawny and big boned
Who proved he was strong, for he always
Won the ram at wrestling.
He was short-shouldered, barrel-chested, and thick
There no door that he could not take off its hinges
Or break through by ramming it with his head.
His beard was as red as any sow or fox,
And very broad, like a spade.
On the end of his nose on the right he had
A wart which was topped by a tuft of hair,
Which was as red as the bristles in a sow's ears.
And his nosehairs were black and thick.
...

He was very good at stealing corn and tripling prices,
Oh, yes, he certainly did have a thumb of gold!

(*Canterbury Tales,*
General Prologue, I (A), 545–66)

Millers in Chaucer's time were objects of general suspicion. Not only were they untrustworthy, swindling their captive clients out of grain or flour, but they were also perceived to be political radicals. Operating literally on the fringes of society—at the outskirts of towns—in general isolation, mills were conversely also meeting places for the exchange of ideas, sometimes heretical ones.

The relative isolation sheltered them from prying eyes, making mills, and the millers who ran them, breeding grounds for seditious ideas. In the aftermath of the Peasant Revolt of 1381, several millers were hanged, an indication of the involvement of millers in dangerous political insurrection.

At the same time, millers maintained an adversarial relationship with the local peasants and, in popular perception, they were considered to be thieves and blackguards. The concept of the "golden thumb" was a common notion, the digit placed conveniently on the scale to make a shorted bag of flour weigh more (*Canterbury Tales*, General Prologue, I (A), 563). Tenants of a particular manor were required to use the local mill to grind their grain; the miller's monopoly on business meant that he was fairly free to cheat and otherwise abuse his clientele. Chaucer's Miller embodies these negative perceptions of medieval millers with his boorish behavior, ugly face, and aggressive attitude:

See also Business and Commerce; Estates; Heresy; Money

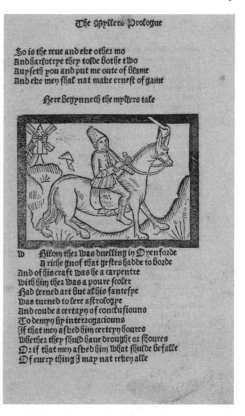

A woodcut of the Miller from a fifteenth-century edition of *The Canterbury Tales*. Courtesy of the Glasgow University Library.

FURTHER READING

Bisson, Lillian M. *Chaucer and the Late Medieval World*. New York: St. Martin's Press, 1998.

Brewer, Derek. *Chaucer and His World*. Cambridge, England: D. S. Brewer, 1978; reprinted 1992.

Britnell, R. H. *The Commercialisation of English Society, 1000–1500*. 2nd ed. New York: Manchester University Press, 1996.

Britnell, Richard, ed. *Daily Life in the Late Middle Ages*. Stroud, England: Sutton, 1998.

Brown, Peter, ed. *A Companion to Chaucer*. Malden, MA: Blackwell, 2002.

Dyer, Christopher. *Making a Living in the Middle Ages: The People of Britain 850–1520*. New Haven, CT: Yale University Press, 2002.

Gies, Frances, and Joseph Gies. *Cathedral, Forge, and Waterwheel*. New York: Harper Collins, 1994.

Monarchy

The system of monarchy was the primary political structure of medieval Europe. Meaning simply "rule by one," a monarchy invests power in a single individual—usually, by laws of primogeniture, the eldest son—who

Tomb of Henry IV at Canterury Cathedral. Courtesy of Lisa Kirchner.

The coronation of Edward III. Courtesy of the Dover Pictorial Archive.

derives power through birth into a ruling family. This system traces its roots to the earliest civilizations and would have been known to people of the Middle Ages through the Old Testament. However, the actual structures that dominated Europe during the medieval period were an amalgamation of the Roman system from the Empire and the structure of the Germanic tribes that succeeded it. From the Romans derived the notion of the king as ruler by divine right. His position was determined by religious means, providing a supernatural basis for his power and authority.

From the Germans came the importance of heredity in ruling, although the German interpretation did not include primogeniture. Germanic kings were chosen from a ruling family—however, it was of primary importance that the king be the best warrior. Therefore, if the next in line to inherit was a child or otherwise unfit to protect the people, a more worthy relative would be chosen to rule.

By the eighth-century rule of the Carolingians, the Roman notion of divine right was given an added layer of symbolism. Basing its validity in the Old Testament, kings in France were anointed with the same holy oil as bishops were at their consecrations. The crowning of a king was also conducted with an elaborate coronation ceremony, befitting the solemnity of the occasion. The idea of the coronation came to England's shores at the start of the tenth century, where it continues to be used today in nearly the same form.

By Chaucer's day, with the changing shape of society affecting the feudal structure, and the middle class gaining in influence and wealth, the monarchy was also undergoing a slow evolution to include the input of the Parliament in its decisions. Any attempts to move backward toward an earlier medieval concept of divine right absolutist kingship were viewed with suspicion and even violent hostility. Two obvious examples of this came during the reign of Richard II, when he was faced with Wat Tyler's Rebellion (the Peasant Revolt of 1381) and his own deposition.

See also Edward III; Estates; John of Gaunt; Peasant Revolt; Richard II

FURTHER READING

Bevan, Bryan. *Edward III: Monarch of Chivalry.* London: Rubicon Press, 1992.

Cantor, Norman. *The Encyclopedia of the Middle Ages.* New York: Viking Press, 1999.

Dunn, Alastair. *The Peasant's Revolt: England's Failed Revolution of 1381.* Stroud, England: Tempus, 2004.

Fraser, Antonia, ed. *The Lives of the Kings and Queens of England.* Rev. ed. Berkeley: University of California Press, 1998.

O'Brien, Mark. *When Adam Delved and Eve Span: A History of the Peasants' Revolt of 1381.* Cheltenham, England: New Clarion, 2004.

Usilton, Larry W. *The Kings of Medieval England, c. 560–1485: A Survey and Research Guide.* Lanham, MD: Scarecrow Press, 1996.

Money

While the use of coins has been a factor of commerce from the beginnings of human history, the extent of that usage has fluctuated wildly in response to economic and political changes in stability and structure. In the early centuries of the Middle Ages, until about the eleventh century, the supply of money in all of Europe was fairly limited, reflecting the low level of economic activity. The eleventh century, however, signaled a turning point, and from this century forward, the use of money became increasingly widespread.

The type of money that was used varied geographically and temporally. However, silver was the most common metal in use everywhere, with gold reserved for the coinage of greatest value. Values were based on the actual weight of the metal, so a larger or thicker coin was worth more. Smaller and thinner coins were more susceptible to coin cropping, a practice that involved cutting small bits from the edges of a coin to save them. Once an ample supply of silver was set aside, one could use the raw silver in trade. This practice dwindled as official coins became the standard for transactions. It was simply too difficult and too complicated to try to weigh a quantity of silver to make a purchase.

Fourteenth century			
Silver	farthing (q)	¼ penny	1 loaf of bread
	halfpenny (ob)	½ penny	1 gallon of small ale
	penny (d)	20 grams	1 pound of butter
			90 percent pure silver
	half-groat	2d	1 day wages for unskilled laborer
	groat	4d	1 day wages for skilled laborer
	shilling (s)	12d	1 day wages for gentleman
Gold	quarter-noble	1s 8d	1 pound of sugar or spice
	half-noble	3s 4d	1 year rent, 1 floor in town-house
	noble	6s 8d	1 day earnings for lord
Moneys of	mark (marc)	13s 4d	
Account	pound (li)	20s	1 carthorse

See also Business and Commerce; Merchant

FURTHER READING
Backman, Clifford R. *The Worlds of Medieval Europe*. New York: Oxford University Press, 2003.
Bisson, Lillian M. *Chaucer and the Late Medieval World*. New York: St. Martin's Press, 1998.
Boitani, Piero, and Jill Mann. *The Cambridge Chaucer Companion*. New York: Cambridge University Press, 1986.
Britnell, R. H. *The Commercialisation of English Society, 1000–1500*. 2nd ed. New York: Manchester University Press, 1996.
Brown, Peter, ed. *A Companion to Chaucer*. Malden, MA: Blackwell, 2002.
Dyer, Christopher. *Making a Living in the Middle Ages: The People of Britain 850–1520*. New Haven, CT: Yale University Press, 2002.
Le Goff, Jacques. *Time, Work, and Culture in the Middle Ages*. Translated by Arthur Goldhammer. Chicago: University of Chicago Press, 1980.
Lerer, Seth, ed. *The Yale Companion to Chaucer*. New Haven, CT: Yale University Press, 2006.
Masschaele, James. *Peasants, Merchants, and Markets: Inland Trade in Medieval England, 1150–1350*. New York: St. Martin's Press, 1997.

Monk

He was a lord ful fat and in good poynt;
His eyen stepe, and rollynge in his heed,
That stemed as a forneys of a leed;

His bootes souple, his hors in greet estaat.
Now certeinly he was a fair prelaat;
He was nat pale as a forpyned goost.
A fat swan loved he best of any roost.

He was a lord all well-fed and in peak condition;
His eyes sparkled and roved about,
As lively as a pot on the boil.
His boots were of supple leather and his horse was of the finest.
Now certainly he was an outstandingly fine prelate.
He was not all pale like a tormented ghost.
And a fat swan was his favorite among any kind of roasted meat.

(*Canterbury Tales,*
General Prologue, I (A), 200–207)

Besides the parish church, monasteries comprised the other form of local Church presence. Designed to enable those who devoted their lives to God to live secluded from the secular world but within communities, monasteries and convents became the alternative to eremitical monasticism, which was based on the solitary life of the hermit and dominated early Church history. The earliest model of true spirituality was of the martyr who died for the faith. As Christianity gained followers and political clout in the third century, the new model was of a monk who died to the secular world, achieving spiritual life through denial, asceticism, and mystical experience.

Early monks, however, were unable to live in total solitude because they became victims of their own holy reputations, attracting followers who sought to learn truth at their feet. Cenobitic monasticism, based on the practice of communal life, soon succeeded eremitic as the dominant form. St. Pachomius (c. 290–346) was the founder of this practice and wrote the first rule for monastic life, emphasizing obedience and manual labor.

In theory, the ideal of communal spiritual life was easy, but in practice monks often fell away from the model. In the sixth century, monasticism underwent a revitalization and rededication thanks to St. Benedict of Nursia (c. 480–c. 543), who wrote what became the guidebook that dominated medieval monastic life for centuries, *The Rule* (*Canterbury Tales,* General Prologue, I (A), 173–76). Like Pachomius, Benedict emphasized obedience to both the abbot (who governed the monastery) and God, as well as hard work, poverty, chastity, and discipline. Monks were restricted in what they could wear, how much they could eat and drink, how much they could talk, and how their day's activities would be structured. Despite the tight control the Rule had over brothers, by the early twelfth century, the monastic ideal had again faltered, in part because of the role monasteries played in the feudal hierarchy. This time, rededication was accomplished by St. Bernard of Clairvaux, founder of the Cistercian order.

While Bernard's Cistericians played a crucial role in the spiritual life of the high Middle Ages, by Chaucer's time, popular opinion of monks was at an ebb. The general questioning of the Church that followed the Black Death focused just as harshly on monastic life, which was considered to be dangerously lax and too worldly. Monks were expected to devote their lives to silent contemplation of God, except when praying during the canonical hours of matins (midnight), lauds (3 A.M.), prime (6 A.M.), terce (9 A.M.), sext (noon), none (3 P.M.), and vespers (6 P.M. or sunset). They were expected to observe vows of poverty and chastity, to eschew gluttony, to promote learning through the copying and preservation of manuscripts, and to generally provide an exemplar of spiritual devotion.

The proverb "The cowl does not make the monk" dates to the late fourteenth century and aptly sums up the problems the cenobitic ideal faced during Chaucer's time. Like the Church in general, monasteries were accused of being too concerned with wealth, a difficult vice to avoid when so many nobles endowed monasteries with funds and building projects to ensure their place in heaven. Although the feudal system was in decline, monasteries were still large landholders and were thus embroiled in the essentially unmonastic task of providing fighting men for battle as well as acting as landlords and managing the operation of connected villages. These tasks alone interfered considerably with time and attention that was supposed to be devoted to spiritual contemplation. Finally, monks were rather notorious for large appetites—for food, drink, and women.

Not only is Chaucer's Monk guilty of these deviations from the ideal, but the monk Daun John of "The Merchant's Tale" is an abysmal example of monastic devotion, cuckolding his best friend and managing a financial swindle of massive proportions. He borrows money from his friend, then loans it to the wife, taking sexual favors as interest. When his friend asks for the money to be returned, John insists he has given it to the wife, who now must hide her adultery and pay back the cash now spent by fulfilling her marital duties with her husband.

Not every monk was tempted by the pleasures of the flesh, but the fact remains that many monks found themselves within the cloistered walls because of a sense of familial duty rather than a deep spiritual calling.

See also Estates; Parson; Prioress; Religion

FURTHER READING

Biller, Peter, and Barrie Dobson, eds. *The Medieval Church: Universities, Heresy, and the Religious Life: Essays in Honour of Gordon Leff.* Rochester, NY: Boydell Press, 1999.

Blumenfeld-Kosinski, Renate. *Poets, Saints, and Visionaries of the Great Schism, 1378–1417.* University Park: Pennsylvania State University Press, 2006.

Foster, Edward E., and David H. Carey, eds. *Chaucer's Church: A Dictionary of Religious Terms in Chaucer.* Brookfield, VT: Ashgate, 2002.

Morocco

In Gernade at the seege eek hadde he be
Of Algezir, and ridden in Belmarye.

In Grenada he had been at the siege
Of Algeciras, and had ridden in Morocco.

(*Canterbury Tales,*
General Prologue, I (A), 56–57)

Chaucer seems to have confused the name of the Marinids (also known as the Banu Marin), the Berber dynasty who ruled Morocco with the name of the country itself. The Marinids established themselves in eastern Morocco in 1248 and conducted a *jihad* into Spain for the next hundred years. The fact that the Knight is said to have campaigned there would indicate that he was operating as a mercenary in the employ of the Spanish monarchy.

See also Knight

FURTHER READING

Cantor, Norman. *The Civilization of the Middle Ages.* Rev. ed. New York: Harper Collins, 1993.

Jones, Terry. *Chaucer's Knight: The Portrait of a Medieval Mercenary.* Baton Rouge: Louisiana State University Press, 1980.

Kaeuper, Richard W. *Chivalry and Violence in Medieval Europe.* New York: Oxford University Press, 1999.

Labarge, Margaret Wade. *Medieval Travellers.* New York: Norton, 1983.

Le Beau, Bryan F., and Menachem Mor, eds. *Pilgrims and Travelers to the Holy Land.* Omaha, NE: Creighton University Press, 1996.

Tyerman, Christopher. *England and the Crusades, 1095–1588.* Chicago: University of Chicago Press, 1988.

Verdon, Jean. *Travel in the Middle Ages.* Notre Dame, IN: University of Notre Dame Press, 2003.

Music

And right anon thanne comen tombesteres
Fetys and smale, and yonge frutesteres,
Syngeres with harpes, baudes, wafereres,
Whiche been the verray develes officeres
To kyndle and blowe the fyr of lecherye,
That is annexed unto glotonye.

> *And then there come the dancing girls,*
> *Small and nimble; and the fruitsellers,*
> *The singers with harps, whose and wayfarers,*
> *Which have been the very devil's officers*
> *To kindle and fan the flames of lechery*
> *Which is annexed onto gluttony.*

> (*Canterbury Tales,*
> "The Pardoner's Tale," VI (C), 477–82)

Although music was perhaps the most popular and widely available pastime of the Middle Ages, much of it has been lost or was never written down. The majority of what has been left behind is church music, as popular tunes were almost never recorded. Even with what survives, we can only guess at how it actually sounded. Differences in inflections, grace notes, mood, and tone all would change the medieval interpretation of a song from our own modern version.

However, we do know that music was very important in the Middle Ages. It was the centerpiece of religious and state ceremonies, village celebrations, and other public events. It was likely enjoyed in private homes, when sundown rendered most other forms of entertainment impossible. It was a constant part of court life, where professional musicians were employed to entertain during banquets, meals, and other occasions when background music was desired. Finally, it was an accompaniment to other entertainments, such as plays or poetry readings.

As an intellectual pursuit, music was included in the quadrivium as one of the seven liberal arts. While it was considered to be the mark of a cultured man to be able to play and sing, as well as write poetry, music in the university was also studied as a branch of arithmetic. The logical structure of a song and the mathematical precision of intervals between notes reflected the logic and harmony of the universe, revealing the emphasis on humanism that was so important in Chaucer's day.

It was believed that God structured the universe to operate in a precise fashion, with the nine spheres controlling the

A sheet of music dating from the late fourteenth century. © Bibliothèque nationale de France.

movement of planets, which in turn controlled, or at least greatly shaped, events on Earth. The music of the spheres, inaudible to human ears yet completely real, was evidence of this motion and harmony. Here on Earth, the fact that music fell into such clearly logical and mathematical patterns was proof that the mysteries of the universe were knowable. Therefore, we find in the structure of much medieval music, particularly of a religious nature, a concentration on the creation of harmonies rather than on melody flow or ease of performance.

Catholics, Jews, and Muslims all included music in their religious services. The best known and earliest examples of Christian sacred music are the Gregorian chants, which are still used today as part of the Catholic liturgy. These chants, claimed by Gregory the Great to have been transmitted directly from God, combine Latin scripture with melodies created with about

An early sixteenth-century illustration of a man playing bagpipes, by Albrecht Durer. Courtesy of the Library of Congress.

half a dozen notes and simple rhythm patterns, all sung a cappella. Over time, Catholic music gained complexity, adding harmony, dissonance, and instruments.

Around the twelfth century, experimentation began that would eventually result in the birth of medieval polyphony. It was also around this time that musical notations began to be systematically recorded, providing us with a fairly complete record of the growth and development of sacred music. By the fifteenth century, popular music would also be more commonly notated.

During the twelfth century, beginning with a plainchant melody, such as one of the Gregorian chants, a composer would add a second identical line an octave lower or higher. This produced a richer, fuller sound, much like what is achieved with a 12-string guitar.

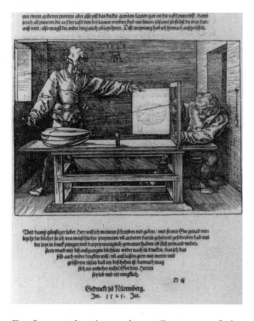

Draftsmen drawing a lute. Courtesy of the Library of Congress.

To this, composers began to experiment with harmonies by employing mathematical structure. A note would be added a third or a fifth away from the starting note, creating a simple chord. This would be performed by voices, a cappella, or by instruments, and, eventually, both. Once harmony was an integral part of sacred music, it did not take long for it to spread to secular music as well, as it provided for endless and beautiful possibilities in the interpretation of a simple starting tune.

While the Church officially frowned upon popular music, it would be the individual clergy, through their love of a good song and dance, who would transmit the ideas of sacred composers to secular music, making the latter more complex and, ultimately, providing it with the means to be preserved for posterity.

Although all levels of society enjoyed secular music, the nobility, by virtue of their wealth and position, were able to do the most to make it important. Often nobles performed music themselves, because music was not only part of the liberal arts life-style, but being able to sing and play were components of being a well-rounded gentleman or lady. Others employed professional musicians, jongleurs, and minstrels, who lived at their courts and performed at all special occasions.

Lower on the social scale, peasants and townspeople enjoyed music in many different forms. They often played and sang for themselves; singing was the cheapest form of musical entertainment. They were also exposed to the professional music of wandering minstrels, who performed a variety of acts including acrobatics and juggling.

Minstrels played a key role in the musical life of the Middle Ages. They spanned many social worlds, performing for royalty and serf alike. They carried tunes, as well as new techniques and ideas, to new places through their travels. The music they performed covered a wide range of subjects, many of them risqué, ranging from drinking to gambling to sex to love affairs, religion, money, or politics.

Female minstrels were not unknown. In fact, there is a record of a woman at Edward II's court in 1316 who was described as being "in the habit of a Minstrel, riding on a great horse, trapped in the minstrel fashion" and who circled the tables then mounted the dais to deliver a petition to the king. His brothers kept a minstrel called Matilda Makejoye in their household.

When a minstrel was employed by a noble, the salary and benefits, so to speak, were substantial for a performance artist. The minstrel received regular payment, plus bonuses for special appearances and travel. In addition, food and clothing, as well as horses, were generally covered by the lord, who would also pay for the purchase and upkeep of the minstrel's instruments. Minstrels also organized themselves into guilds, although this was far more popular on the Continent than it ever was in England. In fact, the only known English example of a minstrels' guild in the fourteenth century is from Tutbury, where John of Gaunt had a castle.

During Lent, the playing of music was strictly forbidden by the Church, leaving minstrels with little to do to earn their living. Therefore, many of them would attend special minstrel schools where they would learn new songs and playing techniques, various tricks such as jumping through hoops and juggling knives, as well as search for and recruit new assistants. There were even specialty schools for specific instruments where minstrels would go in order to master that particular instrument.

While singing was free and easiest to master, the use of instruments was, of course, quite desirable and popular among players and audiences. Early in the Middle Ages, instruments faced Church disapproval, because they were associated with pagan rituals. However, over time, they gained further acceptance and with that, greater varieties came into use.

Horns, drums, and some stringed instruments were used in the early centuries of the Middle Ages, but after the Crusades, more Middle Eastern instruments were imported, such as the lute. Other instruments were developed from Middle Eastern patterns, such as the flute, the bagpipes, and the psaltery. In the tenth century, organs that were operated by a system of levers were introduced and, before long, became a central part of church services.

Instruments generally were divided into two categories. There were the haut—the loud instruments that were played by heralds and waits and could be heard above just about any din. These instruments included the trumpet, nakers, and the shawm. The bas, or soft instruments, were for more intimate, indoor settings, and included string instruments such as the fiddle, harp, gittern, lute, and psaltery. Most popular in folk music were the pipe and tabor, which enabled a musician to create simultaneous melody and rhythm. The pipe and tabor consisted of a three-hold recorder that was played with the left hand while the right beat the tabor, or drum. The bagpipes were popular for outdoor use as they were very loud and therefore easy to hear while dancing. On the quieter end was the shawm, which was the ancestor of the oboe, although made with a double reed. By Chaucer's day, there were some instruments that were considered old fashioned, such as the quadrangular harp known as the rote, or the crowd (or crwyth), which was a small lyre used by the Welsh.

There was a wide variety of string instruments in the Middle Ages. The psaltery consisted of a triangular box with metal strings across it. It was played on the knees or across the chest and could be played with a bow or, more typically, plucked with a pick. The psaltery seems to have been the forerunner of the hammer dulcimer. The harp of the fourteenth century was small so it could be hung from the neck or placed on the knee. It had fewer than 20 gut strings. The lute, which had been brought from the Middle East, had a rounded back, a short neck, a bent peg box, and frets. It had gut strings that could be plucked to create a single-line melody. The gittern, although its name sounds like guitar, more closely resembled the mandolin in that it was plucked and was essentially a smaller version of the lute.

The citole, on the other had, seems to be the forerunner of the modern guitar. It was roughly the size of a modern guitar and was played like one. The citole had frets and metal strings and was played with a quill pick. The fiddle, the forerunner of the modern violin or viola, most resembled the latter in size. It had four or five gut strings which were tuned in an unusual fashion. The top two were in unison, while the bottom two were tuned to the fifth. The flat bridge caused them all to sound in unison.

The forerunners to keyboard instruments were more limited. The organ, as already mentioned, used levers in its earliest stages. Later, it was adapted for the streets to be played with the right hand on a keyboard while the left hand pumped a bellows. The hurdy-gurdy, which was quite popular in street music, required one hand to turn a wheel against the four strings. The general effect was to produce a droning sound that could be stopped abruptly with the use of the other hand, which operated tabs or keys that stopped the top string. The clavichord was similar to the organ and used keys to stop and strike strings.

It is not clear whether Chaucer ever made music himself, and there is no direct evidence that his works were set to music. However, in the Retraction to *The Canterbury Tales* he asks for forgiveness for "many a song and many a lecherous lay," implying that there are such songs to be forgiven for. Whatever the case might be, Chaucer certainly makes many references to music in all of his works, and, judging from the enthusiasm of his examples, he obviously appreciated music. In the General Prologue, we learn that the Miller "A baggepipe wel koude he blowe and sowne" (*he could well play and sound a bagpipe*) and the Squire "koude songes make and wel endite, / Juste and eek daunce, and weel portreye and write" (*could songs make and well perform / and dance, and write and recite poetry*) (*Canterbury Tales,* General Prologue, I (A), 565, 95–96). Chaucer tells us of the Friar:

Somwhat he lipsed, for his wantownesse,
To make his Englissh sweete upon his tonge;
And in his harpyng, whan that he hadde songe
His eyen twynkled in his heed aryght
As doon the sterres in the frosty nyght.

He lisped somewhat, in his strong desire
To make his English sound sweeter upon his tongue;

And when he harped, and was playing a song
His eyes twinkled in his head
Just like the stars twinkling on a frosty night.

(*Canterbury Tales,*
General Prologue, I (A), 264–68)

The harp also appears in *Troilus and Criseyde.* In "The Miller's Tale," both of Alison's suitors, Nicholas and Absolom, play instruments. Absolom plays the gittern, which he uses to woo Alison, while Nicholas plays the psaltery:

And Absolon his gyterne hath ytake
For paramours he thoghte for to wake.
…

And al above ther lay a gay sautrie,
On which he made a-nyghtes melodie
So swetely that all the chambre rong;
And *Angelus ad virginem* he song;
And after that he song the Kynges Noote.
Ful often blessed was his myrie throte.

And Absolon took his cittern
To play for the paramours he thought to woo.
…

And above all there was a gay psaltery
Upon which he would make a melody at night
So sweetly that his chamber rung with the sound
With Angelus ad virginem which he sang.
And after he sang the King's Note
His mighty throat was well blessed.

(*Canterbury Tales,*
"The Miller's Tale," I (A), 3353–54, 3213–18)

In "The Manciple's Tale," Phoebus plays a number of instruments, and Chauntecleer of "The Nun's Priest's Tale" loves to sing to greet the morning. In the brief "Cook's Tale," we learn that Perkyn "Dauncen he koude so wel and jolily / That he was cleped Perkyn Revelour…. / Al konne he pleye on gyterne or ribible" (*He could dance so well and merrily / that he was nicknamed Perkyn the Reveller…. / And well could he play on the cittern or ribible*) (*Canterbury Tales,* "The Cook's Tale," I (A), 4370–71, 4396). Perkyn is a low character and his love of music is mirrored by the low types who play music in "The Pardoner's Tale":

In Flaundres whilom was a compaignye
Of yonge folk that haunteden folye,
As riot, hasard, stywes, and taverns,
Where as with harpes, lutes, and gyternes,
They daunce and pleyen at dees bothe day and nyght,
And eten also and drynken over hir myght
Thurgh which they doon the devel sacrifise
Withinne that develes temple in cursed wise
By superfluytee abhomynable.

In Flanders there was a group
Of young folk who courted folly,
In the form of gambling, dicing, brothels, and taverns,
And they danced and played all day and night
To the sounds of harps, lutes, and gitterns,
While they ate and drank with all their might.
They offered the devil their sacrifices
In the devil's cursed temples
With these abominable excesses.

(*Canterbury Tales,*
"The Pardoner's Tale," VI (C), 463–71)

Finally, "The Knight's Tale" and *The House of Fame* contain extended descriptions of musical performance.

See also Daily Life; Entertainment; Religion

FURTHER READING

Holsinger, Bruce W. *Music, Body, and Desire in Medieval Culture: Hildegard of Bingen to Chaucer.* Stanford, CA: Stanford University Press, 2001.

Smoldon, William L. *The Music of the Medieval Church Dramas.* Edited by Cynthia Bourgeault. New York: Oxford University Press, 1980.

Wilkins, Nigel E. *Music in the Age of Chaucer.* Totowa, NJ: Rowman and Littlefield, 1979.

N

Names

As with clothing and hairstyles, names enjoy periods of fashionableness before they fall into disuse, only to be rediscovered again. During Chaucer's day, certain names were in fashion for new babies, most of which remain popular today. Often the name of the current rulers would be adopted (although the constant popularity of John is not accounted for by the very unpopular King John). The names of saints or apostles were also perennial favorites. And, of course, thanks to the growing popularity of literature and tales of brave knights and beautiful damsels—in particular, the legends of the Knights of the Round Table—knights and famous heroes and heroines of old were popular in Chaucer's day.

By the fourteenth century, surnames had become regularized, which had not been the case in earlier centuries. Often it was enough to identify someone as Hugh, son of Andrew—which, of course, is the origin of Norse names such as Andersson, Magnusson, and Eriksson. "Fitz" plus the father's name denoted the illegitimate children of royalty. Thus, the bastard son of Hugh Despenser would be called Edward Fitz Hugh. Otherwise, people were named by their professions. Roger Cooper would be a barrel maker. Adam Brewer most likely made beer.

Below are some of the more popular names during Chaucer's day and their meanings. While most peasants probably did not understand the origins of what they named their children, it is interesting to note how many boys' names have meanings related to protection and strength. Also, given the popularity of the cult of the virgin it is surprising that the name Mary was not more popular.

Boys' Names

Adam: From Hebrew, meaning "man of God" or "man of the earth"
Alan: Of Celtic/Gaelic origin, meaning "handsome"
Alexander: Greek, meaning "protector of mankind"
Andrew: Of Greek origin, meaning "manly" or "courageous"
Bartholomew: Hebrew, meaning "son of Tolmai"
Brian: From Gaelic, meaning "strong one"
Conan: Of Gaelic origin, meaning "wise"
Daniel: From Hebrew, meaning "God is my judge"
David: Hebrew, meaning "beloved"
Edmund: From Anglo-Saxon, meaning "protector"
Edward: From Anglo-Saxon, meaning "wealthy guardian." Very popular in Chaucer's day because of the Black Prince and the King.
Henry: Of German origin, meaning "ruler of the home"
Hugh: From German, meaning "bright in mind and spirit"
James: Of Hebrew origin, meaning "supplanter"
John: From Hebrew, meaning "God is gracious." Anywhere from one-third to one-half of the English male population was named John or some derivative of it, such as Jack.
Joseph: From Hebrew, meaning "God will increase"
Matthew: Of Hebrew origin, meaning "God's gift"
Nicholas: From Greek, meaning "victorious people"
Peter: Of Greek origin, meaning "a rock"
Philip: From Greek, meaning "lover of horses"
Richard: Of Anglo-Saxon origin, meaning "powerful rich ruler"
Robert: Of Anglo-Saxon origin, meaning "bright fame"
Roger: From German, meaning "fame spear"
Simon: From Hebrew, meaning "it is heard"
Stephen: Of Greek origin, meaning "crowned one"
Thomas: From Greek, meaning "a twin"
Tristan: Of Gaelic origin, meaning "bold and melancholy"
Walter: From German, meaning "army general"
William: From Anglo-Saxon, meaning "protector"

Girls' Names

Agnes: From Greek, meaning "pure"
Alice/Alison: From Greek, meaning "truth, noble"
Annice: An Anglo-Saxon derivative of Agnes
Beatrice: From French, meaning "bringer of joy"
Cecily: Of Gaelic origin, meaning "blind"
Elizabeth: From Hebrew, meaning "consecrated to God"

Emma/Emily: Of Latin origin, meaning "universal"
Isabel: The Spanish version of Elizabeth
Joan: Of Latin origin, meaning "God is good"
Katherine: From Greek, meaning "pure, virginal"
Lucy: From Latin, meaning "bringer of light"
Margaret: Of Latin origin, meaning "a pearl"
Maud: From German, meaning "strength in battle"
Rose: Of Greek origin, from the flower
Sarah: From Hebrew, meaning "princess"

Narcissus

Narcissus was the beautiful son of the river god Cephisus and a nymph named Liriope. Narcissus, because of his exquisite looks, was loved by many but was indifferent to affection. He famously rejected the affections of Echo, who pined away to nothing but a voice. Nemesis, the goddess who punished arrogant lovers for their prideful and selfish natures, made him fall in love with himself. Narcissus died while staring at his reflection in a pool, unable to satisfy his longing. Beautiful flowers sprang up in the spot where he died.

Narcissus admiring his reflection, ca. 1490–1500. Manuscript illustration from *Roman de la Rose* (*The Story of the Rose*) by Guillaume de Lorris and Jean de Meun. © HIP / Art Resource, NY.

And Ecquo died for Narcisus
Nolde nat love hir, and right thus
Hath many another foly doon.

And Echo died for love of Narcissus,
Who did not love her back, and so you see
How many a folly leads to another.

(*Book of the Duchess*, 735–37)

See also Echo

FURTHER READING

Brown, Peter, ed. *A Companion to Chaucer.* Malden, MA: Blackwell, 2002.
Frye, Northrop. *Biblical and Classical Myths: The Mythological Framework of Western Culture.* Buffalo, NY: University of Toronto Press, 2004.
Hansen, William F. *Classical Mythology: A Guide to the Mythical World of the Greeks and Romans.* New York: Oxford University Press, 2005.

Manser, Martin H. *The Facts On File Dictionary of Classical and Biblical Allusions*. New York: Facts On File, 2003.

Morford, Mark P. O. *Classical Mythology*. 7th ed. New York: Oxford University Press, 2003.

Nolan, Barbara. *Chaucer and the Tradition of the Roman Antique*. New York: Cambridge University Press, 1992.

Powell, Barry B. *Classical Myth*. Translated by Herbert M. Howe. 4th ed. Upper Saddle River, NJ: Pearson/Prentice Hall, 2004.

Price, Simon, and Emily Kearns, eds. *The Oxford Dictionary of Classical Myth and Religion*. New York: Oxford University Press, 2003.

Nun

Much like monasteries, convents were designed to provide an opportunity—in this case for women—to live a spiritual ideal in a community. The first convent was founded by the sister of St. Pachomius (c. 290–346) in 320. It was governed by Pachomius, but kept very separate from the

Artémise II depicted as a nun. © Bibliothèque nationale de France.

monastery. Because of a strong emphasis on protecting women, the double model of brother and sister communities became quite common. Typically, the brothers of the monastery would see to the sisters' material needs, but they were strictly cloistered away from one another to prevent any unnecessary temptation.

Like monks, nuns lived together under the direction of a superior, in this case an abbess or prioress. They followed the same spiritual schedule of prayer and mass, getting up several times during the night to follow the canonical hours. Obedience and hard work were also emphasized; however, while for monks labor involved heavier field work as well as the scholarly pursuit of translation and transcription, for nuns work more frequently involved gardening, weaving, spinning, and embroidery. Nuns were required to eschew vanity, wearing habits that covered their closely cropped heads and all but the oval of their faces.

The monastic ideal suffered the same inconsistencies in convents as it did in monasteries, although women were more closely cloistered than men and therefore less exposed to the outside world. Nuns also experienced different kinds of challenges and criticisms because of the Church's generally negative opinion of women.

Rather than being too worldly in their involvement with feudal concerns and wealth, nuns were often criticized for falling prey to vanity, much like Chaucer's Prioress. In all fairness, choices for women were generally limited to either marriage or the cloister. For those who lacked a religious calling but whose parents had made a promise to dedicate a child to the church or who simply lacked marital prospects, a lifetime behind the walls of the convent was the only option.

See also Monk; Prioress; Religion

FURTHER READING

Biller, Peter, and Barrie Dobson, eds. *The Medieval Church: Universities, Heresy, and the Religious Life: Essays in Honour of Gordon Leff.* Rochester, NY: Boydell Press, 1999.

Blumenfeld-Kosinski, Renate. *Poets, Saints, and Visionaries of the Great Schism, 1378–1417.* University Park: Pennsylvania State University Press, 2006.

Foster, Edward E., and David H. Carey, eds. *Chaucer's Church: A Dictionary of Religious Terms in Chaucer.* Brookfield, VT: Ashgate, 2002.

Raguin, Virginia Chieffo, and Sarah Stanbury, eds. *Women's Space: Patronage, Place, and Gender in the Medieval Church.* Albany: State University of New York Press, 2005.

P

Pardoner

His wallet, biforn hym in his lappe,
Bretful of pardoun comen from Rome al hoot.
...

But of his craft, fro Berwyk into Ware
Ne was ther swich another pardoner.
For in his male he hadde a pilwe-beer,
Which that he seyde was Oure Lady veyl;
He seyde he hadde a gobet of the seyl
That Seint Peter hadde, whan that he wente
Upon the see, til Jhesu Crist hym hente.
He hadde a croys of latoun ful of stones,
And in a glas he hadde pigges bones.
But with thise relikes, whan that he fond
A povre person dwellynge upon lond,
Upon a day he gat hym moore moneye
Than that the person gat in monthes tweye;
And thus, with feyned flaterye and japes,
He made the person and the peple his apes.

He had his knap-sack in front of him on his lap
Full of pardons that had come from Rome.
…

But for his trade, from Berwick to Ware
There was not another such pardoner
For in his bag he had a pillow-case
That he said was actually Our Lady's veil;
He said he also had a portion of the sail
That Saint Peter had when he went
Upon the sea, until Jesus Christ found him.
He had a cross of brass, set with stones,
And in a glass he had pig's bones.
With these "relics" when he found a
Poor person dwelling in the country
In that day he'd make more money
Than the parson was likely to make in two months;
Thus with feigned flattery and trickery,
He made the parson and people his apes.

(*Canterbury Tales,*
General Prologue, I (A), 686–706)

A pardoner held an especially important position in the Church in terms of marketing, because he was responsible for raising money by selling papal indulgences. Indulgences were cash donations that granted to the donor a reprieve from penance and a lessening of time in Purgatory. As such, the pardoner not only was a major conduit of important income for the Church, but also was an integral part of the salvation process for parishioners.

A woodcut of the Pardoner from a fifteenth-century edition of *The Canterbury Tales.* Courtesy of the Glasgow University Library.

The nature of the job, however, also lent itself quite easily to fraud and exploitation, as Chaucer's Pardoner demonstrates. He is an unsavory character who carries fake relics to dupe the faithful, not merely by displaying them, but by selling them if he is given the opportunity. He is also in the habit of pocketing the donations of penitents, in effect lining his own purse with the souls of the faithful (*Canterbury Tales,* General Prologue, I (A), 669–714). He works at Rouncivale hospital, which was particularly known for selling indulgences and had been associated multiple times with fraudulent documents.

Catholic legislation seems to bear out the sad fact that the Pardoner was not an anomaly, but a justifiable stereotype. Catholic Church Councils of 1348, 1368, and 1374 declared the following:

Because questors of alms (pardoners) in their preaching advocate many evil practices by which they often deceive the simple-minded and because they distort that which is good by their subtle and fraudulent character and at the same time do much evil through their manifold deceptions, we have determined and do ordain that no pardoners whatever be permitted without letters of their archbishop to their bishop; and that the welfare of souls may the more carefully be provided for, we rule that the words of this decree be inserted in their letters.... Priests who, by any other than the aforesaid way, voluntarily and knowingly permit pardoners to preach are *ipso facto* prohibited for a year from celebrating masses; and the pardoners themselves who attempt to contravene this decree are *ipso facto* excommunicated. If for 40 days they persist in their course, they may, at the command of the bishop, be seized and imprisoned, until such time as their case may otherwise be disposed of by the local diocesan. (Rickert, 379)

Pardoners came under criticism as well because indulgences themselves were increasingly viewed as buying salvation. The situation was compounded by the growing suspicion that pardoners sold counterfeit indulgences by forging the pope's signature. The Pardoner personifies all of the feared vices of illegitimate pardoners: questionable indulgences, which he attempts to sell to the other pilgrims; an open admission of a lack of faith; false relics; and a tale that essentially sums up the very vices he practices.

See also Indulgences; Religion

FURTHER READING

DeWindt, Edwin Brezette, ed. *The Salt of Common Life: Individuality and Choice in the Medieval Town, Countryside, and Church: Essays Presented to J. Ambrose Raftis.* Kalamazoo: Medieval Institute Publications, Western Michigan University, 1995.

Foster, Edward E., and David H. Carey, eds. *Chaucer's Church: A Dictionary of Religious Terms in Chaucer.* Brookfield, VT: Ashgate, 2002.

Needham, Paul. *The Printer & the Pardoner: An Unrecorded Indulgence Printed by William Caxton for the Hospital of St. Mary Rounceval, Charing Cross.* Washington, DC: Library of Congress, 1986.

Rickert, Edith. *Chaucer's World,* ed. Clair Olson and Martin M. Crow. New York: Columbia University Press, 1948; reprint 1968.

Slater, T. R., and Gervase Rosser, eds. *The Church in the Medieval Town.* Brookfield, VT: Ashgate, 1998.

Thomson, John A. F. *Popes and Princes, 1417–1517: Politics and Polity in the Late Medieval Church.* Boston: Allen & Unwin, 1980.

Parson

A good man was ther of religioun,
And was a povre PERSOUN OF A TOUN,
But riche he was of hooly thoght and werk.

He was also a lerned man, a clerk,
That Cristes gospel trewely wolde preche;
His parisshens devoutly wolde he teche.
Benyngne he was, and wonder diligent,
And in adversitee ful pacient,
And swich he was ypreved ofte sithes.
Ful looth were hym to cursen for his tithes,
But rather wolde he yeven, out of doute,
Uunto his povre parisshens aboute
Of his offryng and eek of his substaunce.

A good man there was of religion
Who was a poor Parson of a Town,
But he was rich instead in holy thoughts and work.
He was also a learned man, a clerk,
And would truly preach Christ's gospel;
His parishioners he was dedicated to teaching.
He was quite benign and wonderfully diligent,
And patient in the face of adversity,
For which quality he was quite often praised.
He would not excommunicate when his parishioners couldn't pay their tithes,
But would rather pay them himself, out of doubt,
In order to protect his flock.

(*Canterbury Tales,*
General Prologue, I (A), 478–528)

A parson was, quite simply, a parish priest. In this capacity, the parson was the most important spiritual presence in the life of the typical peasant. He administered sacraments, including baptisms, weddings, and last rites; held mass; visited the sick; and took confession. The parson supported himself through tithes, income from his parish lands, and any fees he collected for specific services rendered.

In Chaucer's *The Canterbury Tales,* the Parson is the one virtuous example of a churchman. He is the counterpoint to the excesses of corruption we see in the Summoner and Pardoner and the love of worldly luxuries so evident in the Prioress, the Monk, and the Friar. He is, therefore, an important character in that he demonstrates that Chaucer was not solely interested in satirizing and criticizing the Church out of hand, but also saw its good points.

However, an equally valid argument could be made against the Parson for abandoning his flock to go on pilgrimage. Furthermore, he is traveling in April so will presumably miss Easter services, the most important holiday in the Catholic calendar. Perhaps he is a much more complex character than he appears at first examination.

See also Friar; Monk; Nun; Religion

FURTHER READING

Biller, Peter, and Barrie Dobson, eds. *The Medieval Church: Universities, Heresy, and the Religious Life: Essays in Honour of Gordon Leff.* Rochester, NY: Boydell Press, 1999.

Blumenfeld-Kosinski, Renate. *Poets, Saints, and Visionaries of the Great Schism, 1378- 1417.* University Park: Pennsylvania State University Press, 2006.

Foster, Edward E., and David H. Carey, eds. *Chaucer's Church: A Dictionary of Religious Terms in Chaucer.* Brookfield, VT: Ashgate, 2002.

Peasant Revolt

Certes, he Jakke Straw and his meynee
Ne made nevere shoutes half so shrille
Whan that they wolden any Flemyng kille,
As thilke day was maad upon the fox.

For certain, Jack Straw and his men
Never made a noise quite so shrill
When they were killing Flemings
As was made this day upon the fox.

(*Canterbury Tales,*
"The Nun's Priest's Tale," VIII, 3394–97)

The Peasant Revolt of 1381 began in Essex in protest of Richard II's standard poll tax and the actions of a very aggressive tax collector. Starting in Brentwood, peasants from Essex and, eventually Kent, banded together to march on London. Things got unruly when the increasingly angry mob began to attack manors, churches, and monasteries along the way. Once they arrived in London, their focus turned political and they burned town halls where taxation records were kept. One of the casualties was Savoy House, which belonged to John of Gaunt.

The young Richard II rose impressively to the occasion and met the peasants at Mile End, just outside of Aldgate, on June 14. He managed to calm the mob and granted their demands for low rent rights, free contract labor, and the abolition of villeinage, the state in which medieval serfs were tied to the overloard's land, bought and sold along with it (although not considered to be property individually in the way a slave would be).

In return, the peasants—led by Wat Tyler—swore their allegiance to Richard. Some of the rebels, however, sensing weakness on the part of the king, decided to push further. They broke into the king's privy chamber, captured Gaunt's physician and the Archbishop of Canterbury, and executed them for treason on Tower Hill.

The death of Wat Tyler. © Bibliothèque nationale de France.

The following day, the peasant rebels met with the king again and demanded the abolition of all nobility except the king and the confiscation and redistribution of Church property. Tyler became rude and aggressive and was pulled from his horse and summarily executed. The rest of the mob dispersed, quickly cowed by royal authority.

The chief impetus behind the rebellion was fair taxation and the abolition of serfdom. Speeches made by Tyler and the radical preacher John Ball all stressed the equality of humanity as descendants of Adam and Eve. The revolt is indicative of the twin strains of social unrest and anticlericalism that were leading to the end of the medieval worldview.

It is unknown whether Chaucer was there and, if so, how much he saw of the Peasant Revolt. But "The Nun's Priests's Tale" contains lines describing the rebellion, suggesting he might have witnessed the great news event of his day (*Canterbury Tales,* "The Nun's Priest's Tale," VIII, 3394-97).

See also Aldgate; Estates; John of Gaunt; Richard II

FURTHER READING

Cantor, Norman. *The Encyclopedia of the Middle Ages.* New York: Viking Press, 1999.

Dunn, Alastair. *The Peasant's Revolt: England's Failed Revolution of 1381.* Stroud, England: Tempus, 2004.

Fraser, Antonia, ed. *The Lives of the Kings and Queens of England.* Rev. ed. Berkeley: University of California Press, 1998.

O'Brien, Mark. *When Adam Delved and Eve Span: A History of the Peasants' Revolt of 1381.* Cheltenham, England: New Clarion, 2004.

Philosophy

A CLERK ther was of Oxenford also,
That unto logyk hadde longe ygo.
As leene was his hors as is a rake,
And he nas nat right fat, I undertake,

But looked holwe, and therto sobrely.
Ful thredbare was his overeste courtepy,
For he hadde geten hym yet no benefice,
Ne was so worldly for to have office.
For hym was levere have at his beddes heed
Twenty bookes, clad in blak or reed,
Or Aristotle and his philosophie
Than robes riche, or fithele, or gay sautrie.
But al be that he was a philosophre.
Yet hadde he but litel gold in cofre;

There was a scholar from Oxford too,
Who was studying logic, but had not taken his
degree.
His horse was as lean as a rake,
And the scholar himself was not fat either, let me
tell you.
He looked hollow and, because of it, serious and
sober.
His overcoat was threadbare
Because he had not yet gotten himself an income,
Being too devoted to study to find an office.
For he would much rather have at the head of his
bed
Twenty books, bound in black or red leather,
By Aristotle and his philosophy
Than to have rich robes, or a fiddle, or even a
beautiful psaltery.
Although he was a man of philosophy,
He had little in the way of money in his coffers.

The visions of St. Benedict and St. Paul; from *Devotional and Philosophical Writings,* ca. 1325–1345. Courtesy of the Glasgow University Library.

(*Canterbury Tales,*
General Prologue, I (A), 285–98)

Medieval philosophy has long been interpreted as the philosophy of the so-called Dark Ages, in between the decline of the ancient pagan traditions and the rebirth of thinking known as the Renaissance. Like any generalization, this attitude falls woefully short of explaining the richer tradition that existed during the long centuries of the Middle Ages.

At its core, medieval philosophy was a product of three very different traditions: Jewish, Latin Christian (from those areas controlled by the later Western Roman Empire), and Muslim. The amalgamation was made possible by the efforts of the monks who translated works from their various languages and preserved them for later generations. And, as has been famously pointed out by Thomas Cahill, the monks who played a pivotal role in this preservation were the Irish. Most instrumental was John Scot Erigena, who taught at the court of Charles the Bold during the ninth century. It was his work in synthesizing the Stoic tradition with Aristotelian and Platonic philosophy that carried the greatest impact on medieval philosophy and added a Christian stamp to the thoughts of earlier pagans.

Plato (427–347 B.C.) provided the idea that the soul exists after the death of the body, an obviously appealing notion to Christian thinkers and one that was easily assimilated into medieval philosophy. As such, he dominated medieval thinking until about the twelfth century, when Aristotle (384–322 B.C.) was "rediscovered." Because he wrote about so many varied and disparate topics, it is impossible to overexaggerate the importance of Aristotle, although it would be a mistake to claim that all of medieval philosophy was merely the reshaping of Aristotelian thought. While he was notoriously vague on the idea of the soul, Aristotle was important morally for his writings on ethics, among other topics.

Also important in shaping medieval philosophical thought were St. Augustine of Hippo (354–430), Pseudo-Dionysus (fifth century), and Boethius (c. 480–545/526)—so crucial to Chaucer. Of these three, Augustine probably had the greatest impact on medieval thought and its particularly Christianized version of pagan ideas. In particular, Augustine's *Confessions* provided medieval philosophers with a framework for understanding the self and its quest for goodness and truth in a world that was hopelessly flawed.

Plato, Seneca, and Aristotle; from *Devotional and Philosophical Writings*, ca. 1325–1345. Courtesy of the Glasgow University Library.

Boethius is crucial both for his *Consolation of Philosophy* and for his translations of and commentaries on earlier thinkers. His work enabled his contemporaries and successors to gain access to writings that perhaps might otherwise have been lost or were unreadable and provided a framework for thinking about them. The *Consolation*, in addition, was written during his yearlong imprisonment awaiting trial and execution. It is modeled on the Roman form of Menippean satire, which blends prose and verse.

The book is a conversation between himself and Lady Philosophy, who attempts to lead Boethius to the conclusion that happiness must come from inside himself and not from material success. If he follows this advice, Dame Fortune cannot take anything away from him. Boethius's discussion attempts to answer religious questions in a purely secular, philosophical fashion, bringing faith and reason into harmony. He addresses questions of free will, predestination, virtue, and justice and attempts to reveal why goodness is no guarantee of success while evil behavior does not condemn one to failure.

It is impossible to overestimate Boethius's influence on Chaucer. Not only did Chaucer translate the *Consolation* into Middle English, but many of his concepts and characters are direct references to Boethius's work. Nature in *The Parliament of Fowls* is the literary daughter of Lady Philosophy. Furthermore, Boethius's use of Dame Fortune and his emphasis on patience and steadfastness find their way into all of Chaucer's works.

Around the twelfth century, philosophy underwent important developments that reflected the benefits of the revival in education as well as a new emphasis on logic. Perhaps the most important figure of the earlier part of this change would be Peter Abelard. Certainly, his personal life made him one of the more legendary figures of his time. Abelard for the first time created a methodology for philosophy, a means for attempting to arrive at absolutes, or to refute them entirely. His *Sic et non* provided contradictory problems that could only be resolved through the use of reason and rational thought.

After Abelard, during the later twelfth and thirteenth centuries, the rediscovery of Greek texts, and access to Islamic manuscripts as well, enabled medieval philosophers to expand their framework of thought to include disputations with their Jewish and Muslim counterparts. Beginning in Sicily and Italy, where Arabic and Greek medical and mathematical texts were being translated for use in the universities, the rise of these three intertwined intellectual traditions followed the rise of the university system, and philosophy became a very academic pursuit. The systematic study of the history of philosophical thought there, which was made possible by access to better libraries, and the proximity of masters with a seemingly endless stream of students, forged new directions in medieval philosophy that bore fruit during the Renaissance. It also paved the way for a more modern conception of thought and the movement away from philosophical questions that only addressed man's relation to the divine.

See also Boethius; Clerk; Education; Medicine; Science

FURTHER READING

Biller, Peter, and Barrie Dobson, eds. *The Medieval Church: Universities, Heresy, and the Religious Life: Essays in Honour of Gordon Leff.* Rochester, NY: Boydell Press, 1999.

Bisson, Lillian M. *Chaucer and the Late Medieval World.* New York: St. Martin's Press, 1998.

Boitani, Piero, and Jill Mann. *The Cambridge Chaucer Companion.* New York: Cambridge University Press, 1986.

Brown, Peter, ed. *A Companion to Chaucer.* Malden, MA: Blackwell, 2002.

Copeland, Rita. *Pedagogy, Intellectuals, and Dissent in the Later Middle Ages: Lollardy and Ideas of Learning.* New York: Cambridge University Press, 2001.

Gersh, Stephen, and Bert Roest, eds. *Medieval and Renaissance Humanism: Rhetoric, Representation and Reform.* Boston: Brill, 2003.

Gray, Douglas, ed. *The Oxford Companion to Chaucer.* New York: Oxford University Press, 2003.

MacDonald, Alasdair A., and Michael W. Twonmey, eds. *Schooling and Society: The Ordering and Reordering of Knowledge in the Western Middle Ages.* Dudley, MA: Peeters, 2004.

Miller, Mark. *Philosophical Chaucer: Love, Sex, and Agency in the* "Canterbury Tales." New York: Cambridge University Press, 2004.

Minnis, A. J. *Chaucer's Boece and the Medieval Tradition of Boethius.* Rochester, NY: D. S. Brewer, 1993.

Physician

In al this world ne was ther noon hym lik,
To speke of phisik and of surgerye,
For he was grounded in astronomye.
He kepte his pacient a ful greet deel
In houres by his magyk natureel.

In all this world there was none other like him
To speak of medicine and surgery
For he was well-taught in astronomy.
He kept his patients in good health
By the use of his natural magic.

(*Canterbury Tales,*
General Prologue, I (A), 412–16)

According to John Arderne's code of ethics, a doctor should follow these precepts: never boast, offend servants, eye the ladies of the house, or speak ill of other doctors, speak; seldom laugh and joke; and always study, take payment in advance, and keep clean hands, good manners and patients' secrets. Arderne, a physician in the train of Henry of Lancaster (the future Henry IV) wrote this advice in 1376, roughly a decade before the time Chaucer was writing *The Canterbury Tales.* Although the character of the Doctour of Phisik is not so fully drawn as some others, he seems to embody the spirit of this practical advice, as well as certain other notions of physicians of the time.

University-trained physicians were the elite of the medieval medical profession. They were respected for their education, their reliance on theory and philosophy, and their knowledge of Latin. They were known as theorizers and philosophers, unlike surgeons who worked with their hands. Physicians could diagnose a patient based merely on the alignment of the heavens, by the color and smell of a flask of urine, or by the actions of a goldfinch. For the most part, they did not sully their hands with physical exams, bloodletting, or other surgical business.

Doctors offered advice and prescriptions for treatments that were then undertaken by apothecaries, surgeons, barber-surgeons, and barber-tonsors. Their purpose was to care for patients through knowledge, not necessarily to cure disease. The theoretical focus of their approach is evident in the lack of separate medical facilities at either Oxford or Cambridge until the early to mid-fourteenth century.

That a physician needed a wide range of knowledge is clear in Chaucer's description of the Doctour of Phisik of whom he writes. Because of their high status, many became wealthy. Others used their position if not actually to trade in the spices they prescribed, to profit mutually from the business they sent to the apothecaries who often were very much involved in mercantile activities:

In sangwyn and in pers he clad was al,
Lyned with taffata and with sendal.
And yet he was but esy of dispence;
He kepte that he wan in pestilence.
For gold in phisik is a cordial,
Therfore he lovede gold in special.

In red and Prussian blue he was all dressed
Lined with taffeta and fine sarcenet.
And yet, he was not one to spend elaborately.
He kept all of the money he earned from treating disease
For gold in medicine is the best cordial,
Therefore, he loved gold best of everything.

(*Canterbury Tales,*
General Prologue, I (A), 439–444)

Chaucer makes note of this focus on money and profit, which undercuts his prior statements regarding the intellectual gifts of the Doctour. The general impression left is that the medical profession was also facing the kind of resentment leveled at the Church, which was perceived as being more concerned with profiteering than care of individuals.

See also Black Death; Four Humors; Medicine

FURTHER READING

French, Roger. *Canonical Medicine: Gentile da Foligno and Scholasticism.* Boston: Brill, 2001.

French, Roger, Jon Arrizabalaga, Andrew Cunningham, and Luis García-Ballester, eds. *Medicine from the Black Death to the French Disease.* Aldershot, England: Ashgate, 1998.

Gottfried, Robert S. *Doctors and Medicine in Medieval England*, 1340–1530. Princeton, NJ: Princeton University Press, 1986.

Hildegard of Bingen. *On Natural Philosophy and Medicine: Selections from "Case et Cure."* Translation and introduction by Margret Berger. Cambridge, England: D. S. Brewer, 1999.

Kibre, Pearl. *Studies in Medieval Science: Alchemy, Astrology, Mathematics, and Medicine.* London: Hambledon Press, 1984.

Pilgrimage

She hadde passed many a straunge strem;
At Rome she hadde been, and at Boloigne,
In Galice at Seint-Jame, and at Coligne.
She koude muchel of wandrynge by the weye.

She had passed over many a foreign stream;
She had been at Rome and at Bologne,
In Galicia at Saint Iago de Campostela, and at Cologne.
She had done much wandering by the way.

(*Canterbury Tales,*
General Prologue, I (A), 464–67)

Pilgrimage was a movement in its zenith by Chaucer's day; however, it remained an important impulse in the greater movement that would eventually lead to the end of the domination of the Catholic Church over the religious and political life of Europe. This development is ironic, because beginning roughly in the eleventh century the Church strongly recommended the use of pilgrimage as a form of penance or devotion, a way to seek absolution for sins or to demonstrate the willingness to sacrifice comfort, income, and even safety to visit places associated with the lives or deaths of important saints or Christ.

As years progressed and dissatisfaction with the Church grew, pilgrimage evolved into a means of controlling one's own salvation. An individual did not need the intercession of a priest in order to visit Jerusalem; he or she only required the desire to make the visit. Thus, pilgrimage ultimately became a step in the general movement toward the Protestant Reformation.

Pilgrimage itself was predicated on the notion of making effort and personal sacrifice to journey to a location that was in some sense holy. The relics of famous saints and their tombs were some of the most popular destinations, as the pilgrims of *The Canterbury Tales* demonstrate (*Canterbury Tales,* General Prologue, I (A), 12). Dubious claims of the miraculous healing powers of particular saints sometimes created a deluge of visitors to tiny churches that were unprepared for the influx of ailing pilgrims.

For those who could not afford an expensive transcontinental journey to a foreign location, the association of a particular locale in one's own country provided a means to the end of showing devotion on a smaller scale. For the very devout, however, nothing short of a visit to Rome, Santiago de Compostela in Spain, or the Holy Land would suffice.

These were the holiest places in the world for a Christian, and all three presented challenges in travel for the average English pilgrim. No matter the destination, solitary travel could be dangerous, expensive,

An undated illustration of the Pilgrims from Chaucer's *The Canterbury Tales*. © Art Resource, NY.

and lonely, inspiring many pilgrims to band together. They could provide protection for one another, especially at night when lack of inns meant camping outdoors.

Over time, however, the inhabitants in and around popular pilgrimage sites began to realize there was a lucrative market to be exploited through catering to pilgrims (*Canterbury Tales*, General Prologue, I (A), 685). Pilgrims usually brought money, and they often wanted to bring back souvenirs of their travels. For the average peasant, a lifetime was typically bounded by the limits of the village. A man or woman could be born, baptized, married, and buried all in the shadow of the local church.

Any travel at all was uncomfortable and expensive. Many peasants did not even own a horse for riding, so all travel had to be undertaken on foot. Add to this the fact of little free time and it becomes clear why few peasants left their villages. In a time before mass communication and media, they had no connection to a world beyond the village border; and in a world before advertising, they had no desire for goods beyond what was available in that village. Everything they needed, including friends, family, and marital prospects, were there.

By the late thirteenth and early fourteenth centuries, however, the growth of a rudimentary middle class (mostly through trade and mercantilism) and the expansion of urban centers meant increased opportunities for travel and communication. Perhaps the average peasant

A woodcut of the Pilgrims from a fifteenth-century edition of *The Canterbury Tales*. Courtesy of the Glasgow University Library.

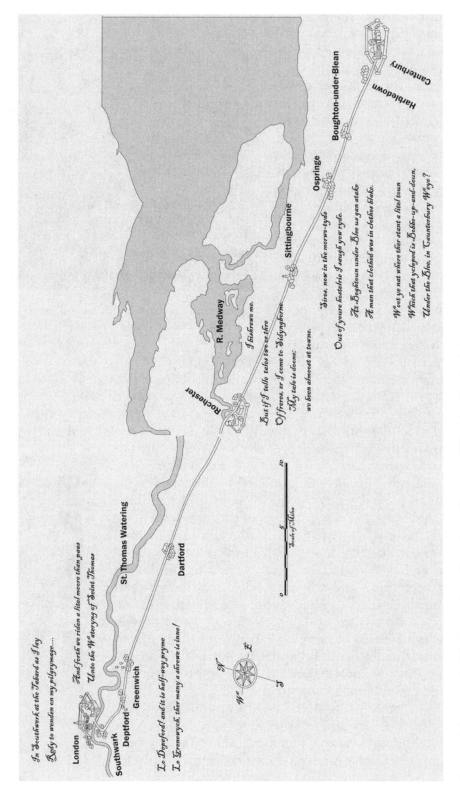

A map of the route the Pilgrims took to Canterbury. Courtesy of Ricochet Productions.

remained tied to the land, but some of his relatives were moving beyond the village, and those who traveled through villages brought tales of other places. Thus, visiting "foreign" locales—even those in the next county—became more conceivable and desirable. Pilgrimage presented the opportunity to travel and see new, interesting places under the socially laudable guise of religious devotion. Certainly there were many people in the Age of Faith who went on pilgrimage solely for reasons of spiritual commitment. However, as was the case with the Crusades, there were many who were motivated by personal gain, even if it was only entertainment or escapism.

With this in mind, it is easy to understand the somewhat cynical impulse on the part of those who sought to benefit financially from the influx of travelers to a particular locale. With thousands of pilgrims visiting a spot every year, enhancing the experience could be an economic boon to poor villages. Inns and taverns popped up along common pilgrimage routes, providing food and shelter to weary travelers. Their presence altered some trade routes as merchants discovered comfortable way stations along the roads between, for example, London and Cornwall. Within villages, souvenir stands appeared, selling trinkets associated with a particular saint, such as rosaries or bogus relics:

For in his male he hadde a pilwe-beer,
Which that he seyde was Oure Lady veyl;
He seyde he hadde a gobet of the seyl
That Seint Peter hadde, what that he wente
Upon the see, til Jhesu Crist hym hente.
He hadde a croys of latoun ful of stones,
And in a glas he hadde pigges-bones.
But with thise relikes, what that he fond
A povre person dwellynge uon lond,
Upon a day he gat hym moore money
Than that the person gat in monthes tweye.

For in his bag he had a pillow-case
That he said was actually Our Lady's veil;
He said he also had a portion of the sail
That Saint Peter had when he went
Upon the sea, until Jesus Christ found him.
He had a cross of brass, set with stones,
And in a glass he had pig's bones.
With these "relics" when he found a
Poor person dwelling in the country
In that day he'd make more money
Than the parson was likely to make in two months.

(*Canterbury Tales,*
General Prologue, I (A), 694–704)

Other enterprising souls created maps of pilgrimage routes to guide travelers along their way between sites. The increased capital was also frequently applied toward building a new church, upon the construction of which some dedicated pilgrims would assist.

As we can see from Chaucer's *The Canterbury Tales,* pilgrimage brought together a wide variety of people with disparate backgrounds and economic classes. Although there are a fair number of religious people in the party, they are balanced not only by their own questionable devoutness but also by the characters such as the Reeve and Miller, who seem as far removed from genuine spiritual contrition as one could possibly be. The rollicking nature of many of the tales and the general air of frivolity provides a tangible clue to the reality of fourteenth-century pilgrimages as breaks from the monotony of everyday life.

See also Canterbury; Religion; Thomas à Becket

FURTHER READING

Blick, Sarah, and Rita Tekippe, eds. *Art and Architecture of Late Medieval Pilgrimage in Northern Europe and the British Isles.* Boston: Brill, 2005.

Dyas, Dee. *Pilgrimage in Medieval English Literature, 700–1500.* Rochester, NY: D. S. Brewer, 2001.

Finucane, Ronald C. *Miracles and Pilgrims: Popular Beliefs in Medieval England.* New York: St. Martin's Press, 1995.

Labarge, Margaret Wade. *Medieval Travellers.* New York: Norton, 1983.

Lambdin, Laura C., and Robert T. Lambdin, eds. *Chaucer's Pilgrims.* Westport, CT: Praeger, 1999.

Le Beau, Bryan F., and Menachem Mor, eds. *Pilgrims and Travelers to the Holy Land.* Omaha, NE: Creighton University Press, 1996.

Swatos, Jr., William H., and Luigi Tomasi, eds. *From Medieval Pilgrimage to Religious Tourism: The Social and Cultural Economics of Piety.* Westport, CT: Praeger, 2002.

Verdon, Jean. *Travel in the Middle Ages.* Notre Dame, IN: University of Notre Dame Press, 2003.

Webb, Diana. *Medieval European Pilgrimage, c. 700–c. 1500.* New York: Palgrave, 2002.

———. *Pilgrimage in Medieval England.* New York: Hambledon and London, 2000.

———. *Pilgrims and Pilgrimage in the Medieval West.* New York: I. B. Tauris, 2001.

Priapus

The son of Venus and Bacchus, Priapus was the god of creation and procreation in the human, animal, and plant worlds. He was also the patron god of horticulture. Depicted as an ugly little man with enormous genitals that signified his creative powers, he was known for his lustful nature.

One legend describes his profound physical longing for an unwilling nymph. When he tried to sneak up on her while she was asleep, an ass brayed, awakening the other nymphs and gods who all laughed at his sexual arousal. Chaucer mentions him in this particularly embarrassing moment in *The Parliament of Fowls:*

The god Priapus saw I, as I wente,
Withinne the temple in sovereyn place stonde,
In swich aray as whan the asse hym shente
With cri by nighte, and with hys scptre in honde.
Ful besyly men gonne assaye and fonde
Upon his hed to sette, of sondry hewe,
Garlondes ful of freshe floures newe.

The god Priapus I saw, when I
Entered the temple, standing as the focus of worship
In just such a condition as when the ass brayed
That night and startled him. He had his scepter in his hand.
Before me men had gone and paid tribute,
Setting garlands of flowers, fresh and multi-colored,
Upon his head to honor him.

(*Parliament of Fowls*, 253–59)

Priapus is also amusingly alluded to in "The Merchant's Tale" in the description of the garden in which January likes to have sex with his disgusted wife (*Canterbury Tales*, "The Merchant's Tale," IV (E), 2034–37).

FURTHER READING

Brown, Peter, ed. *A Companion to Chaucer.* Malden, MA: Blackwell, 2002.

Frye, Northrop. *Biblical and Classical Myths: The Mythological Framework of Western Culture.* Buffalo, NY: University of Toronto Press, 2004.

Hansen, William F. *Classical Mythology: A Guide to the Mythical World of the Greeks and Romans.* New York: Oxford University Press, 2005.

Manser, Martin H. *The Facts On File Dictionary of Classical and Biblical Allusions.* New York: Facts On File, 2003.

Morford, Mark P. O. *Classical Mythology.* 7th ed. New York: Oxford University Press, 2003.

Nolan, Barbara. *Chaucer and the Tradition of the Roman Antique.* New York: Cambridge University Press, 1992.

Powell, Barry B. *Classical Myth.* Translated by Herbert M. Howe. 4th ed. Upper Saddle River, NJ: Pearson/Prentice Hall, 2004.

Price, Simon, and Emily Kearns, eds. *The Oxford Dictionary of Classical Myth and Religion.* New York: Oxford University Press, 2003.

Prioress

Ther was also a Nonne, a PRIORESSE,
That of hir smylyng was ful symple and coy;
Hire gretteste ooth was but by Seinte Loy;
And she was cleped madame Eglentyne.
Ful weel she soong the service dyvyne,
Entuned in hir nose ful semely;
And Frenssh she spak ful faire and fetisly,
After the scole of Stratford atte Bowe,
For Frenssh of Parys was to hire unknowe.
At mete wel ytaught was she with alle;
She leet no morsel from hir lippes falle,
Ne wette hir fyngres in hir sauce depe;
Wel koude she carie a morsel and wel kepe
That no drope ne fille upon hire brest.
In curteisie was set ful muchel hir lest.
Hir over-lippe wyped she so clene
That in hir coppe ther was no ferthyng sene
Of grece, whan she drunken hadde hir draughte.
Ful semely after hir mete she raughte.
And sikerly she was of greet desport,
And ful plesaunt, and amyable of port,
And peyned hire to countrefete cheere
Of court, and to been estatlich of manere,
And to ben holden digne of reverence.
But for to speken of hire conscience,
She was so charitable and so pitous
She wolde wepe, if that she saugh a mous
Kaught in a trappe, if it were deed or bledde.
Of smale houndes hadde she that she fedde
With rosted flessh, or milk and wastel-breed.
But soore wepte she if oon of hem were deed,
Or if men smoot it with a yerde smerte;
And al was conscience and tendre herte.
Ful semyly hir wympul pynched was,
Hir nose tretys, hir eyen greye as glas,
Hir mouth ful smal, and therto softe and reed.
But sikerly she hadde a fair forheed;
It was almoost a spanne brood, I trowe;
For, hardily, she was nat undergrowe.
Ful fetys was hir cloke, as I was war.
Of small coral aboute hire arm she bar
A peire of bedes, gauded al with grene,
And theron heng a brooch of gold ful sheene,
On which ther was first write a crowned A,
And after *Amor vincit omnia.*

There was also a nun, a Prioress,
Her smile was very natural and demure,
Her strongest oath was "by Saint Elegius!"
And she was called Madame Eglantyne.
She sung the liturgy quite well,
Through her nose, prettily intoned.
And she spoke French equally well and learnedly
In the style of the school at Stratford-at-Bow
For the French of Paris was unknown to her.
At the table she was well-taught to behave
She let no morsel fall from her lips,
And she never dipped her fingers in the sauce
She carried each morsel daintily up to her mouth
So that no drop of sauce fell upon her breast.
She kept her upper lip so clean
That in her cup there was not a speck of grease seen
When she had drunk from it.
And she so politely reached for what she wanted at the table.
Her demeanor was very pleasant
She was kind and courtly to all,
Very pleasant and amiable
And acted in such a way as to mimic the manners
Of court, so much so that she was thought to
Be a person of much renown.
But to speak of her conscience,
She was so charitable and so full of pity
That she would weep if she saw a mouse
Caught in a trap, if it was dead or had bled.
She kept many small hounds that she fed
On roasted meat and fine white bread.
And she wept bitterly if one were dead,
Or if a man were to beat it.
She was very sympathetic and tender-hearted.
Her wimple was pleated quite fetchingly
Her nose nicely shaped and her eyes grey as glass
Her mouth was small, soft and red.
She had a beautiful forehead
Nearly a span in width, I'd bet
For she was certainly not overly petite.
Her cloak, I noticed, was very elegant
She had a coral rosary, with gauds of green
That she carried on her arm.
And from there she hung a brooch of shining gold.
On which there was written at first a crowned "A"
And underneath, "love conquers all."

(*Canterbury Tales*,
General Prologue, I (A), 118–62)

The Prioress is one of Chaucer's most fully drawn characters and emerges, despite her physical beauty and breeding, as one of the least attractive. She represents in the broadest sense the decline in spirituality of the medieval church and, more narrowly, someone who has undertaken a calling for which she is completely unsuited and to which she has little dedication, despite her position of authority.

It is unclear why Madame Eglantyne entered the convent in the first place. Women joined nunneries for a number of reasons. Some girls were promised by their families, much as a younger son would be placed in a monastery, in order to forge a connection with the Church. Making the sacrifice of consecrating a marriageable daughter as a perpetual virgin was believed to obtain her family important blessings. Some women had a genuine vocation and entered convent life voluntarily. Others entered as a last resort—being either under-dowered or unattractive, they were considered unmarriageable.

Because Chaucer specifically mentions that Eglantyne is attractive and her manners are exceedingly courtly, it is unlikely that her family was too poor to dower her or that she had no marital prospects. She may have entered at a very young age, the youngest of several daughters. However, she seems by her habits to have lived outside of a convent for most of her life. Her daily habits indicate clearly an exposure to secular life as well as the unlikelihood that she entered willingly due to a spiritual need to devote her life to the contemplation of God.

Chaucer's characterization of the Prioress might possibly be satirical, because her flaws are counter to what was expected from a religious person. Her manners are genteel and suited to court life and she speaks French. She worries about her appearance, smiling sweetly, making sure her clothing is flattering, her wimple nicely pleated, and her brooch displaying the motto *Amor vincit omnia*. Finally, she keeps pets, little dogs that she lavishes with affection and attention. None of these things should have occupied her attention, because a nun, above all, should be concerned with God.

Not only is the Prioress a poor excuse for a nun, but her position as head of the convent makes her character more questionable. Although the specific duties of a prioress varied greatly from house to house, generally speaking the prioress was responsible for disciplining the novices and sisters, meeting with visiting churchmen and dignitaries, choosing sisters for administrative positions within the convent, and the general spiritual well-being of the convent.

The prioress was usually someone from a noble background—the position was often political as well as spiritual. However, it was expected that the prioress would be dedicated to the church. It is clear that Madame Eglantyne has other things on her mind.

And yet, she was no doubt not the only one of her vocation who strayed from the strict Benedictine expectations of conduct. Accumulation of wealth and high prestige meant that many monasteries and convents wielded considerable worldly power and influence, two inevitabilities that, combined with the aforementioned lack of vocation on the part of many within the walls, meant that standards were often lax in Chaucer's day. Prioresses were known to attend weddings and dance upon occasion.

While all of these activities were out of keeping with proper nunly behavior, the one reason for breaking cloister that was strictly frowned upon was going on pilgrimage. As late as 1318, the archbishop of York declared that nuns who went on pilgrimage were "to say as many psalters as it would have taken to perform the pilgrimage so rashly vowed." Therefore, more than any of her other questionable activities, Eglantyne's decision to travel to Canterbury is the most damning evidence that she is not a committed and devoted religious woman.

See also Estates; Monk; Nun; Religion

FURTHER READING

Biller, Peter, and Barrie Dobson, eds. *The Medieval Church: Universities, Heresy, and the Religious Life: Essays in Honour of Gordon Leff.* Rochester, NY: Boydell Press, 1999.

Blumenfeld-Kosinski, Renate. *Poets, Saints, and Visionaries of the Great Schism, 1378–1417.* University Park: Pennsylvania State University Press, 2006.

Foster, Edward E., and David H. Carey, eds. *Chaucer's Church: A Dictionary of Religious Terms in Chaucer.* Brookfield, VT: Ashgate, 2002.

Gies, Frances, and Joseph Gies. *Women in the Middle Ages.* New York: Harper, 1978.

Riches, Samantha J. E., and Sarah Salih, eds. *Gender and Holiness: Men, Women, and Saints in Late Medieval Europe.* New York: Routledge, 2002.

Private Houses

A povre wydwe, somdeel stape in age,
Was whilom dwellyng in a narwe cotage,
Biside a grove, stondynge in a dale.
This wydwe, of which I telle yow my tale,
Syn thilke day that she was last a wyf
In pacience ladde a ful symple lyf,
For litel was hir catel and hir rente
By housbondrie of swich as God hire sente
She foonde hirself and eek hir doghtren two.

A poor widow, well advanced in age,
Lived in a narrow little cottage,
In the middle of a dale, beside a grove of trees.
This widow, of whom I tell my tale,
Ever since the last day that she was a wife

Had lived a good and simple life.
She had few needs, and only a little money for her rent
And by careful husbandry she made the most of what God sent her
To take care of herself and her two daughters.

(*Canterbury Tales,*
"The Nun's Priest's Tale," VII, 2821–29)

Although medieval people had a much looser interpretation of privacy than we might today—with activities such as sleeping, eating, procreating, birthing, and eliminating all taking place with a good deal of openness—their homes were in many ways rather similar to our own. The quality of a home was controlled in great part by economic status and social rank. And yet, with our dependence on running water, appliances, and central heat, most of us would find even the noblest castle or lordly manor to be drafty, cold, inconvenient, and dirty.

While the day-to-day lives of peasants have not been well documented, we fortunately know a surprising amount about their homes thanks to remaining physical evidence. Rural peasants lived in villages or small towns that surrounded their lord's manor. Most of them occupied small one- to three-room, one-story cottages. The typical cottage had two rooms and measured roughly 15 feet square.

The frame was built of joined timber, and the walls were filled with wattle and daub—mud that was thickened and given substance and insulation with straw and sticks. Roofs were generally made of thatch, unless the cottage was located in an area where slate was cheap and plentiful. The latter posed much less of a fire hazard, an important consideration given the presence of daily open fires within the cottage walls.

The floors were usually packed dirt. Sometimes a second floor loft was created for a separate sleeping area by using boards to create flooring and stairs. Windows were merely slits to provide light and fresh air, but glass would have been out of the economic reach of the peasantry. Therefore, in colder months, peasants stuffed rags in the holes to stop the flow of air. The rags could be removed if more light was desired or if the fire was especially smoky. Prosperous peasants had shutters over their window slits.

The typical medieval home had little in the way of furniture and, as expected, peasants had less than the higher classes. Most had a storage chest or two that doubled as seating and a table if the family lacked a separate table. Beds might be a cot topped with a straw mattress or a pallet on the floor or sacks of straw on the floor. For the "kitchen"—located in the center of the room around the fire—there might be a few iron pots for cooking soup or porridge. The fire, in fact, was the central element in the home, and was placed in the center of the room on a raised platform, with a hole directly above it in the ceiling to draw smoke up and out. The fire provided warmth and light and the ability to cook. In the wintertime, the family would sleep near the fire, and the livestock often joined them inside for additional warmth. To supplement the light of the fire, tallow candles (made from animal fat) were used sparingly, providing weak yellowish light and producing an unpleasant smell.

The urban working class lived in similar dwellings in the cities and towns. Urban homes usually measured about 12 feet by 20 feet, but were in actuality far larger than the rural cottages because they were two or three floors rather than one. They were also more nicely appointed inside. There would be a shop on the first floor (if the house belonged to an artisan or craftsman), with a door fronting the street. Downstairs would be a cellar for storage, and the floor would be made of wood or slate instead of dirt. Additionally, because these houses tended to be built in attached rows, making them natural fire hazards, the roofs were made of slate or tile rather than thatch. The kitchen would have a fireplace, and, depending on the prosperity level of the tenant, there might be a fireplace elsewhere to heat other floors.

Aristocratic homes, as one would expect, were larger and more comfortable. Their quality varied with the income of the occupant, but they typically were comprised of several rooms with a clear delineation between public and private spaces. Stone was the preferred material for building, although brick was not unknown. Wattle and daub also was used in the walls but was made of better materials, making a smoother, more attractive wall with more efficient insulating properties—although homes were still drafty and cold with poor circulation of the heat source. Over the wattle and daub was plaster and whitewash for a brighter, cleaner appearing interior. Floors were made of wood, while the roofs were made of tile or slate.

The most important room in the house would be the hall, a feature that was adapted from the great hall of castles and incorporated into more modest aristocratic manors. Here the household had its core. Public business was transacted in the hall, banquets and entertainments were held there, and all the formal daily meals were eaten there. The area was partitioned with wooden screens to block drafts. The hall was divided into a high end, where those of higher rank and the family dined, and the low end. The low end was nearest the kitchen, providing it with perhaps a bit of ambient heat, but also exposing it to the smells, bustle, and potential smoke. The high end was closest to the family's private chambers and the solarium. In some cases, the manor house was at the center of a group of other buildings that housed facilities to make the things necessary for the house, such as a brewing shed, a buttery, and a honey house.

To light and heat their homes, the nobility used beeswax candles and fires from their fireplaces. Firewood was essential, although in London charcoal was more common. Unlike peasants, the nobility had glass windows in their homes. Despite these many comforts, the wealthy might still find their homes drab or drafty. Therefore, they hung wall hangings such as tapestries or painted cloths to insulate and decorate. The wooden floors, which could be chilly in cooler weather, were covered with rush mats dusted with flowers and herbs.

Aristocratic manors also had more and nicer furniture. There were chairs as well as storage chests, tables, and beds. Mattresses were stuffed with a variety of materials from wool to cotton. The main mattress was covered with a second smaller one, stuffed with feathers. A bolster provided a pillow. The best beds had curtained hangings around them, often elaborately embroidered. In case one awakened with an urge to empty one's bladder, a chamber pot was placed under the bed for convenience. Nobody, after all, wants to use an outhouse in the middle of the night if it is not necessary.

See also Daily Life; Estates; Furniture

FURTHER READING

Bowden, Muriel. *A Reader's Guide to Geoffrey Chaucer.* Syracuse, NY: Syracuse University Press, 2001.

Brewer, Derek. *Chaucer and His World.* Cambridge, England: D.S. Brewer, 1978; reprinted 1992.

Britnell, Richard, ed. *Daily Life in the Late Middle Ages.* Stroud: Sutton Pub., 1998.

DeWindt, Edwin Brezette, ed. *The Salt of Common Life: Individuality and Choice in the Medieval Town, Countryside, and Church: Essays Presented to J. Ambrose Raftis.* Kalamazoo, MI: Medieval Institute Publications, Western Michigan University, 1995.

Duby, Georges. *The Three Orders: Feudal Society Imagined.* Translated by Arthur Goldhammer. Chicago: University of Chicago Press, 1980; reprinted 1982.

Dyer, Christopher. *Making a Living in the Middle Ages: The People of Britain 850–1520.* New Haven: Yale University Press, 2002.

Emery, Anthony. *Greater Medieval Houses of England and Wales, 1300–1500.* New York: Cambridge University Press, 1996.

French, Katherine L. *The People of the Parish: Community Life in a Late Medieval English Diocese.* Philadelphia: University of Pennsylvania Press, 2001.

Masschaele, James. *Peasants, Merchants, and Markets: Inland Trade in Medieval England, 1150–1350.* New York: St. Martin's Press, 1997.

Morgan, Gwyneth. *Life in a Medieval Village.* New York: Cambridge University Press, 1975.

Power, Eileen. *Medieval People.* New York: Barnes and Noble, 1924; reprinted 1968.

Quiney, Anthony. *Town Houses of Medieval Britain.* New Haven: Yale University Press, 2003.

Schofield, John. *Medieval London Houses.* New Haven: Yale University Press, 1994.

Singman, Jeffrey L., and Will McLean. *Daily Life in Chaucer's England.* Westport, CT: Greenwood Press, 1995.

Swabey, Ffiona. *Medieval Gentlewoman: Life in a Gentry Household in the Later Middle Ages.* New York: Routledge, 1999.

Wood, Margaret. *The English Mediaeval House*. London: Bracken Books, 1983; reprinted 1985.

Prussia

Ful ofte tyme he hadde the bord bigonne
Aboven alle nacions in Pruce.

There was many a time that he had taken the highest seat at the table
Above all of the knights of other nations in Prussia.

(*Canterbury Tales*,
General Prologue, I (A), 52–54)

Slavic tribes first populated the area of modern Germany known as Prussia, situated to the north and east of the Russian border. In the seventh and eighth centuries, Germanic tribes invaded and settled the area. Prussia became a Christian kingdom in 1226 when it was conquered by the Teutonic knights, who converted the inhabitants. The conquest was especially brutal, and the Prussians were enslaved by the knights.

In 1309, the knights moved their headquarters to Malbork castle, located south of Gdansk (Danzig), and fourteenth-century Prussia became an important staging ground for the raids made by the Teutonic knights on Russia and Lithuania. Both the Pope and the Holy Roman Emperor, with the purpose of converting the inhabitants to Christianity, sanctioned this activity.

Many bachelor knights from England and France, including Chaucer's Knight, joined the Order on these raids as mercenaries, finding it to be potentially lucrative work: England would eventually ban travel to the area from 1385 to 1388. The Prussians finally overthrew the crusading invaders in 1454 with aid from Lithuania and Poland. Prussia is mentioned in passing *The Book of the Duchess*, when the Black Knight mentions that his lady was not of the kind to send men out to distant lands, such as Prussia (*Book of the Duchess*, 1025).

See also Knight

FURTHER READING

Cantor, Norman. *The Civilization of the Middle Ages*. Rev. ed. New York: Harper Collins, 1993.

Jones, Terry. *Chaucer's Knight: The Portrait of a Medieval Mercenary*. Baton Rouge: Louisiana State University Press, 1980.

Kaeuper, Richard W. *Chivalry and Violence in Medieval Europe*. New York: Oxford University Press, 1999.

Labarge, Margaret Wade. *Medieval Travellers.* New York: Norton, 1983.

Le Beau, Bryan F., and Menachem Mor, eds. *Pilgrims and Travelers to the Holy Land.* Omaha, NE: Creighton University Press, 1996.

Tyerman, Christopher. *England and the Crusades, 1095–1588.* Chicago: University of Chicago Press, 1988.

Verdon, Jean. *Travel in the Middle Ages.* Notre Dame, IN: University of Notre Dame Press, 2003.

R

Reeve

The REVE was a sclendre colerik man.
His berd was shave as ny as ever he kan;
His heer was by his erys ful round yshorn;
His top was dokked lyk a preest biforn.
Ful longe were his legges and ful lene,
Ylyk a staf; ther was no calf ysene.
Wel koude he kepe a gerner and a bynne;
Ther was noon auditour koude on him wynne.
Wel wiste he by the droghte and by the reyn
The yeldynge of his seed and of his greyn.
His lordes sheep, his neet, his dayerye,
His swyn, his hors, his stoor, and his pultrye
Was hooly in this Reves governynge,
And by his covenant yaf the rekenynge,
Syn that his lord was twenty yeer of age.
Ther koude no man brynge hym in arrerage.
Ther nas bailiff, ne hierde, nor oother hyne,
That he ne knew his sleighte and his covyne;
They were adrad of hym as of the deeth.

His wonyng was ful faire upon an heeth;
With grene trees yshadwed was his place.
He koude bettre than his lord purchace.
Ful riche he was astored pryvely.
His lord wel koude he plesen subtilly,
To yeve and lene hym of his owene good,
And have a thank, and yet a cote and hood.
In youthe he hadde lerned a good myster:
He was a wel good wrighte, a carpenter.

The Reeve was a slender, choleric man.
His beard was shaved as close as he could get it
His hair was cut quite short around his ears,
With the top shorn like a priest's.
His legs were very long and lean
And, like a stick, he didn't have a calf.
He kept his granary and bins well stocked;
No auditor could get one over on him.
He could tell in advance by drought and by rain
What his seed and grain would yield.
His lord's sheep, cattle, dairy,
His wine, his horses, his poultry, and livestock
Was entirely in the Reeve's governance,
And by his covenant he had given a reckoning
Since his lord was twenty years of age.
There was no man who could catch him in arrears,
There was no bailiff, herdsman, or farm-boy
Whose actions he did not know.
They were all as afraid of him as of the plague.
His house was well-placed upon a heath
With green trees shading it well.
He was better at managing business than was his lord
He had stored away a pile of riches on the side.
He was talented at making his lord happy by
Lending him his own property,
And by this method earned his thanks, as well as a coat and a hood
As a youth he had learned to master a useful trade,
He was a wood-worker, a carpenter.

(*Canterbury Tales,*
General Prologue, I (A), 587–614)

A medieval reeve was employed by the lord of the manor to manage the land and the surrounding village. The reeve acted as a steward or bailiff (or in much the same capacity as did the manciple in his milieu), overseeing production and supervising the peasants to make sure that they worked and did not steal from the landlord. In most cases, the lord chose the reeve, but infrequently the reeve was a democratic choice of the peasants.

In either case, the reeve faced a number of challenges. He was a peasant like those he oversaw. As with any boss, the reeve's authority made him unpopular with some of his charges, and his social ranking as their equal made his position one that was often fraught with tension.

However, as the fourteenth century progressed, and the prestige of the office increased, many reeves found themselves to be respected, if not liked, within their villages. For those whose wages did not keep up with their level of prestige, however, the job could be expensive. If the manor did not meet its goals of production, the reeve was expected to make up the shortfall from his own pocket.

Manor courts were held once yearly to determine amounts owed and to hear grievances from both the reeve and the peasants he oversaw. If he was lax in his duties or abused his power, he would be held accountable. Conversely, if he was resourceful and good at his job, he would be more susceptible to cheating his lord because he was smart enough to realize the importance of covering himself from any eventual losses that might be incurred through events out of his control, such as bad weather.

Chaucer's Reeve is canny and crafty. He is good at his job, terrifying the peasants with his knowledge of every blade of grass that grows on the manor. He keeps them working up to capacity so that he does not need to dip into his own reserves to make up for their laziness. He also has feathered his own nest well by being better at business than his lord:

Ful riche he was astored pryvely.
His lord wel koude he plesen subtilly,
To yeve and lene hym of his owene good,
And have a thank, and yet a cote and hood.

He had stored away a pile of riches on the side.
He was talented at making his lord happy by
Lending him his own property,
And by this method earned his thanks, as well as a coat and a hood/

(*Canterbury Tales,*
General Prologue, I (A), 609–12)

In short, while he is not an especially attractive character, the Reeve is important because he demonstrates Chaucer's apparent belief that peasants could command substantial native intelligence and that nobility does not automatically confer sharp wits.

And yet, because the Reeve uses his talents in a somewhat negative way, his portrayal is a warning for what can happen when natural ability is constrained by the system or, perhaps, when it appears in someone who does not have the breeding or inborn *gentilesse* to handle it properly and morally.

A more upright man might not live as comfortable a life, but still would be able to manage the manor to best production.

See also Business and Commerce; Estates

FURTHER READING

Bisson, Lillian M. *Chaucer and the Late Medieval World.* New York: St. Martin's Press, 1998.

Brewer, Derek. *Chaucer and His World.* Cambridge, England: D. S. Brewer, 1978; reprinted 1992.

Britnell, R. H. *The Commercialisation of English Society, 1000–1500.* 2nd ed. New York: Manchester University Press, 1996.

Britnell, Richard, ed. *Daily Life in the Late Middle Ages.* Stroud, England: Sutton, 1998.

Brown, Peter, ed. *A Companion to Chaucer.* Malden, MA: Blackwell, 2002.

Dyer, Christopher. *Making a Living in the Middle Ages: The People of Britain 850–1520.* New Haven, CT: Yale University Press, 2002.

Gies, Frances, and Joseph Gies. *Cathedral, Forge, and Waterwheel.* New York: Harper Collins, 1994.

Religion

A good man was ther of religioun,
And was a povre PERSOUN OF A TOUN,
But riche he was of hooly thoght and werk.
He was also a lerned man, a clerk,
That Cristes gospel trewely wolde preche;
His parisshens devoutly wolde he teche.
Benygne he was, and wonder diligent,
And in adversitee ful pacient,
And swich he was ypreved ofte sithes.
Ful looth were hym to cursen for his tithes,
But rather wolde he yeven, out of doute,
Unto his povre parisshens aboute
Of his offryng and eek of his substaunce.

A good man there was of religion
Who was a poor Parson of a Town,
But he was rich instead in holy thoughts and work.
He was also a learned man, a clerk,
And would truly preach Christ's gospel;
His parishioners he was dedicated to teaching.
He was quite benign and wonderfully diligent,
And patient in the face of adversity,
For which quality he was quite often praised.
He would not excommunicate when his parishioners couldn't pay their tithes,

But would rather pay them himself, out of doubt,
In order to protect his flock.

(*Canterbury Tales,*
General Prologue, I (A), 478–528)

The Catholic Church, until the Protestant Reformation of the sixteenth century, was the only sanctioned and legal form of Christian worship in the world. This had been the case since its ultimate rise to power upon the fall of the Roman Empire, at which time it became the unifying political and religious force in Europe. In the role, it had experienced ultimate power with the corruption that brings as well as spiritual and doctrinal challenges that redefined and reshaped the core beliefs of the Christian faith.

By the fourteenth century, these challenges included worldly popes chosen from powerful families for their political connections, the Great Schism, heretical movements, and issues involving the proper conduct of monastics and priests. The medieval Catholic Church perhaps was not in as bad of a condition as the negative commentary of Chaucer and his contemporaries would indicate.

Yet, it is popular perception that creates a certain reality, and if the men of the fourteenth century believed the church to be in a moral and spiritual decline and they acted independently to assure their salvation by other methods, then certainly the decline of the Church was in part hastened by those who believed, justly or unjustly, that the institution had failed them. Whether one's struggle with faith involved a movement toward or away from the Church, the fact remained that it was a powerful and pervasive influence in the life of every soul in fourteenth-century Europe.

The medieval calendar was controlled by the seasons and the Catholic Church. Since agriculture was the dominant economic driver of the Middle Ages, seasonal changes dictated

A close view of the figurines at Chartres Cathedral. Courtesy of Lisa Kirchner.

A close view of the figurines at Chartres Cathedral. Courtesy of Lisa Kirchner.

The tomb of Archbishop Henry Chichele, founder of All Soul's College in Oxford. Courtesy of Lisa Kirchner.

in some fashion the daily activities and diet of nearly every member of society. The Church controlled the spiritual progress of the year and of each individual's life. It was, in essence, the central focus of medieval communal life. One entered the world with the Church's blessing through baptism, married under its auspices, kept one's soul clean through confession and penance, and died and entered the afterlife with its last rites. In short, it shaped life from womb to tomb.

The seven sacraments were defined in the twelfth century as outward symbols of God's grace that were imperative for salvation. Baptism signified one's membership in the church. By the beginning of the twelfth century, it was generally believed that the unbaptized were not saved. Given the high infant mortality rates during the Middle Ages, parents were strongly encouraged to baptize their newborns as soon as possible. Informal ceremonies administered by midwives and to be followed in early childhood by an official baptism had persisted through the eleventh century, but starting in the twelfth, the Church wanted some kind of official regulation of the definition of a proper baptism. The ceremony was removed from the home and took place soon after the baby's birth in the parish church or cathedral.

Marriage also did not become an official sacrament until the twelfth century. The Church had historically followed Paul's teachings on the glorified state of celibacy; however, the clergy realized that the creation of new generations was necessary to society's continuation. By making marriage a sacrament, they were able to imbue the necessity of sex in the procreation process with sanctity and dignity.

Marriage was also viewed as a necessary building block for society in terms of creating stability. For the aristocracy especially, wealth was consolidated and land was passed through family hands. Dynasties and political alliances had long been an underlying motivation behind marital choices. Yet the openly accepted practice of noblemen keeping concubines had long disturbed the Church.

A decorated cross depicting the Bishop of Limoges. © Bibliothèque nationale de France.

In addition, in previous centuries it had been relatively easy for a man to divorce his wife. This sometimes resulted in property issues and often had larger political repercussions. By making the act of marriage something more than a financial contract, and by providing a blessing from a higher power, the Church hoped to make medieval marriages more stable and perhaps even happy.

The other sacraments that affected daily life concerned one's spiritual health. The taking of the Eucharist was considered to be the highest sacrament of the church. In the early days of the Church, it was celebrated as the communal taking of wine and bread to symbolize the body and blood of Christ. By the eleventh and twelfth centuries, the Eucharist had taken on supernatural overtones through the miracle of transubstantiation, the literal transformation into body and blood. Despite its growing importance, communion was a fairly rare occurrence for the average Catholic. So rare, in fact, that in 1215 a church council decreed that all

The tomb of Archibishop John Stratford. Courtesy of Lisa Kirchner.

Eleanor Cross in Northampton. Courtesy of Corbis.

Christians must partake of it at least once per year. It was one of the important parts of the expression of faith that enabled the laity to participate in the mysteries of the church.

Confession was also crucial for atoning for one's sins and doing penance to demonstrate contrition. Unlike the relative anonymity of a confessional booth in modern times, medieval confessors knelt at the altar while the priest pulled his hood down to cover his eyes. Penance was assigned relative to the severity of the penitent's sins. Confirmation was regularized for older children in the thirteenth century, and Mass was made mandatory on Sundays and festivals. It was, of course, conducted completely in Latin. Finally, extreme unction, or last rites, required the sinner to demonstrate proper remorse at death in order to obtain final forgiveness and salvation. By the late twelfth century, last rites were required for a soul to enter heaven.

Days off were observed around the calendar of saints' days. In fact, the word "holiday" originates with "holy day." These were times that were intended for quiet contemplation, as on every Sunday, along with church attendance and communal activity. The three most important holy days were Christmas, Easter, and Pentecost (50 days after Easter). The major feasts combined elements of both pagan and Christian holy days—especially Christmas, which incorporated not only the general timing of the winter solstice, but also mistletoe and yule logs from pagan Germanic and Celtic celebrations of the shortest day of the year.

The local church formed the hub around which the community turned, and at the center of the hub was the parish priest. He was provided with a house in the parish and was supported by tithes, fees for services rendered, and rent from any land that he had in the parish. He used his income for upkeep of the church, providing for the poor, and providing hospitality to travelers. In most rural areas, the parish priest was of common birth; however, it was extremely rare that he would be of the lower peasant class.

The need for a certain degree of education obviated the possibility that someone of impoverished beginnings could rise to such an important position within the medieval hierarchy. As dissatisfaction with abuses by the church grew, this perceived disparity between the relatively high place of the priest as opposed to the majority of his parishioners led to tension be-

The Temple Church in London. Courtesy of Lisa Kirchner.

tween shepherd and flock, a tension that was often heightened in times of scarcity by the practice of tithing.

Tithing was a system requiring each person to give one-tenth of his or her income to the church. Because the fourteenth century was not yet fully a cash economy, many tithes were paid in kind—a bag of grain, a chicken, or an article of craftsmanship. For many, there were times when the pressure of paying a tithe plus rental to an overlord in goods left the family in want. When a peasant's children were hungry and dressed in rags while the priest looked well fed and warmly dressed, it is easy to see where resentment against the structure of the Church had its most fundamental roots.

The church provided spiritual guidance in the form of weekly masses and the availability of the priest for consultation. In addition, the church provided important functions of entertainment and commerce. Since the church was usually located centrally in a village, right on the village square, up until Chaucer's day it was the focal point for weekly markets. Often a cut of the proceeds from the markets was taken by the church for its own expenses, and the privilege of holding a market was strictly regulated by the king. By the fourteenth century, while markets generally were still held in cathedral towns, their auspices were purely secular.

The church also provided the only venue for theater in the form of instructional entertainment, the mystery and miracle plays. These plays took the form of cycles, with a new chapter enacted each time, portraying key stories from the Bible, and were performed either in the churchyard or on its porch.

See also Baptism; Calendar; Cathedrals; Great Schism; Heresy; Indulgences; Marriage; Monk; Nun; Parson; Prioress; Sex

FURTHER READING

Biller, Peter, and Barrie Dobson, eds. *The Medieval Church: Universities, Heresy, and the Religious Life: Essays in Honour of Gordon Leff.* Rochester, NY: Boydell Press, 1999.

Blumenfeld-Kosinski, Renate. *Poets, Saints, and Visionaries of the Great Schism, 1378–1417.* University Park: Pennsylvania State University Press, 2006.

Foster, Edward E., and David H. Carey, eds. *Chaucer's Church: A Dictionary of Religious Terms in Chaucer.* Brookfield, VT: Ashgate, 2002.

Raguin, Virginia Chieffo, and Sarah Stanbury, eds. *Women's Space: Patronage, Place, and Gender in the Medieval Church.* Albany: State University of New York Press, 2005.

An undated illumination of Charles VI, Isabelle, and Richard II. © Bibliothèque nationale de France.

Richard II

Richard II (1367–1400), second born and eldest surviving son of Edward the Black Prince, ascended the throne in 1377 upon the death of his grandfather Edward III. His uncle, the unpopular but very powerful John of Gaunt, was Richard's most loyal supporter, protector, and advisor over the next two decades. Neither of Richard's two marriages, to Anne of Bohemia (1366–94) in 1382 and Isabella of Valois (1387–1410) in 1396, produced heirs.

Richard came to a throne left in disarray by his ailing and apathetic grandfather, beset by contentious barons eager to wrest control from the boy king. Making things worse for Richard was the changing social world he entered, one where commoners were increasingly questioning the aristocracy's right to rule. Unfortunately for him, Richard clung to the earlier medieval notion that a king is God's appointed leader.

Fourteen-year-old Richard's handling of the Peasant Revolt of 1381 (Wat Tyler's Rebellion) was perhaps the high point of his reign. Showing remarkable courage, he rode to Mile End with a small company of nobles to meet Wat Tyler and the peasant rebels. His concessions were more than fair, and Richard granted the rebels all of their demands. When Tyler, made reckless by his success, made more demands, the king's company seized and killed him. The remaining peasants immediately surrendered, and Richard concluded the business by not following through on any of his promised concessions.

The lessons he carried away from this incident made an already weak ruler a devious and prideful one as well, a fatal combination in the end. His

Richard II on the throne in England; from a painting in Westminster Abbey. Courtesy of the Library of Congress.

failed expedition to Scotland in 1385 underscored perceptions of his lack of military prowess. Furthermore, Richard's attempts to end the Hundred Years War in 1396 by negotiations were met with criticism. Peace without victory went against medieval notions of chivalry and bravery. Like Edward II before him, Richard was also believed to shower too much attention on his favorites. The growing discontent within Parliament led to the attack upon the king's councilors in 1388 known as the Merciless Parliament. Those who had not fled were found guilty of treason.

Richard nursed his grievances for the remainder of his reign, and his wrath reached a head in 1397 when he had the leaders of the Merciless Parliament (including Henry of Bolingbroke, Gaunt's son and the future Henry IV) exiled, murdered, or executed. With his enemies dispatched,

Richard was free to wield the unquestioned power he believed was his right. His megalomania pushed tolerance to the limits, tolerance that was only held in check by John of Gaunt.

When Gaunt died in February 1399, Richard's final tie to reason was severed and Bolingbroke decided to stake his claim to the throne. Richard's attempt to flee to north Wales ended with his capture and forced abdication in favor of Henry. In 1400 he was secretly murdered in Pontefract Castle.

In "Lak of Stedfastnesse," one of Chaucer's short poems, the poet addresses the beleaguered Richard II, telling him to hold fast to principles.

See also John of Gaunt; Peasant Revolt

FURTHER READING

Bennett, Michael. *Richard II and the Revolution of 1399.* Gloucestershire, England: Sutton, 1999.

Bevan, Bryan. *Edward III: Monarch of Chivalry.* London: Rubicon Press, 1992.

Cantor, Norman. *The Encyclopedia of the Middle Ages.* New York: Viking Press, 1999.

Collins, Hugh E. L. *The Order of the Garter, 1348–1461: Chivalry and Politics in Late Medieval England.* New York: Oxford University Press, 2000.

Dunn, Alastair. *The Peasant's Revolt: England's Failed Revolution of 1381.* Stroud, England: Tempus, 2004.

Fraser, Antonia, ed. *The Lives of the Kings and Queens of England.* Rev. ed. Berkeley: University of California Press, 1998.

O'Brien, Mark. *When Adam Delved and Eve Span: A History of the Peasants' Revolt of 1381.* Cheltenham, England: New Clarion, 2004.

Staley, Lynn. *Languages of Power in the Age of Richard II.* University Park: Pennsylvania State University Press, 2005.

Rooster and Hen

In al the land, of crowyng nas his peer.
His voys was murier than the murie orgon
On messe-dayes that in the chirche gon.
...

His coomb was redder than the fyn coral,
And batailled as it were a castel wal;
His byle was blak, and as the jeet it shoon;
Lyk asure were his legges and his toon;
His nayles whitter than the lylye flour,
...

fair damoysele Pertelote.
Curteys she was, discreet, and debonaire,
And compaignable, and bar hyrself so faire

Syn thilke day that she was seven nyght oold
That trewely she hath the herte in hoold
Of Chauntecleer.

In all of the land, he had no peer in crowing.
His voice was mellower than the mellow organ
That on mass days was heard in the church
...

His comb was redder than fine coral,
And crenellated just like a castle wall;
His beak was black and shone just like jet
Azure blue were his legs and toes
And his nails were whiter than the lily-flower.
...

His fair wife Pertelote
Was courteous, gentle and kind,
With friendly ways, and was herself so beautiful
Even since the day she turned seven nights old
That she truly held the heart
Of Chauntecleer.

(*Canterbury Tales,*
"The Nun's Priest's Tale," VII, 2850–52, 2859–
63, 2870–75)

Chickens are the main characters in Chaucer's "The Nun's Priest's Tale," a story that interestingly portrays poultry in the guise of a noble knight and his lady fair. Symbolically, the rooster was considered to be intelligent, watchful, and vigilant, announcing the dawn and often the death of a man. However, the lengths to which Chaucer goes to make his chickens appear aristocratic and philosophical is an extended literary joke that makes this story one of the most delightful in *The Canterbury Tales*.

Because the rooster crows to welcome the dawn, he was long considered to be a bird of cleverness, even of prescience. His attentive nature enables him to determine when the sun will rise and, for the ancients in particular, his loud crow chased away the darkness. In a Christian context, the cock crowed three times before Peter denied Christ, a fulfilled prophecy that made the bird the emblem of St. Peter.

"The Nun's Priest's Tale" features Chauntecleer the rooster and his bride Pertelote. She is one of seven in his flock, and the most beautiful and noble. Through the tale of the proud rooster, literally henpecked into placing himself into danger, and ultimately besting the wily fox, Chaucer provides a parody of the kind of courtly literature served up by the Squire. The language is of the troubadours, but Chaucer never lets us forget that these are chickens in a barnyard.

See also Animals; Birds

FURTHER READING

Rowland, Beryl. *Blind Beasts: Chaucer's Animal World*. Kent, OH: Kent State University Press, 1971.

Salisbury, Joyce E., ed. *The Medieval World of Nature: A Book of Essays*. New York: Garland, 1993.

Strickland, Debra Higgs. *Medieval Bestiaries: Text, Image, Ideology*. New York: Cambridge University Press, 1995.

Telesko, Werner. *The Wisdom of Nature: The Healing Powers and Symbolism of Plants and Animals in the Middle Ages*. New York: Prestel, 2001.

Russia

In Lettow hadde he reysed and in Ruse,
No Cristen man so ofte of his degree.

In Lithuania he had raised and in Russia
There was no Christian man who had fought there so often.

(*Canterbury Tales*,
General Prologue, I (A), 54–55)

Russia, in the medieval period, developed as a loosely affiliated group of states, all of Eastern Slavic ethnicity, which fused Byzantine culture with its own through the 988 conversions to Christianity initiated by the Byzantine Empire. By the thirteenth century, however, the Mongolian Tatars had begun to dominate Russia, demanding tribute money from individual princes to continue to rule in relative independence.

Although some princes turned to the Tatars for assistance in resisting Lithuanian and Swedish encroachments, as well as invasions by the Teutonic knights (of which the Knight was a part), once Mongolian domination began to demonstrate signs of weakening, the grand princes of Russia rose up in open opposition (*Canterbury Tales,* General Prologue, I (A), 52–54). In 1380, the khan was defeated, shifting the balance of power in Russia.

See also Knight

FURTHER READING

Cantor, Norman. *The Civilization of the Middle Ages*. Rev. ed. New York: Harper Collins, 1993.

Jones, Terry. *Chaucer's Knight: The Portrait of a Medieval Mercenary*. Baton Rouge: Louisiana State University Press, 1980.

Kaeuper, Richard W. *Chivalry and Violence in Medieval Europe*. New York: Oxford University Press, 1999.

Labarge, Margaret Wade. *Medieval Travellers*. New York: Norton, 1983.

S

Science

———————

Unslekked lym, chalk, and gleyre of an ey,
Poudres diverse, asshes, donge, pisse, and cley,
Cered pokkets, sal peter, vitriole,
And diverse fires maad of wode and cole;
Sal tartre, alkaly, and sal preparat,
And combust materes and coagulat;

  …

I wol yow telle, as was me taught also,
The foure spirites and the bodies sevene,

  …

The firste spirit quyksilver called is,
The seconde orpyment, the thridde, ywis,
Sal armonyak, and the ferthe brymstoon.
The bodyes sevene eek, lo, hem heere anoon:
Sol gold is, and Luna silver we threpe,
Mars iren, Mercurie quyksilver we clepe,
Saturnus leed, and Juppiter is tyn,
And Venus coper, by my fader kyn!

I could tell you of unslaked lime, the chalk, and the white of an egg,
The many different powders, the dung, the piss, and the clay,

The waterproofed bags, the saltpeter, and the vitriol,
And all of the fires made of wood and coal.
And there is the salt of tartar and the alkali, and the common salt,
That combusts and coagulates.

…

And I will tell you, as it was told to me,
Of the four spirits and the bodies seven.

…

The first spirit is called quicksilver,
And the second orpiment, the third,
Sal ammoniac, and the fourth brimstone.
The bodies seven; listen! Here they are:
Gold is the sun, and silver is the moon,
Mars iron, and Mercury is quicksilver we say.
Saturn is lead, and Jupiter is tin,
And Venus is copper, by my father's teaching!

(*Canterbury Tales,*
"The Canon's Yeoman's Tale," VIII (G), 806–97)

Although most people think of the Middle Ages as a period dominated by crushing religious superstition and authority, preventing any scientific growth from occurring, this is an extreme view and, surprisingly, more scientific achievement came out of the later medieval period than one might suppose. The most important thing to keep in mind is that scientific freedom of inquiry and experimentation varied with time and place. And the development of science also reflected the domination of the two movements of scholasticism and humanism, providing differing emphases depending on which school of thought one followed. However, the unifying thread for all was the emphasis on studying the Greek masters.

Medieval scientists, scholasticists and humanists alike, looked to Plato and Aristotle especially for understanding cosmology and natural philosophy, while they turned to Archimedes and Euclid for math. They studied medicine, biology, and botany from Hippocrates, Galen, and Aristotle. Ptolemy helped them to comprehend astronomy.

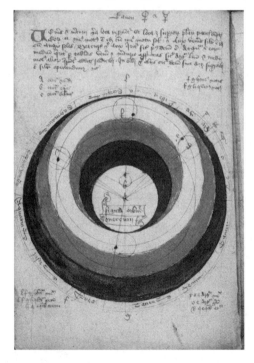

The Orbit of Mercury as depicted in a late-fourteenth-century French text. Courtesy of the Glasgow University Library.

All of these past scholars provided a theoretical background for understanding the world. Because of his range of writings, Aristotle was easily the most important influence on the scientists of the Middle Ages. As one scholar has noted, "Although many medieval scholars were determined to apply themselves to the whole range of classical natural sciences, they worked within a tradition (classical) and a context (Christian) that identified certain problems as critical ones, demanding attention. Because Aristotle's works were central to the curriculum of the universities, practically every subject he addressed attracted scholarly interest." Later in the period, his ideas would be increasingly challenged and supplemented by empirical research or observation.

The works of the classical Greeks had made their way into Europe around the twelfth century, when the Spanish conquered Muslim Spain. The Arabs of Spain had carried these works with them and had used them to supplement their own learning. Through trade, they came into contact with Christian Europe and traded information along with goods. Later, after the conquest, the Greek works they studied were translated into Latin, enabling Christian scientists to read them easily and benefit from the ideas. This translation of major Greek works was one of the more important developments in the thirteenth century for the evolution of science.

The other major development of the time was the growth of the university. Universities provided places where scholars could devote their lives to ideas, freeing them of other obligations and distractions while they explored the intellectual life. With their emphasis on celibacy for the teachers, and the single-minded devotion to one pursuit, universities were not terribly different from monasteries.

Because the Church had such influence over every facet of life and thought, it is only natural that medieval scientists would seek to reconcile Christianity with the pagan authors and new ideas they were uncovering. One of the largest stumbling blocks, and one that has of course influenced our perception of how much scientific work was conducted during the Middle Ages, was whether it was worth the potential jeopardy to one's soul to even study science. Not only were the authors in question pagans and therefore sinners, but the material itself revealed things about the nature of the universe that perhaps man was not really meant to understand.

Fortunately, universities eventually decided that it was indeed worth it and stood firm when the Church attempted to limit what they could and could not study there. For instance, the Church attempted to forbid the University of Paris from teaching Aristotle's "books on nature" early in the thirteenth century. The university initially took this prohibition to heart, but later fought against it. By the end of the century, scholars were regularly at loggerheads with churchmen, but maintained their intellectual integrity, refusing to allow spiritual pronouncements to influence their curriculum.

This firm stand was made easier by the writings of men like Roger Bacon, a Franciscan friar who spent a great deal of his professional life attempting to ease the tensions between the scientific world and the religious by finding ways to make the first serve the purposes of the second. His ideas would ultimately triumph, and, by the start of the fourteenth century, not only had natural sciences become a central part of the university curriculum, but the Church had become a major patron of the educational system. Only a few areas of inquiry, such as the origin of the universe and the nature of the soul, remained off limits or severely restricted. Otherwise, scientists were essentially free to explore whatever paths they wished.

Although they were strongly discouraged from questioning the origin of the cosmos, they did debate its nature. They did so within a Christian framework, taking God's role as a given but moving outward from that to more complex ideas. Most educated people by Chaucer's day believed that the cosmos was a sphere and that the Earth was at its center. The Earth as well was believed to be round, its microcosm mirroring the macrocosm of the universe at large.

In addition to dispelling myths of a flat earth, medieval scientists also made significant contributions to other realms of scientific thought. For instance, they developed extremely refined theories on the nature of light and vision, some of which are still in currency today. The kinematics of motion were developed during Chaucer's day at Oxford and Paris and were so influential that they informed and shape Galileo's theories on falling bodies nearly three centuries later.

Finally, in response to the Black Death, the study of medicine was refined and improved, with doctors eventually focusing on patients rather than restricting their practice to theoretical beliefs about the nature of urine or the four humors. For much of the Middle Ages, scholastic medicine dominated the field.

Based on the universal belief in the superiority of philosophy as a means of comprehending the world, scholasticism depended on the Socratic method of inquiry. Issues were debated based on theory and ancient experts were cited, but very little in the way of practical medicine was accomplished. For scholastic doctors, using one's hands in the way of barbers and surgeons was degrading manual labor. Instead, scholastic physicians based their knowledge on the old masters—Hippocrates, Aristotle, and Galen, with a bit of Pliny thrown in for good measure. It was Aristotle who provided what was the most basic of medical doctrines, the one by which nearly every ailment could be explained, diagnosed, and treated: the four humors.

Galen provided a great many specifics about the human body, such as his hypothesis on blood flow: "Ne Dedalus with his playes slye; / Ne hele me may no phisicien, / Noght Ypocras ne Galyen" (*Neither Daedalus with his playing sly / nor the help of any physician / Such as Hippocrates or Galen*) (*Book of the Duchess*, 570–72). According to Galen, blood is a by-product of digestion and begins in the stomach, where food is converted to *chyle*. While part of the chyle goes to the spleen, becomes bile, and returns to the stomach, the rest travels to the liver, where it is converted to blood and moves through the vessels to the right ventricle. From the right side of the heart, the blood divided, with half going to the left ventricle and the other half to the lungs where it mixed with *pneuma* or "vital spirit." From there it was distributed to the organs and provided warmth and energy to the body. Any residue was excreted as sweat. This was the prevalent theory until William Harvey's discoveries in 1628. Alchemy, of which Chaucer writes so thoroughly in "The Canon's Yeoman's Tale," through the work of Paracelsus, was also an important influence on medical developments.

See also Alchemy; Astrology and Astronomy; Black Death; Education; Four Humors; Medicine; Religion

FURTHER READING

Astell, Ann W. *Chaucer and the Universe of Learning.* Ithaca, NY : Cornell University Press, 1996.

Brown, Peter, ed. *A Companion to Chaucer.* Malden, MA: Blackwell, 2002.

French, Roger. *Canonical Medicine: Gentile da Foligno and Scholasticism.* Boston: Brill, 2001.

French, Roger, Jon Arrizabalaga, Andrew Cunningham, and Luis García-Ballester, eds. *Medicine from the Black Death to the French Disease.* Aldershot, England: Ashgate, 1998.

Gottfried, Robert S. *Doctors and Medicine in Medieval England, 1340–1530.* Princeton, NJ: Princeton University Press, 1986.

Gray, Douglas, ed. *The Oxford Companion to Chaucer.* New York: Oxford University Press, 2003.

Hildegard of Bingen. *On Natural Philosophy and Medicine: Selections from "Case et Cure."* Translation and introduction by Margret Berger. Cambridge, England: D. S. Brewer, 1999.

Jeffery, Paul. *The Collegiate Churches of England and Wales.* London: Robert Hale, 2004.

Kibre, Pearl. *Studies in Medieval Science: Alchemy, Astrology, Mathematics, and Medicine.* London: Hambledon Press, 1984.

King, Margot, H., and Wesley M. Stevens, eds. *Saints, Scholars, and Heroes: Studies in Medieval Culture in Honor of Charles W. Jones.* Collegeville, MN: Hill Monastic Manuscript Library, Saint John's Abbey and University, 1979.

Kircher, Timothy. *The Poet's Wisdom: The Humanists, the Church, and the Formation of Philosophy in the Early Renaissance.* Boston: Brill, 2006.

MacDonald, Alasdair A., and Michael W. Twonmey, eds. *Schooling and Society: The Ordering and Reordering of Knowledge in the Western Middle Ages.* Dudley, MA: Peeters, 2004.

Orme, Nicholas. *English Schools in the Middle Ages.* London: Methuen, 1973.

Scrope-Grosvenor Trial

The Scrope-Grosvenor trial concerned the right of one family over another to use a particular coat of arms. The 1385 suit was brought to the Earl

Marshall's Court by Lord Richard Le Scrope, Chief Justice of the Kings Bench, against Sir Robert Grosvenor and was the second such case in which Scrope had been involved that year. Previously, William Carminow, the Sheriff of Cornwall, brought suit against Scrope, claiming that his family had rights to the same coat of arms dating back to a since-lost charter from King Arthur.

Although Scrope's claim only dated to the Conquest, he won the case, apparently thanks in part to his powerful friends, but also to the dubious nature of Carminow's claim. In the next case, Scrope discovered that Grosvenor was also using the same coat of arms, although Grosvenor maintained that the replication was unintentional.

Both the Scropes and the Grosvenors were powerful families in four-teenth-century England; the Scropes, however, were more influential. When both were called to arms for one of Richard II's Scottish campaigns, they noticed that they were showing the same coat of arms. A conflict ensued, with both men demanding the other desist in using the arms.

The ensuing lawsuit lasted for five long years, with each man producing depositions from the rich and powerful to support them. Scrope's claims were bolstered when a seal from the Franciscan friary of Richmond was submitted bearing the same arms (a blue shield with a golden bend). The friary was closely connected with the Scrope family and had acquired land from Richard Scrope to enlarge its facilities. They were also strengthened by testimony from royal witnesses, most notably John of Gaunt and Owain Glyndwr.

Chaucer was a witness, and his deposition provides an interesting look into the case specifically and the nature of medieval trials generally:

> Being asked whether he had ever heard of any interruption or challenge made by Sir Robert Grosvenor or his ancestors, said no, but that he was once in Friday Street, London, and walking through the street, he observed a new sign hanging out with these arms thereon, and inquired "what inn that was that had hung out these arms of Scrope?"

> And one answered him, saying, "They are not hung out, Sir, for the arms of Scrope, nor painted there for those arms, but they are painted and put there by a Knight of the county of Chester, called Sir Robert Grosvenor;" and that was the first time that he ever heard speak of Sir Robert Grosvenor, or his ancestors, or of any one bearing the name of Grosvenor (Chaucer's Deposition, October 15, 1386).

Scrope was ultimately successful and Grosvenor was ordered to alter his own coat of arms by adding a *bordure argent*. Richard II, upon direct appeal from Grosvenor, altered the court's decision. Grosvenor's complaint was that a *bordure* was a sign of relatedness. Richard II agreed and Grosvenor adopted an entirely different coat of arms, a blue shield with a wheat-sheaf.

See also Animals; Heraldry; Knight

FURTHER READING

Coss, Peter, and Maurice Keen, eds. *Heraldry, Pageantry, and Social Display in Medieval England.* Rochester, NY: Boydell Press, 2002.

De Pisan, Christine. *The Book of Deeds of Arms and of Chivalry.* Translated by Sumner Willard. Edited by Charity Cannon Willard. University Park: Pennsylvania State University Press, 1999.

Sex

Herkne eek, lo, which a sharp word for the nones,
Biside a welle, Jhesus, God and man,
Spak in repreeve of the Samaritan;
"Thou has yhad fyve housbondes," quod he,
"And that ilke man that now hath thee
is noght thyn houbonde," thus seyde he certeyn.
What that he mente thereby, I can nat seyn;
But that I axe, why that the fifthe man
Was noon housbonde to the Samaritan?
How manye myghte she have in mariage?
Yet herde I nevere tellen in myn age
Upon this nombre diffinicioun.
...

What rekketh me, thogh folk seye vileynye
Of shrewed Lameth and his bigamye?
I woot wel Abraham was an hooly man,
And Jacob eek, as ferforth as I kan;
And ech of hem hadde syves mo than two,
And many another holy man also.
Wher can ye seye, in any manere age,
That hye God defended mariage
By expres word? I pray yow, telleth me.
Or where comanded he virginitee?

I was told to hearken too, the sharp words
That Jesus, who was both God and man,
Spoke in reproof to the Samaritan;
"You have had five husbands," he said,
"and that man who you have now
is not your husband," so he said with certainty,
but what he meant by it, I cannot really say.
But I will still ask, why the fifth man
Was not considered to be her husband?
How many men might she wed?
In all my years, I have never

Heard this number defined precisely.

…

What do I care, even if folks say it is villainy
That Lamech committed with his bigamy?
I know well that Abraham was a holy man,
And Jacob too, so far as I can tell;
And both of them had more wives than two,
As did many another holy man.
Where can you say, in any age,
That God forbade marriage
By any express word? I pray you to tell me
Where he commanded virginity.

(*Canterbury Tales,*
"The Wife of Bath's Tale," III (D), 14–25, 53–62)

In medieval society, so morally dominated by the precepts of the Church, marriage was a state inferior to virginity. Following the writings of Paul, those who wanted to be considered perfect should join a celibate order and live in perpetual state of virginity. Those who could not manage this life-long commitment needed to find a way to end their celibacy without condemning themselves to hell.

The answer was in marriage—better to marry than burn. This was true for both men and women.

However, for women, the state of virginity until marriage was of especially high importance. Her chastity before and within the marriage was the most important thing about a woman. While men were not expected to hold themselves to such high standards, they still faced dangers, spiritual and physical, if they overindulged themselves sexually. There were also legal ramifications for both men and women if they engaged in premarital sex. Because fornication was a moral offense, it was punishable in ecclesiastical courts and, therefore, the responsibility of the Summoner to issue summonses to the guilty parties.

Not only was a woman expected to maintain chastity before and after marriage, but also in widowhood. It was generally accepted that a good Christian would only marry once. This was particularly true for women. A second marriage was an indication that a woman was not really concerned about her spiritual development and understanding divine love. She was instead concentrating on the rewards of physical love in this world.

This is the Wife of Bath's situation, albeit to an exaggerated degree. She has married five times, which indicates level of sensuality that might have been found threatening to men and women of her time. Indeed, she asks why God would have given us pleasure in our sex organs if he didn't intend us to use them. to justify her decisions, or at least to establish credible precedence, her prologue refers to several Old Testament figures who married many times (*Canterbury Tales,* "The Wife of Bath's Tale," III (D), 14–25, 53–62).

As the Wife implies in her prologue, while sex outside of marriage was forbidden, within marriage it was a complicated situation. The law of the Church obligated husbands and wives to have sex with one another upon demand—known as payment of the marital debt—but also restricted the number of times they should be having it in order to prevent excessive demand and lechery in the marital bed. The Wife used her claim to the debt to control her husbands. If they desired sex, she withheld it, complaining of excessive use. If they respected her wishes, she responded by demanding sex, claiming they were feeble and could not fill her needs.

The payment of the marital debt was tricky for women, for moral reasons. For example, the Wife is viewed as a trifle wild because she knows the market value of sex and she freely admits its pleasurable appeal. For men, the danger came from the physical demands of sex. Because seminal fluid was believed to be in limited supply—a man was thought to be born with a certain amount of it and, when it was used up, there would be no more. Worse yet, as semen contained a man's life force, when the supply dwindled, so did his energy. Therefore, indiscriminate sex could foreshorten a man's life and was particularly risky for older men, who were weakened already through the passage of time.

And yet the eagerness of men for the very dangerous act of copulation was a standard stock comic motif of literature and music. Not only was there the stereotypical young groom who is so enthusiastic for his wedding night that he wishes the day away, but there is the other end of the spectrum of which Chaucer makes particular use: the *Senex amans,* or old man in love. These men are just as eager for their wedding nights, yet they are so feeble one fears they might not survive. Because they are ancient and nearly doddering, the audience knows that they will not be able to satisfy their young wives, who inevitably will stray and betray them.

The most comic of these is the figure of January in "The Merchant's Tale," who foolishly weds young May, a lusty girl who not only cuckolds him, but does it under his nose and outwits him about it with her quick thinking and smooth tongue. January's eagerness for his wedding night makes him an object of mockery, as does his desire for frequent intercourse in inventive places:

════════════════

This Januarie is ravysshed in a traunce
At every tyme he looked on hir face;
But in his herte he gan hire to manace
That he that nyght in armes wolde hire streyne
Harder than evere Parys dide Eleyne.
   ...

And Januarie hath faste in armes take
His fresshe May, his paradys, his make.
He lulleth hire; he kisseth hire ful ofte;
With thikke brustles of his berd unsofte,
Lyk to the skyn of houndfyssh, sharp as brere—
For he was shave al newe in his manere—
He rubbeth hire aboute hir tendre face,
And seyde thus, "Allas! I moot trespace
To yow, my spouse, and yow greetly offende
Er tyme come that I wil doun descende."
  …

And upright in his bed thanne sitteth he,
And after that he sang ful loude and cleere,
And kiste his wyf, and made wantown cheere.
He was al coltissh, ful of ragerye,
And ful of jargon as a flekked pye.
The slakke skyn aboute his nekke shaketh
Whil that he sang, so chaunteth he and craketh.
  …

Anon he preyde hire strepen hire al naked
He wolde of hire, he seyde, han som plesaunce,
  …

And she obeyeth, be hire lief or looth.
  …

He made a gardyn, walled al with stoon;
So fair a gardyn woot I nowher noon.
For, out of doute, I verraily suppose
That he that wroot the Romance of the Rose
Ne koude of it the beautee wel devyse;
Ne Priapus ne myght nat suffise,
  …

And whan he wolde paye his wyf hir dette
In somer seson, thider wolde he go,
And May his wyf, and no wight but they two;
And thynges whiche that were nat doon abedde,
He in the gardyn parfourned hem and spedde.

This January was struck dumb in a trance
Every time he looked into her face;
But in his heart he began to imagine
That he would that night hold her in his arms and
Strain her harder than Paris ever strained Helen.
  …
And January passionately into his arms
Took his May, his paradise, his mate.
He lulled her and kissed her often
With the bristles of his beard harsh—

Like the skin of a shark, sharp as briars
For he was freshly shaved, after his fashion—
He rubbed them against her tender face,
And said to her, "Alas! I must trespass
Upon you, my spouse, and I fear I might
Greatly offend you now that the time
Has come for me to descend."
...

Then he sat upright in bed,
And began to sing loud and clear
And kissed his wife and acted friskily.
He was all coltish and full of lechery,
And as full of chatter as a magpie.
The slack skin around his neck shook
While he sang, so croakingly like a frog.
...

And then he asked her to strip herself naked
He would ask of her, he said, some pleasure,
...

And she obeyed him, whether she liked it or not.
...

He made a garden, walled with stone
So fair a garden was nowhere to be seen
Without a doubt, I honestly believe
That he who wrote the Romance of the Rose
Could not accurately depict its beauty;
Nor might even Priapus be able to.
...

And when he would pay his wife her debt
In summer season, there he would go
And May his wife, and no-one but the two of them.
And all those things that were not done in bed,
He would perform in the garden.

(*Canterbury* Tales,
"The Merchant's Tale," IV (E), 1750–54,
1821–50, 1958–61, 2029-34, 2048–52)

The Merchant says he knows not whether May found this heaven or hell, but the fact that January is made so ridiculous that she endeavors to have sex in a tree with his squire is ample testament to the sad fact that January cannot satisfy his wife, despite his creative quests for amorous locales.

See also Marriage; Priapus; Religion

FURTHER READING

Bullough, Vern L. *Sexual Practices and the Medieval Church*. Buffalo, NY: Prometheus Books, 1982.

Duby, Georges. *Love and Marriage in the Middle Ages*. Translated by Jane Dunnett. Chicago: University of Chicago Press, 1988; reprinted in translation 1994.

Hawkes, Gail. *Sex and Pleasure in Western Culture*. Malden, MA: Polity, 2004.

Jacobs, Kathryn Elisabeth. *Marriage Contracts from Chaucer to the Renaissance Stage*. Gainesville: University Press of Florida, 2001.

McCarthy, Conor. *Marriage in Medieval England: Law, Literature, and Practice*. Woodbridge, VT: Boydell Press, 2004.

Miller, Mark. *Philosophical Chaucer: Love, Sex, and Agency in the "Canterbury Tales."* New York: Cambridge University Press, 2004.

Mitchell, Linda Elizabeth. *Portraits of Medieval Women: Family, Marriage, and Politics in England, 1255–1350*. New York: Palgrave Macmillan, 2003.

Smith, Warren S., ed. *Satiric Advice on Women and Marriage: From Plautus to Chaucer*. Ann Arbor: University of Michigan Press, 2005.

Wilson, Katharina M., and Elizabeth M. Makowski. *Wykked Wyves and the Woes of Marriage: Misogamous Literature from Juvenal to Chaucer*. Albany: State University of New York Press, 1990.

Sheep

Symbolically opposite the wolf is its hapless and placid ovine victim, the sheep. The two stages of the sheep's life cycle, youth and adulthood, carried different symbolic connotations. The lamb had direct connections with Christian mythology and had long been a symbol of Christ himself, evoking innocence, purity, and sacrifice. It was unheard of to depict a lamb in any negative sense because it was too closely connected with the "lamb of God."

The sheep, on the other hand, had a greater range of allegorical uses, moving beyond the religious to wider symbolism. The most common, however, remained the use of the sheep as representative of the religious flock. The priest—the shepherd—was responsible for protecting the flock from outside harm:

He sette nat his benefice to hyre
And leet his sheep encombred in the myre
And ran to Londoun unto Seinte Poules
To seken hym a chaunterie for soules,
Or with a bretherhed to been withholde;
But dwelte at hoom, and kepte wel his folde,
So that the wolf ne made it nat myscarie;
He was a shepherde and nought a mercenarie.

He would not hire out his benefice to others
Or allow his sheep to wander freely in the muck
In order to run to Saint Paul's in London
To seek a chantry for other souls,
Or to enter a brotherhood.
Instead he stayed at home and kept watch over his fold
So that the wolf would not prey upon it
He was a shepherd, not a mercenary.

(*Canterbury Tales,*
General Prologue, I (A), 507–14)

The ram specifically could also symbolize sexual virility, and it appears to be a duality of this nature that Chaucer plays upon in his description of the Parson:

For if a preest be foul, on whom we truste,
No wonder is a lewed man to ruste;
And shame it is, if a prest take keep,
A shiten shepherde and a clene sheep.
Wel oghte a preest ensample for to yive,
By his clennesse, how that his sheep sholde lyve.

For if a priest, who we trust in for our salvation, is dirty
No wonder that regular men are led to lewd acts.
And what a shame it is—you priests take note—
To see a beshitted shepherd and a clean sheep.
The priest ought to set the example
By his own clean living for how his sheep should live.

(*Canterbury Tales,*
General Prologue, I (A), 501–6)

An illumination of medieval butchers slaughtering and selling sheep. © Bibliothèque nationale de France.

While he does not seem to imply that the Parson is in any way guilty of impure or inappropriate thoughts and actions, Chaucer's characterization of other religious characters makes it clear that he views many of them to be far too worldly in many cases, poor shepherds for their innocent and vulnerable flocks.

FURTHER READING

Rowland, Beryl. *Blind Beasts: Chaucer's Animal World*. Kent, OH: Kent State University Press, 1971.

Salisbury, Joyce E., ed. *The Medieval World of Nature: A Book of Essays*. New York: Garland, 1993.

Strickland, Debra Higgs. *Medieval Bestiaries: Text, Image, Ideology*. New York: Cambridge University Press, 1995.

Telesko, Werner. *The Wisdom of Nature: The Healing Powers and Symbolism of Plants and Animals in the Middle Ages*. New York: Prestel, 2001.

Shipman

A SHIPMAN was ther, wonynge fer by weste;
For aught I woot, he was of Dertemouthe.
He rood upon a rouncy, as he kouthe,
In a gowne of faldyng to the knee.
 …
And certainly he was a good felawe.
Ful many a draughte of wyn had he ydrawe
Fro Burdeux-ward, whil that the chapman sleep.
Of nyce conscience took he no keep.
If that he faught and hadde the hyer hond,
By water he sente hem hoom to every lond.
But of his craft to rekene wel his tydes,
His stremes, and his daungers hym besides,
His herberwe, and his moone, his lodemenage,
Ther nas noon swich from Hulle to Cartage.
Hardy he was and wys to undertake;
With many a tempest hadde his berd been shake.

A Shipman was there, hailing from the west,
For all I know he was from Dartmouth.
He rode upon a rouncy, as he knew how,
In a gown of wool that hung to the knee.
 …
And certainly he was a good fellow
Full many a drought of wine had he drawn
From Bordeaux, while the merchant was sleeping.
He really had no use for a nice conscience.

If he fought and gained the upper hand,
He would send them to their deaths by water
every time.
But as for his seacraft he knew well the tides,
The currents, and all the dangers there besides,
His harbor, his moon, and his navigational skill,
There was no other from Hull to Carthage.
He was hardy and wise,
And in many tempests had his beard been
shaken.

(*Canterbury Tales,*
General Prologue, I (A), 388–410)

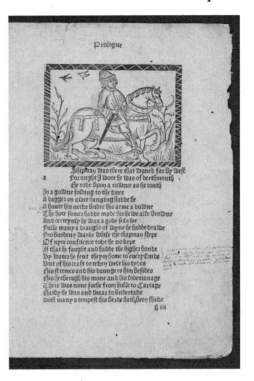

A woodcut of the Shipman from a fifteenth-century edition of *The Canterbury Tales.* Courtesy of the Glasgow University Library.

During the Middle Ages, shipman was a generic term. It could refer to either a common sailor or to the higher status of a ship's captain. In either capacity he would be involved in the shipment of goods from or to other countries. Chaucer initially leaves his definition of the term a bit vague, but his description indicates that the Shipman holds the higher status of captain.

His clothes are well-worn, but of good quality and he rides a cob, not a common nag. His character is mixed. He will not take prisoners at sea and he appears to be a good companion. However, he likes his wine enough to steal from merchants and is not above committing a little piracy when he can. He appears to be a little exotic and a little dangerous if one were to get on his wrong side.

See also Business and Commerce; Merchant

FURTHER READING

Backman, Clifford R. *The Worlds of Medieval Europe.* New York: Oxford University Press, 2003.

Bisson, Lillian M. *Chaucer and the Late Medieval World.* New York: St. Martin's Press, 1998.

Britnell, R. H. *The Commercialisation of English Society, 1000–1500.* 2nd ed. New York: Manchester University Press, 1996.

Brown, Peter, ed. *A Companion to Chaucer.* Malden, MA: Blackwell, 2002.

Dyer, Christopher. *Making a Living in the Middle Ages: The People of Britain 850–1520.* New Haven, CT: Yale University Press, 2002.

Le Goff, Jacques. *Medieval Callings.* Translated by Lydia G. Cochrane. Chicago: University of Chicago Press, 1980.

Masschaele, James. *Peasants, Merchants, and Markets: Inland Trade in Medieval England, 1150–1350.* New York: St. Martin's Press, 1997.

Shoes and Footwear. *See* Fashion

Sittingbourne

Located in the county of Kent, Sittingbourne was originally a Roman settlement, situated on Watling Street, midway along the main route between London and Dover. The name derives from the Anglo-Saxon *Sædingburga,* meaning "hamlet by the borne." The town enjoyed a fair amount of attention during Chaucer's time. Located along the route to Canterbury, Sittingbourne became an important way station for pilgrims, boasting two inns for travelers. It also was home to a number of the peasants involved in Wat Tyler's Rebellion in 1381.

The Canterbury pilgrims arrive here at the end of "The Summoner's Tale":

My tale is doon; we been almost at towne.

My tale is done; and we are almost at Sittingbourne town.

(*Canterbury Tales,*
"The Summoner's Tale," III (D), 2294)

See also London; Southwark

FURTHER READING

Archer, Lucy. *Architecture in Britain and Ireland, 600–1500.* London: Harvill Press, 1999.

Brewer, Derek. *Chaucer and His World.* Cambridge, England: D. S. Brewer, 1978; reprinted 1992.

Hanawalt, Barbara A., ed. *Chaucer's England: Literature in Historical Context.* Minneapolis: University of Minnesota Press, 1992.

Lambdin, Laura C., and Robert T. Lambdin, eds. *Chaucer's Pilgrims.* Westport, CT: Praeger, 1999.

Webb, Diana. *Medieval European Pilgrimage, c. 700-c. 1500.* New York: Palgrave, 2002.

———. *Pilgrimage in Medieval England.* New York: Hambledon and London, 2000.

———. *Pilgrims and Pilgrimage in the Medieval West.* New York: I. B. Tauris, 2001.

Southwark

Southwark is most important to *The Canterbury Tales* as the location of the Tabard Inn, from which the pilgrims set forth:

Bifil that in that seson on a day,
In Southwerk at the Tabard as I lay
Redy to wenden on my pilgrymage
To Caunterbury with ful devout corage,
At nyght was come into that hostelrye
Wel nyne and twenty in a compaignye
Of sondry folk, by aventure yfalle
In felaweshipe, and pilgrimes were they alle,
That toward Caunterbury wolden ryde.

…

Why that assembled was this compaignye
In Southwerk at this gentil hostelrye
That highte the Tabard, faste by the Belle.

And in that season on a day
In Southwark at the Tabard Inn as I stayed
Ready to set out on my pilgrimage
To Canterbury with full devotion,
That night were come into the hostelry
A company of twenty nine
Sundry folk who by chance fell
Into fellowship, and pilgrims were they all
Riding as well toward Canterbury.
…
And why the company was assembled together
In Southwark at this fine inn
That was called the Tabard, located next to the
Bell.

(*Canterbury Tales*,
General Prologue, I (A), 19–27, 717–19)

The tomb of John Gower, poet laureate to Richard II. Courtesy of Lisa Kirchner.

Southwark is the oldest of London's boroughs, located on the southern side of the Thames and pre-existing Roman rule.

In order to cross the river and sack the city in 43 A.D., the Romans built the first London Bridge at this natural crossing place for the Thames, forever linking Southwark with the rest of London. The

Southwark Cathedral. Courtesy of Lisa Kirchner.

name Southwark is first mentioned by the Saxons in 944, when they built a bridge at the military encampment of *Suðringagewoerc*. During this period, Southwark was the trading center of England. It continued to dominate and, until 1295, it was the only town outside of London to send two representatives to Parliament.

See also London; Sittingbourne

FURTHER READING

Archer, Lucy. *Architecture in Britain and Ireland, 600–1500*. London: Harvill Press, 1999.

Brewer, Derek. *Chaucer and His World*. Cambridge, England: D. S. Brewer, 1978; reprinted 1992.

Carlin, Martha. *Medieval Southwark*. Rio Grande, OH: Hambledon Press, 1996.

Southwark Fair is an engraving by William Hogarth, originally called the *Humours of the Fair*. The engraving was based on a 1733 painting of the 1732 Southwark Fair. Courtesy of the Library of Congress.

Hanawalt, Barbara A., ed. *Chaucer's England: Literature in Historical Context.* Minneapolis: University of Minnesota Press, 1992.

Lambdin, Laura C., and Robert T. Lambdin, eds. *Chaucer's Pilgrims.* Westport, CT: Praeger, 1999.

Webb, Diana. *Medieval European Pilgrimage, c. 700–c. 1500.* New York: Palgrave, 2002.

————. *Pilgrimage in Medieval England.* New York: Hambledon and London, 2000.

————. *Pilgrims and Pilgrimage in the Medieval West.* New York: I. B. Tauris, 2001.

Sports. *See* Games

Squire

With hym ther was his sone, a yong SQUIER,
A lovyere and a lusty bacheler,
With lokkes crulle as they were leyd in presse.
...

Of his stature he was of evene lengthe,
And wonderly delyvere, and of greet strengthe.
And he hadde been somtyme in chyvachie
In Flaundres, in Artoys, and Pycardie,
And born hym weel, as of so litel space,
In hope to stonden in his lady grace.
Embrouded was he, as it were a meede
Al ful of fresshe floures, whyte and reede.
Syngynge he was, or floytynge, al the day
He was as fressh as is the month of May.
Short was his gowne, with sleves longe and wyde.

With him he had his son, a young Squire,
Who was a lover and a high-spirited bachelor
With hair so curly it seemed it had been pressed in an iron.
...

He was of about average height
And wonderfully athletic, and of great strength.
He had spent some time doing chivalric deeds,
In Flanders, Artois, and Picardy
And he had born himself well, in so little time
In the hopes of winning his lady's favor.
His clothes were richly embroidered, like those of a maid,
With flowers of red and white.
He sang all of the time and played the flute all day long

Squire

He was as fresh as the month of May.
His gown was short with long, wide sleeves.

(*Canterbury Tales,*
General Prologue, I (A), 79–100)

Medieval squires were essentially knights in training. Having passed through the process of serving as a page from the ages of about 7 to 14—learning basic serving skills, falconry, and care of weaponry—a boy would be assigned to a particular knight to serve as his personal assistant or squire. In this capacity, he learned fighting techniques as preparation for the day when he would become a knight himself. He also learned the practice of the code of chivalry that demanded honor, loyalty, and courtesy. Finally, he served the knight in a practical fashion, dressing and arming him for battle and cleaning and taking care of his horse and armor.

Once the squire had completed sufficient training (and, as the Middle Ages progressed, once he had enough money to buy equipment of his own), he could be dubbed a knight. This generally occurred between the ages of 17 and 21, but there are some who remained lifelong squires, thanks to a system of indenture that developed late in the thirteenth century. A contract drawn between John of Gaunt and Symkyn Molyneux indicates that Molyneux's was a permanent position:

> The said Symkyn is retained and will remain with our said lord for peace and for war for the term of his life, as follows: that is to say, the said Symkyn shall be bound to serve our said lord as well in time of peace as of war in whatsoever parts it shall please our said Lord, well and fitly arrayed. And he shall be boarded as well in time of peace as of war. And he shall take for his fees by the year, as well in time of peace as of war, ten marks sterling from the issues of the Duchy of Lancaster.... And his year of war shall begin the day when he shall move from his inn towards our said Lord by letters which shall be sent to him thereof. (Rickert, 139)

Chaucer's Squire is the son of the Knight, an unusual occurrence because boys usually served knights in different households. He is flashy where the knight is somber, his clothing at the very height of fashion, and his interest in bravery, courtly love, music, and gallantry makes him very nearly a caricature of the romanticized knight of the late Middle Ages.

Chaucer describes him in terms more suited to a young woman—"embroidery," "fresh as the month of May"—making him seem slightly effeminate and ridiculous. Furthermore, despite his varied experience and proven valor, the fact that his father is the Knight, whose economic status is questionable, indicates that he might be too impoverished to afford the equipment necessary when attaining knighthood status. Therefore, his description is even more ironic, given his showy appearance.

See also Chivalry; Courtly Love; Feudalism; Knight

FURTHER READING

Ainsworth, Peter F. *Jean Froissart and the Fabric of History: Truth, Myth, and Fiction in the* "Chroniques." New York: Oxford University Press, 1990.

Alexander, Jonathan, and Paul Binski, eds. *Age of Chivalry: Art in Plantagenet England, 1200–1400.* London: Royal Academy of Arts in association with Weidenfeld and Nicholson, 1987.

Barber, Richard. *The Reign of Chivalry.* Rochester, NY: Boydell Press, 2005.

Barker, Juliet R. V. *The Tournament in England, 1100–1400.* Wolfeboro, NH: Boydell Press, 1986.

Broughton, Bradford B. *Dictionary of Medieval Knighthood and Chivalry. Concepts and Terms.* Westport, CT: Greenwood Press, 1986.

Bumke, Joachim. *Courtly Culture.* New York: Overlook Press, 2000.

Chickering, Howell, and Thomas H. Seiler, eds. *The Study of Chivalry: Resources and Approaches.* Kalamazoo: Medieval Institute Publications, Western Michigan University, 1988.

De Pisan, Christine. *The Book of Deeds of Arms and of Chivalry.* Translated by Sumner Willard. Edited by Charity Cannon Willard. University Park: Pennsylvania State University Press, 1999.

Jones, Terry. *Chaucer's Knight: The Portrait of a Medieval Mercenary.* Baton Rouge: Louisiana State University Press, 1980.

Kaeuper, Richard W. *Chivalry and Violence in Medieval Europe.* New York: Oxford University Press, 1999.

Laing, Lloyd Robert. *Medieval Britain: The Age of Chivalry.* New York: St. Martin's Press, 1996.

Rickert, Edith. *Chaucer's World,* ed. Clair C. Olson and Martin M. Crow. New York: Columbia University Press, 1948; reprint 1968.

Trim, D.J.B., ed. *The Chivalric Ethos and the Development of Military Professionalism.* Boston: Brill, 2003.

St. Augustine

What sholde he studie and make hymselven wood,
Upon a book in cloystre alwey to poure,
Or swynken with his handes, and laboure,
As Austyn bit? How shal the world be served?
Lat Austyn have his swynk to hym reserved!

Why should he study and bore himself stiff,
Pouring over a book hidden away in a cloister,
Or slave away with his hands, laboring,
As Saint Augustine bid? How would that serve the world?
Let Augustine have his work all for himself!

(*Canterbury Tales,*
General Prologue, I (A), 184–88)

Augustine was both the first archbishop of Canterbury and the Apostle of the English. His general date of birth is unknown, although we know

St. Augustine's Abbey. Courtesy of Lisa Kirchner.

that he died May 26, 604. Little is known of his early life beyond that he became a monk at the monastery of St. Andrew's in Rome, where he was a devoted follower of the Rule of Saint Benedict. Through his talents and dedication, Augustine was eventually elected prior. It was through this position that he drew the notice and friendship of Gregory the Great.

Gregory had determined that it was crucial to the Church to convert the pagans of Britain. The only problem was in finding missionaries to travel there and do the work. The Anglo-Saxons, whose paganism had caused a serious decline in Christianity on the island, had recently conquered England. However, the ascension of King Æthelbert to the control not only of Kent but Essex, Mercia, and East Anglia changed the religious mood in England.

In order to gain international influence, Æthelbert had arranged a marriage to Bertha, the Christian daughter of Charibert of Paris. One stipulation of the marriage contract was that Bertha be allowed to practice her religion freely. While Æthelbert was never an enthusiastic promoter of Christianity, he did open the door to Gregory's attempts to convert the island. Augustine arrived in Kent on the Isle of Thanet in 597, where he was warmly welcomed by Æthelbert and Bertha, the king even traveling to greet the missionaries in person.

Æthelbert allowed the missionaries to establish a home base in Canterbury, from which location Augustine set about preaching to the Anglo-Saxons, being careful to approach them in a manner that would neither offend nor create outright hostility. One of his most effective methods was to use old pagan temples as sites for new churches, as well as to incorporate other pagan aspects, such as holy days, into the Christian celebratory calendar. He had converted the king and many of his subjects by 601 and was rewarded with the archbishopric of Canterbury. His success cemented Canterbury as the pre-eminent religious site in England.

In addition, Augustine attempted to impose uniformity of practice throughout the isles, which met with limited success. One major bone of contention between English Christians and Celtic Christians was in the determination of the dating of Easter, a debate that continued beyond Augustine's life to finally be resolved at the Synod of Whitby in 664 by Bishop Wilfrid.

Augustine is mentioned in *The Canterbury Tales* in the Monk's description, the character's disparagement for the great churchman's rule a clue to what a poor monastic he is (*Canterbury Tales*, General Prologue, I (A), 185–88). Later, the host Harry Bailey swears by him at end of "The Shipman's Tale:" "The monk putte in the mannes hood an ape, / And in his wyves eek, by Seint Austyn!" (*The monk surely made a monkey of that man, / And his wife as well, by Saint Augustine!*) (*Canterbury Tales*, "The Shipman's Tale," VII, 440–41).

See also Canterbury; Religion; St. Benedict

FURTHER READING

Collinson, Patrick, Nigel Ramsay, and Margaret Sparks, eds. *A History of Canterbury Cathedral*. New York: Oxford University Press, 1995.

Lyle, Marjorie. *Canterbury: 2000 Years of History*. Rev. ed. Stroud, England: Tempus, 2002.

Paola, Suzanne. *The Lives of the Saints*. Seattle: University of Washington Press, 2002.

Riches, Samantha J. E., and Sarah Salih, eds. *Gender and Holiness: Men, Women, and Saints in Late Medieval Europe*. New York: Routledge, 2002.

Slavitt, David R. *Lives of the Saints*. New York: Atheneum, 1989.

Whatley, E. Gordon, Anne B. Thompson, and Robert K. Upchurch, eds. *Saints' Lives in Middle English Collections*. Kalamazoo: Medieval Institute Publications, Western Michigan University, 2004.

St. Benedict

The rule of Seint Maure or of Seint Beneit—
By cause that it was old and somdel streit
This ilke Monk leet olde thynges pace,
And heeld after the newe world the space.

The rule of Saint Maurus or of Saint Benedict,
Because they were so old and straightlaced,

St. Benedict

This monk let old things fall by the wayside
And instead let modern ideas guide him.

(*Canterbury Tales*,
General Prologue, I (A), 173–76)

Benedict of Nursia (ca. 480–543) was the founder of western cenobitic monasticism, which emphasized communal living over solitary hermitage. He is the author of *The Rule*, which became the authoritative text on proper monastic behavior, emphasizing silence, work, and abstinence from food, drink, sex, etc.

He was born into a noble family in Nursia. He was educated in Rome, which disgusted him with its excess. His precise age when he experienced his epiphany is a matter of some debate. There are some sources that place his conversion at age 14. However, his primary biography, written by St. Gregory, puts him at 19 or 20. Whatever his age, he was old enough to comprehend the emptiness of the dissolute lives of his peers. Turning away from this seemingly meaningless aristocratic life-style into which he had been born, around the year 500 Benedict became a hermit, inhabiting a cave (according to legends) on the outskirts of the city for three years. He did not apparently originally intend to become a hermit, but instead only wanted to find a place away from the city and, to that end, took with him his nurse to live in Enfide. However, when he worked his first miracle, his fame drove him to flee Enfide as he had Rome. The miracle involved fixing a wheat-sifter that his nurse had broken.

The fame of his holy ways while living in the cave led many followers to visit his cave, and eventually Benedict was forced to rethink the benefits of solitude. This reconsideration was compounded by the community's invitation to take over as abbot of their monastery. Early in his tenure there, he came to believe that social life is essential to religious life and that the pursuit of complete solitude is only attainable for a very few. However, social behavior inevitably leads one's focus away from strict contemplation of the divine. Therefore, it is crucial to regulate every moment of the monastic day. He attempted to completely discipline the monastery to such a degree that the monks tried to poison him, driving him to flee back to his cave.

However, reports of his miracles became so frequent that he was once again entreated to leave his hermitage and enter the world of men. He founded 12 monasteries and took over a thirteenth himself. While governing these, he arrived at a plan for keeping the monks on a straight spiritual and disciplinary plan. Monks under the Benedictine rule were limited as to the amount of food and wine they were allowed to consume each day, when and where they should pray, and how much they were allowed to speak. Work was a crucial part of the monk's life, as it forced discipline and reminded one to always be obedient. Labor was thought to cleanse and strip one of vanity. Private ownership of anything was forbidden, and strict poverty was imperative. Overall, Benedict's Rule was intended to keep monks humble and focused on the contemplation of the divine, rather than the pleasures of this world.

Chaucer's very modern Monk, finding Benedict's rules to be too restrictive, eschews its demands for his order, a blatant indication that he is not a dedicated religious (*Canterbury Tales,* General Prologue, I (A), 173–76). The carpenter also swears by him in "The Miller's Tale": "'Jhesu Crist and Seinte Benedight, / Blesse this house from every wikked wight'" ("*Jesus Christ and Saint Benedict / Bless this house from every wicked man!*") (*Canterbury Tales,* "The Miller's Tale," I (A), 3483–84).

See also Monk; Religion

FURTHER READING

Paola, Suzanne. *The Lives of the Saints.* Seattle: University of Washington Press, 2002.

Riches, Samantha J. E., and Sarah Salih, eds. *Gender and Holiness: Men, Women, and Saints in Late Medieval Europe.* New York: Routledge, 2002.

Slavitt, David R. *Lives of the Saints.* New York: Atheneum, 1989.

Whatley, E. Gordon, Anne B. Thompson, and Robert K. Upchurch, eds. *Saints' Lives in Middle English Collections.* Kalamazoo: Medieval Institute Publications, Western Michigan University, 2004.

St. Bernard

Bernard, the son of Burgundian nobility, was born in 1090, near Dijon, France. In 1113, he joined the monastery of Cîteaux, which had been founded in 1098 with the purpose of rededicating the Rule of St. Benedict. In 1115, Bernard was sent to found a new house that he named Clairvaux at Vallée d'Absinthe, which would become one of the most influential monasteries of the Middle Ages. During Bernard's tenure there, news arrived from the Holy Land that several crusader states were being threatened by the Seljuk Turks.

Upon the pope's command in 1134, Bernard preached the Second Crusade. It was answered by King Louis of France, who was accompanied on crusade by his wife, the legendary Eleanor of Aquitaine. The Crusade was an unfortunate disaster, and Bernard spent his last years questioning his role in that failure. In addition to his connection with the Crusades, Bernard was also influential in the shaping of Christian thought during the twelfth century. He was a trusted advisor to the pope. He shaped the new emphasis of the Church on forgiveness that ran concurrently with the growth of cathedrals, contributing to the rise of the cult of the Virgin Mary and the growth of personalized mysticism. He died at Clairvaux in 1153.

See also Monk; Religion

FURTHER READING

Paola, Suzanne. *The Lives of the Saints*. Seattle: University of Washington Press, 2002.

Riches, Samantha J. E., and Sarah Salih, eds. *Gender and Holiness: Men, Women, and Saints in Late Medieval Europe*. New York: Routledge, 2002.

Slavitt, David R. *Lives of the Saints*. New York: Atheneum, 1989.

Whatley, E. Gordon, Anne B. Thompson, and Robert K. Upchurch, eds. *Saints' Lives in Middle English Collections*. Kalamazoo: Medieval Institute Publications, Western Michigan University, 2004.

St. Cecilia

This mayden bright Cecilie, as hir lif seith,
Was comen of Romayns and of noble kynde,
And from hir cradel up fostred in the feith
Of Crist, and bar his gospel in hir mynde.
She nevere cessed, as I writen fynde,
Of hir preyere and God to love and drede,
Bisekynge hym to kepe hir maydenhede.

This bright maiden Cecilia, as is recounted in her "Life"
Was of noble, Roman birth.
From her cradle she had been raised to be a
Christian, and to accept Christ's gospel in her mind.
She never ceased, as I have read,
To pray and to love and fear God,
Beseeching him to let her keep her maidenhead.

(*Canterbury Tales*,
"The Second Nun's Tale," VIII (G), 120–26)

Cecilia is one of the most venerated martyrs of early Christian history and is the patron saint of church music. Although her actual feast date in earlier years is a matter of debate, it is clear that she was celebrated during the fourth century almost immediately after her death.

Cecilia was the daughter of a fourth-century Roman senatorial family and was raised a Christian. She was contracted in marriage by her parents to Valerianus, the son of a prominent noble, but pagan, family. Desiring to retain her virginity, on her wedding night Cecilia told her new husband that an angel—to whom she was mystically betrothed—guarded her body. Therefore, any attempts to deflower her would be at the risk of his life. In answer to his wish to see the angel, Cecilia sent Valerianus along the Via Appia, where he met Pope Urbanus. There at the third milestone, Urbanus baptized Valerianus, who went home to his wife a new Christian.

Upon his return, an angel appeared to the couple and crowned them with roses and lilies. Their zeal for the faith also attracted Valerianus's brother, who converted and proceeded to proselytize and administer to the bodies of murdered Christian martyrs. These activities caught the attention of the Roman prefect, who ordered the death of Valerianus, his brother, and, eventually, Cecilia. The brothers won a minor victory prior to their executions when they converted their executioner, who finished his life a martyr with the two men. When Cecilia buried their bodies together, she was pursued by the prefect, captured, and ordered to die.

Her death was gruesome and prolonged and demonstrated proof of her sanctity. She had been condemned to be smothered in her own bath. However, as she remained unhurt despite the executioner's attempts, he instead tried to decapitate her. The sword fell three times, but Cecelia's head would not fall. She lived for three days, covered in her own blood, during which she made provisions for the poor and stipulated that her house should be consecrated as a church.

"The Second Nun's Tale" is entirely devoted to an account of Cecelia's life. It focuses on Cecilia's saintly chastity and is indicative of the proper kind of tale someone in her position would tell. It reveals more about her than the short introduction in the General Prologue and sets her in contrast with the Prioress, who tells a tale of another saint who is tinged with anti-Semitism and intolerance.

See also Monk; Religion

FURTHER READING

Paola, Suzanne. *The Lives of the Saints.* Seattle: University of Washington Press, 2002.

Riches, Samantha J. E., and Sarah Salih, eds. *Gender and Holiness: Men, Women, and Saints in Late Medieval Europe.* New York: Routledge, 2002.

Slavitt, David R. *Lives of the Saints.* New York: Atheneum, 1989.

Whatley, E. Gordon, Anne B. Thompson, and Robert K. Upchurch, eds. *Saints' Lives in Middle English Collections.* Kalamazoo: Medieval Institute Publications, Western Michigan University, 2004.

St. Christopher

St. Christopher was and continues to be one of the most popular Catholic saints. However, almost nothing is known about his life. It is presumed that he was a martyr who lived in the third century. The legend of his life maintains that he was the son of the Christian wife of a pagan king of Canaan or Arabia. In answer to her prayers to the Virgin Mary, the boy was born, named Offro, and dedicated to Apollo and Machmet. As he grew, Offro became an imposing man, of huge stature and strength. Although he promised himself to both a powerful king and to the devil, he quickly grew disenchanted with their cowardice.

His search for someone new to serve brought him to a hermit who encouraged him to take Jesus Christ as his master. Offro was baptized

Christopher and expressed his devotion to Christ by carrying people across a stream. One day he carried a very heavy child who made him feel as if the entire world was on his shoulders. The child eventually identified himself as God and ordered Christopher to plant his staff in the ground as proof of who he was. The next morning, the staff was in full flower, laden with fruit. The miracle won countless followers but cost Christopher his head, because he was arrested and condemned to death.

He is the patron of several German cities, as well as of bookbinders, gardeners, and mariners. He is invoked against a wide range of potential maladies and disasters, including storms and lightning, epilepsy, and pestilence. The Yeoman wears a silver St. Christopher medal around his neck (*Canterbury Tales,* General Prologue, I (A), 115).

See also Religion

FURTHER READING

Paola, Suzanne. *The Lives of the Saints.* Seattle: University of Washington Press, 2002.

Riches, Samantha J. E., and Sarah Salih, eds. *Gender and Holiness: Men, Women, and Saints in Late Medieval Europe.* New York: Routledge, 2002.

Slavitt, David R. *Lives of the Saints.* New York: Atheneum, 1989.

Whatley, E. Gordon, Anne B. Thompson, and Robert K. Upchurch, eds. *Saints' Lives in Middle English Collections.* Kalamazoo: Medieval Institute Publications, Western Michigan University, 2004.

St. Cuthbert

"Now, Symond," seyde John, "by Seint Cutberd,
Ay is thou myrie, and this faire answerd."

*"Now Simon," said John, "by Saint Cuthbert,
You have us there, and you'll get your answer!"*

(*Canterbury Tales,*
"The Reeve's Tale," I (A), 4127–28)

Cuthbert, patron of Durham and Bishop of Lindisfarne, was born around 635. His feast day is March 20. We have no information about his earliest years, although it is believed that he was of English birth. According to Bede, he was most likely born near Melrose into a peasant family. We know that we worked as a shepherd as a boy, and it was in this capacity that his epiphany occurred.

While he was a young boy, a playmate (probably an angel) foretold that Cuthbert would grow up to become a bishop. This prophecy deeply affected him, and he grew up to be very devout and spiritual. While tending his sheep in 651, Cuthbert saw a vision of St. Aiden of Lindisfarne being carried to heaven by angels. He was prompted by this particular experience finally to enter the monastery of Melrose. He was, however, delayed in this decision by the instability of the times. He seems to have spent the next four years as a soldier in the service of Oswin of Deira in his struggle against Penda of Mercia.

After the battle of Winwidfield, Cuthbert was able to lay down his weapons and enter the monastery, where he would be renowned for both his holiness and his miracles. He was involved in the Synod of Whitby and won himself great favor with Canterbury by abiding by the decision to calculate Easter by Roman tradition rather than Celtic.

In 676, Cuthbert retired to an island near Lindisfarne to take up solitary contemplation. He was eventually recalled from his retirement and consecrated bishop of Lindisfarne in 685, in which capacity he served for the two years prior to his death. In 686, at Christmastime, his impending death prompted him to return to his cell on Farne Island, where he died two months later. He was buried at the monastery at Lindisfarne, becoming famous almost immediately for his miracles, which were so numerous that he quickly earned the nickname "Wonder-worker of England."

His reputation was enhanced by the discovery of his incorrupt body during his 698 translation. In 1104, during his final translation to Durham cathedral, his body was again found to be incorrupt, interred with the head of St. Oswald, which had been placed with Cuthbert's body for safekeeping.

See also Religion; St. Augustine

FURTHER READING

Paola, Suzanne. *The Lives of the Saints.* Seattle: University of Washington Press, 2002.

Riches, Samantha J. E., and Sarah Salih, eds. *Gender and Holiness: Men, Women, and Saints in Late Medieval Europe.* New York: Routledge, 2002.

Slavitt, David R. *Lives of the Saints.* New York: Atheneum, 1989.

Whatley, E. Gordon, Anne B. Thompson, and Robert K. Upchurch, eds. *Saints' Lives in Middle English Collections.* Kalamazoo: Medieval Institute Publications, Western Michigan University, 2004.

St. Denis

A marchant whilom dwelled at Seint-Denys,
That riche was, for which men helde hym wys.
    …

For which he hath to Parys sent anon
A messager, and preyed hath daun John
That he sholde come to Seint-Denys to pleye
With hym and with his wyf a day or tweye

...

And unto Seint-Denys he comth anon.

...

I clepe hym so, by Seint Denys of Fraunce,
To have the moore cause of aqueyntaunce
Of yow, which I have loved specially
Aboven alle wommen, sikerly.

...

The Sonday next the marchant was agon,
To Seint-Denys ycomen is daun John
With crowne and berd al fressh and newe yshave.

...

To Seint-Denys he gan for to repaire,
And with his wyf he maketh feeste and cheere

There was a merchant who lived in Saint-Denis.
He was very rich, so everyone thought he was wise.

...

And so he sent to Paris a messenger
To convince Don John
To come to Saint-Denis to relax
With him and his wife a day or two

...

And to Saint-Denis he eventually came.

...

I so named him, by Saint Denis of France,
To have the greater opportunity to know you,
Who I have loved especially well
Above all other women, I assure you.

...

The next Sunday the merchant was gone, and so
To Saint-Denis Don John came
With his beard and crown washed and freshly shaved.

...

He went home to Saint-Denis
And feasted and partied with his wife.

(*Canterbury Tales,*
"The Shipman's Tale," VII, 1–2, 57–60, 67,
151–54, 307–9, 326-27)

———————

St. Denis, bishop of Paris, was born in Italy sometime during the third century. His feast day is celebrated on October 9. He is usually represented carrying his severed head as, according to his legend, when he was beheaded and martyred for his beliefs, he rose and walked with his head in his

St. Denis Cathedral. Courtesy of Lisa Kirchner.

hands. By the seventh century, he had become a national figure for France and an object of much devotion.

Denis was especially important in the conversion of the French, building a church in the Isle de France, which he used as a base of operations in converting the pagans. His efforts led him to become hated by the local pagan priests. These priests encouraged the local population to make life difficult for the Christians by rioting, and they eventually convinced the governor to order Denis to stop teaching the faith.

He would not stop, and so he was captured, tortured, and eventually beheaded. According to some sources, the torture included racking, scourging, and prison. The execution itself—by beheading—was immediately preceded by other seemingly deadly punishments such as burning at the stake and being fed to wild animals. His body was collected by a Christian woman who buried it and marked the grave with a small shrine. Over time the shrine grew to include a church and a Benedictine monastery, which rose to prominence during the seventh century.

The merchant of "The Shipman's Tale" lives in a town named for St. Denis, and the cuckolding monk Brother John swears by the saint. The juxtaposition of the town's name with the swearing by a very bad monk makes for comic effect along with biting satire on the state of the Church.

See also Monk; Religion

Stained glass in St. Denis Cathedral. Courtesy of Lisa Kirchner.

FURTHER READING

Paola, Suzanne. *The Lives of the Saints*. Seattle: University of Washington Press, 2002.

Riches, Samantha J. E., and Sarah Salih, eds. *Gender and Holiness: Men, Women, and Saints in Late Medieval Europe*. New York: Routledge, 2002.

Slavitt, David R. *Lives of the Saints*. New York: Atheneum, 1989.

Whatley, E. Gordon, Anne B. Thompson, and Robert K. Upchurch, eds. *Saints' Lives in Middle English Collections*. Kalamazoo: Medieval Institute Publications, Western Michigan University, 2004.

St. Dunstan

And somtyme be we servant unto man,
As to the erchebisshop Seint Dunstan.

And sometimes we are servants of men,
As we are to the archbishop Saint Dunstan.

(*Canterbury Tales,*
"The Friar's Tale," III (D), 1501–2)

Dunstan was one of the most revered saints of the early Anglo-Saxon Church. His birth occurred sometime in the early tenth century to a noble Glastonbury family. The exact year is debated in the hagiographies written about him, although the general consensus seems to be that he was born prior to 925. His later sanctity was foretold before his birth by a miraculous extinguishing and relighting of candles. His mother, known for her Christian devotion, was in a church on Candleday, when all of the candles suddenly went out. Then the candle she held in her hand relit itself. Everyone in the church relit their own candles by her holy light, which demonstrated that the child she carried would be "the minister of eternal light" for the English Church.

As a child he experienced an illness that nearly killed him, and a number of religious visions, including one of an abbey restored to glory. At an early age, he was accepted into minor orders at the church of St. Mary. His devotion quickly enabled him to rise to prominence, and he eventually was in a position to influence kings. He died peacefully in 988, after a vision of angels foretold that he had three days to live.

Dunstan is the patron of goldsmiths and was said to control devils, as Satan notes in "The Friar's Tale."

See also Friar; Religion

FURTHER READING

Paola, Suzanne. *The Lives of the Saints*. Seattle: University of Washington Press, 2002.

Riches, Samantha J. E., and Sarah Salih, eds. *Gender and Holiness: Men, Women, and Saints in Late Medieval Europe*. New York: Routledge, 2002.

Slavitt, David R. *Lives of the Saints*. New York: Atheneum, 1989.

Whatley, E. Gordon, Anne B. Thompson, and Robert K. Upchurch, eds. *Saints' Lives in Middle English Collections*. Kalamazoo: Medieval Institute Publications, Western Michigan University, 2004.

St. Edward

Edward the Confessor (1003–1066) was the son of King Æthelred II (Æthelred the Unready) and Emma of Normandy. As a child, he was sent to Normandy to be raised at his uncle's court and, during his absence, Cnut of Denmark conquered England. Emma married the new king and bore him a son, Harðacnut. When Cnut died in 1035, he was succeeded after minor familial scuffling by Harðacnut, whom Emma supported over her sons by her first husband.

Harðacnut died suddenly of acute alcohol poisoning at a family wedding in 1042 and half-brother Edward was recalled by the English to take the throne. Edward married Edith, daughter of Earl Godwin, who had been instrumental to his return to the throne. When the union resulted in no issue, word was given out that the couple had opted for celibacy from the outset of the marriage.

It is this devotion to God that helped to earn Edward his sainthood; yet in his day, the absence of heirs was a dangerous political weakness. It could be taken by the devout as a sign that God had not blessed Edward's reign. Therefore, his claims to celibacy could very well be interpreted as a canny political ploy to turn a disadvantage into a strength.

Upon Edward's death, the throne was contested by Edward's cousin, William of Normandy, and Edith's brother, Harold Godwinsson. Both men claimed to have been promised the crown by Edward. Harold, by luck of proximity, had himself quickly crowned but was killed on the battlefield at Stamford Bridge (the Battle of Hastings, October 14, 1066), when William invaded and seized the crown—in turn to be known as William the Conqueror.

Chaucer's Monk plans to provide a tale about the saintly king in his prologue (*Canterbury Tales,* "The Monk's Tale," VIII, 1970).

See also Religion

FURTHER READING

Paola, Suzanne. *The Lives of the Saints.* Seattle: University of Washington Press, 2002.

Riches, Samantha J. E., and Sarah Salih, eds. *Gender and Holiness: Men, Women, and Saints in Late Medieval Europe.* New York: Routledge, 2002.

Slavitt, David R. *Lives of the Saints.* New York: Atheneum, 1989.

Whatley, E. Gordon, Anne B. Thompson, and Robert K. Upchurch, eds. *Saints' Lives in Middle English Collections.* Kalamazoo: Medieval Institute Publications, Western Michigan University, 2004.

St. Eligius

St. Eligius (or St. Eloi in his native French) was born near Limoges in 590 to Roman parents. At an early age, he was sent by his father to work at the mint at Limoges. His talent and honesty there enabled him to gain a commission to make a golden, jewel-encrusted throne for king Clothaire II. He was rewarded for this work by eventually being made master of the king's mint. After Clothaire's death, his son and successor Dagobert made Eligius his chief councilor.

In every promotion, Eligius used his rising influence and power to enhance the position of the Church. During his tenure at the mint, he founded several monasteries and endowed many churches, including several in honor of St. Martin of Tours and St. Denis. He also built St. Paul's basilica in Paris. Upon Dagobert's death in 639, Eligius left court and took the orders of priesthood. In 640 he was elected bishop of Noyon-Tournai, which was dominated by pagans, whose conversion he made his first and most energetically undertaken priority. He continued for 20 years in this position until his death in 660.

Eligius is the patron saint of metalworkers, especially goldsmiths and blacksmiths. He has also been adopted by cabmen, which might explain his evocation by the carter in "The Friar's Tale" (*Canterbury Tales*, "The Friar's Tale," III (D), 1564). He is also the subject of the Prioress's strongest oath "By Saint Loy!" (*Canterbury Tales*, General Prologue, I (A), 120).

See also Religion; St. Denis

FURTHER READING

Paola, Suzanne. *The Lives of the Saints*. Seattle: University of Washington Press, 2002.

Riches, Samantha J. E., and Sarah Salih, eds. *Gender and Holiness: Men, Women, and Saints in Late Medieval Europe*. New York: Routledge, 2002.

Slavitt, David R. *Lives of the Saints*. New York: Atheneum, 1989.

Whatley, E. Gordon, Anne B. Thompson, and Robert K. Upchurch, eds. *Saints' Lives in Middle English Collections*. Kalamazoo: Medieval Institute Publications, Western Michigan University, 2004.

St. Frideswide

This carpenter to blessen hym bigan,
And seyde, "Help us, Seinte Frydeswyde!
A man woot litel what hym shal bityde.
This man is falle, with his astromye,
In some woodnesse or in some agonye.
I thoghte ay wel how that it sholde be!"

The carpenter began to bless himself,
And said, "Help us, Saint Frideswide!
A little knows what has happened to him.
This man has fallen, though his astronomy,
Into madness or agony.
I suspected too well how it might be!"

(*Canterbury Tales,*
"The Miller's Tale," I (A), 3448–53)

Known for her miraculous healing powers, this virgin and patroness of Oxford was born around 650. According to her legend, Frideswide—or Fritha—was the daughter of King Didan of lower Mercia. Frideswide was known far and wide for her remarkable beauty, which drew the attention of Prince Ælfgar of the royal Mercian house. Despite her wish to remain unwed, Ælfgar pursued her relentlessly and asked for her hand in marriage.

She refused him, explaining her desire to preserve her virginity. When he refused to take no for an answer, Frideswise fled to Oxford, hiding herself in a solitary cell. When Ælfgar still attempted to pursue her, coming to her cell to plead his case, he was miraculously struck blind.

Frideswide took pity on him and healed his blindness, which won him to her cause and he agreed to no longer trouble her. In return for her kindness and devotion, he enabled a convent to be built on the spot of her cell and allowed her to live out her life in peace there.

The carpenter of "The Miller's Tale" calls upon Frideswide to help them in the face of the coming flood—an ironic twist to ask the assistance of a sainted virgin, given the fact that the flood is a ploy concocted on the part of Nicholas the Oxford student to sleep with the Miller's wife:

See also Religion

FURTHER READING

Paola, Suzanne. *The Lives of the Saints.* Seattle: University of Washington Press, 2002.

Riches, Samantha J. E., and Sarah Salih, eds. *Gender and Holiness: Men, Women, and Saints in Late Medieval Europe.* New York: Routledge, 2002.

Slavitt, David R. *Lives of the Saints.* New York: Atheneum, 1989.

Whatley, E. Gordon, Anne B. Thompson, and Robert K. Upchurch, eds. *Saints' Lives in Middle English Collections.* Kalamazoo: Medieval Institute Publications, Western Michigan University, 2004.

St. Giles

Giles was a seventh-century abbot who was born in Athens to noble parents. Rather like St. Benedict, Giles sought spiritual fulfillment that he was unable to find in his native land. He traveled to Gaul, where he lived as a hermit in the wilderness near the Rhone. Like so many others before him, news of his sanctity and wisdom spread far and wide and he soon found himself besieged by legions of the faithful. Over the years, he retreated further and further into the wilderness to escape his admiring crowds, ending his sojourn in the forest near Nimes, where he lived for several years with a pet hind.

According to the legend, King Wamba of the Visigoths sought him out here and convinced the saintly Giles to found a monastery, to be governed under the Rule of St. Benedict. Another version of the legend recounts a hunting accident in which Wamba shot at the hind but wounded Giles instead, crippling the saint.

In either case, Giles agreed to build a monastery in the valley of Nimes, which he placed under St. Benedict's Rule. While there, his reputation for miracles and saintly behavior grew. Upon his death, word of Giles's miracles spread quickly throughout Europe, causing the foundation and rededication of many churches in his name.

The Dreamer evokes him during one of his dreams in *The House of Fame:* "For whi me thoughte, be Seynt Gyle, / Al was of ston of beryle, / Bothe the castel and the tour, / And eke the halle and every bour" (*For which I thought, by Saint Giles, / everything was of beryl stone, / Both the castle and the tower / and every hall and every bower*) (*House of Fame*, Book III, 1183–86).

See also Religion

FURTHER READING

Paola, Suzanne. *The Lives of the Saints.* Seattle: University of Washington Press, 2002.

Riches, Samantha J. E., and Sarah Salih, eds. *Gender and Holiness: Men, Women, and Saints in Late Medieval Europe.* New York: Routledge, 2002.

Slavitt, David R. *Lives of the Saints.* New York: Atheneum, 1989.

Whatley, E. Gordon, Anne B. Thompson, and Robert K. Upchurch, eds. *Saints' Lives in Middle English Collections.* Kalamazoo: Medieval Institute Publications, Western Michigan University, 2004.

St. Jerome

And eek ther was somtyme a clerk at Rome,
A cardinal, that highte Seint Jerome,
That made a book agayn Jovinian;
In which book eek ther was Tertulan,
Crisippus, Trotula, and Helowys,
That was abbesse nat fer fro Parys,

And there was once a clerk at Rome,
A cardinal who was called Saint Jerome,
Who made a book against Jovinian
And there were also books by Tertullian,
Chrysippus, Trotula, and Heloise,
Who was an abbess not far from Paris.

(*Canterbury Tales,*
"The Wife of Bath's Tale," III, 673–76)

Jerome was born in a small town in Dalmatia around 341. For his time, he accomplished an impressive amount of traveling, all of it to enhance his spirituality and learning. Around the age of 20, he traveled to Rome and was baptized, then continued on to Trier to undertake study in theology. In the year 373, he decided to travel the east, a plan that brought him into contact with important Church thinkers of the time, while alerting him to various troubling controversies within the Church.

He lived for a time in Antioch, where he was ordained as a priest, then moved to Constantinople in 380, where he struck up an important friendship with St. Gregory of Nazianzus. Finally in 382 he returned to Rome, where he remained for three years. His time there was truncated by the machinations of his enemies who, after the death of St. Gregory, conspired to ruin Jerome's reputation.

He eventually settled in Bethlehem, where he lived in a monastery until the end of his life, reading and writing on the issues that troubled him much of his life. His contemplations of these controversies formed a significant portion of his later written work, but Jerome is most famous for his translation of the Old Testament into Latin, upon which he began work in 382 when he returned to Rome. His translations were instrumental to the development of the Church in the West and were used for a large part of the Middle Ages. He continued to visit both translation and analysis for the rest of his life, dying in 420 in Bethlehem.

In the prologue to "The Wife of Bath's Tale", Jankyn's book of wicked wives contains passages from Jerome, among others. Chaucer also mentions Jerome in "The Tale of Melibee" and in "The Parson's Tale," in both of which his sayings are recounted.

See also Religion

FURTHER READING

Paola, Suzanne. *The Lives of the Saints.* Seattle: University of Washington Press, 2002.

Riches, Samantha J. E., and Sarah Salih, eds. *Gender and Holiness: Men, Women, and Saints in Late Medieval Europe.* New York: Routledge, 2002.

Slavitt, David R. *Lives of the Saints.* New York: Atheneum, 1989.

Whatley, E. Gordon, Anne B. Thompson, and Robert K. Upchurch, eds. *Saints' Lives in Middle English Collections.* Kalamazoo: Medieval Institute Publications, Western Michigan University, 2004.

St. Julian

A FRANKELEYN was in his compaignye;
Whit was his berd as is the dayesye;
Of his complexioun he was sangwyn.
Wel loved he by the morwe a sop in wyn;
To lyven in delit was evere his wone,
For he was Epicurus owene sone,
That heeld opinioun that pleyn delit
Was verray felicitee parfit
An housholdere, and that a greet, was he;
Seint Julian he was in his contree.
His breed, his ale was alweys after oon;

A bettre envyned man was nowher noon.
Withoute bake mete was nevere his hous,
Of fissh and flessh, and that so plentevous
It snewed in his hous of mete and drynke;
Of alle deyntees that men koude thynke,
After the sondry sesons of the yeer,
So chaunged he his mete and his soper.

A Franklin was in the company;
His beard was as white as a daisy
And his complexion was sanguine.
He loved a sop of bread in wine in the morning;
And to live the good life was forever his goal,
For he was Epicurus's own son,
Who help the opinion that plain delight
Was the epitome of perfection
His house was always open and lavishly provisioned;
A veritable Saint Julian was he in his county.
His bread and his ale were always of top quality
There was not a better wine cellar known.
His house was never without roasted meat and fish
And it was so plenteous there that it
Seemed that it snowed meat and drink in his home,
As well as any delicacies that a man could imagine.
During each season of the year
He changed his supper menu to reflect what was in season.

(*Canterbury Tales,*
General Prologue, I (A), 331–49)

———————————————

Julian is the patron saint of travelers, boatmen, and innkeepers and is thus connected with hospitality. His legend in some ways mirrors the history of Oedipus up to a point. According to legend, Julian was a nobleman. While out hunting one day as a young man, Julian was told by a stag that he would murder his own parents. Horrified, he resolved to alter his fate through action. He quickly left his home and moved far away, not telling his family where he went or even why. His parents, however, were grief stricken to lose him and spent great energy to locate their beloved son.

When they eventually found him, they decided to pay him a surprise visit. By this time, he was married and had undertaken a fulfilling life in his new town. When his parents arrived, Julian was not at home. His wife, however, equally unaware of the stag's prophecy, was thrilled to finally meet her in-laws and assumed her husband would be happy to see his long-lost parents. Lacking better accommodations, she offered them her husband's bed to sleep in while he was absent. In the morning, he had still not returned from his errand. Blissfully unaware, his wife went to church, leaving her in-laws to sleep peacefully.

Julian returned and, finding strangers in his bed, deduced that his wife had been unfaithful to him while he was away. He promptly killed his parents in the bed where they lay, fulfilling the stag's prophecy. Upon discovering his mistake, Julian and his wife made a pilgrimage to Rome as penance, and then founded a hospital for the poor where he devoted the rest of his life to their care.

His legend is probably no more than a pious fiction. His reputation for hospitality, however, is invoked perhaps ironically in relation to the Franklin, whose board is always groaning and whose door is always open.

See also Religion

FURTHER READING

Paola, Suzanne. *The Lives of the Saints.* Seattle: University of Washington Press, 2002.

Riches, Samantha J. E., and Sarah Salih, eds. *Gender and Holiness: Men, Women, and Saints in Late Medieval Europe.* New York: Routledge, 2002.

Slavitt, David R. *Lives of the Saints.* New York: Atheneum, 1989.

Whatley, E. Gordon, Anne B. Thompson, and Robert K. Upchurch, eds. *Saints' Lives in Middle English Collections.* Kalamazoo: Medieval Institute Publications, Western Michigan University, 2004.

St. Loy. *See* St. Eligius

St. Neot

The details of Neot's life are extremely uncertain and vague. He was probably a monk who lived at Glastonbury during the ninth century. It is believed that he eventually left the monastery and traveled to Cornwall to live in solitude at the place now known as St. Neot.

At some point during his life it is assumed that Neot made a pilgrimage to Rome, where the pope instructed him to found a college for training clergymen in Cornwall. He is perhaps most famous for his appearance in the story of Alfred the Great and the cakes, as retold by Asser in his biography of the king:

> There is a place in the remote parts of English Britain far to the west, which in English is called Athelney and which we refer to as "Athelings' Isle"; it is surrounded on all sides by vast salt marshes and sustained by some level ground in the middle. King Alfred happened unexpectedly to come there as a lone traveller. Noticing the cottage of a certain unknown swineherd (as he later learned), he directed his path towards it and sought there a peaceful retreat; he was given refuge, and he stayed there a number of days, impoverished, subdued and content with the bare necessities. Reflecting patiently that these things had befallen him through God's just judgement, he remained there awaiting God's mercy through the intercession of His servant Neot; for he had conceived from Neot the hope

that he nourished in his heart. "Whom the Lord loveth", says the apostle, "He chastiseth; He scourgeth every son whom He adopteth" (Hebrews xii, 61). In addition to this, Alfred patiently kept the picture of Job's astonishing constancy before his eyes every day. Now it happened by chance one day, when the swineherd was leading his flock to their usual pastures, that the king remained alone at home with the swineherd's wife. The wife, concerned for her husband's return, had entrusted some kneaded flour to the husband of sea-borne Venus. As is the custom among countrywomen, she was intent on other domestic occupations, until, when she sought the bread from Vulcan, she saw it burning from the other side of the room. She immediately grew angry and said to the king (unknown to her as such): "Look here, man, You hesitate to turn the loaves which you see to be burning, Yet you're quite happy to eat them when they come warm from the oven!" But the king, reproached by these disparaging insults, ascribed them to his divine lot; somewhat shaken, and submitting to the woman's scolding, he not only turned the bread but even attended to it as she brought out the loaves when they were ready. (*Alfred the Great*, 197–98)

In "The Miller's Tale," the blacksmith Gervaise swears by Neot: "By Seint Note, ye woot wel what I mene" (*By Saint Neot, you know quite well what I mean*) (*Canterbury Tales*, "The Miller's Tale," I (A), 3771).

See also Religion

FURTHER READING

Alfred the Great: Asser's Life of King Alfred *and Other Contemporary Sources*, trans. and introd. Simon Keynes and Michael Lapidge. New York: Penguin, 1983.

Paola, Suzanne. *The Lives of the Saints*. Seattle: University of Washington Press, 2002.

Riches, Samantha J. E., and Sarah Salih, eds. *Gender and Holiness: Men, Women, and Saints in Late Medieval Europe*. New York: Routledge, 2002.

Slavitt, David R. *Lives of the Saints*. New York: Atheneum, 1989.

Whatley, E. Gordon, Anne B. Thompson, and Robert K. Upchurch, eds. *Saints' Lives in Middle English Collections*. Kalamazoo: Medieval Institute Publications, Western Michigan University, 2004.

St. Ronan

St. Ronan of Iona is named by Bede as one of the practitioners of the Roman custom of calculating the date of Easter as against the Irish tradition. As a moveable feast, the issue of when to celebrate the most important holy day in the Christian calendar was long debated. Ronan's practice of siding with Rome—which eventually won the debate—brought him into conflict with St. Finan, Bishop of Lindisfarne. Because Ronan was also an Irishman, the issue took on a certain political significance, one that might anachronistically be termed as nationalism. In 664's Synod of Whitby, the Roman tradition was upheld as correct and Ronan was vindicated.

He is invoked by the Pardoner in response to Harry Bailly's exasperation at the close of "The Doctour of Phisik's Tale" (*Canterbury Tales*, "The Doctour of Phisik's Tale," VI (C), 310).

See also Religion; St. Augustine; St. Cuthbert

FURTHER READING

Paola, Suzanne. *The Lives of the Saints*. Seattle: University of Washington Press, 2002.

Riches, Samantha J. E., and Sarah Salih, eds. *Gender and Holiness: Men, Women, and Saints in Late Medieval Europe*. New York: Routledge, 2002.

Slavitt, David R. *Lives of the Saints*. New York: Atheneum, 1989.

Whatley, E. Gordon, Anne B. Thompson, and Robert K. Upchurch, eds. *Saints' Lives in Middle English Collections*. Kalamazoo: Medieval Institute Publications, Western Michigan University, 2004.

St. Valentine

For this was on Seynt Valentyne's day,
Whan every foul cometh there to chese his make.

For this was on Saint Valentine's Day,
When every bird comes out to choose his mate.

(*Parliament of Fowls*, 309–10, 683–86)

There are at least three St. Valentines in Catholic records and legends, all of whom have stories of questionable authenticity and none of whom are directly connected with anything resembling love or romance.

Two of the Valentines were martyrs of the third century and were beheaded on February 14 of their respective years. The first of these was a Roman priest who helped Christians during the persecutions under emperor Claudius II. For his crimes, he was martyred in 270. The second was a bishop from Terni in Italy who appears to have been martyred sometime between 273 and 275. Nothing further is known of why precisely he was beheaded. The third Valentine was an itinerant bishop in Italy from the seventh century. Nothing more is known of his life or martyrdom.

The connection between St. Valentine's Day and romance appears to have been a popular medieval notion that birds begin choosing their mates on this day. For this reason Chaucer chooses St. Valentine's Day for *The Parliament of Fowls* (*Parliament of Fowls*, 309–10, 683–86). He also mentions the day in the prologue to *The Legend of Good Women*, writing "And songen, 'Blessed be Seynt Valentyn, / For on his day I chees yow to by myn, / Withouten repenting, myn herte swete!'" (*And he sang, "Blessed be*

Saint Valentine, / For on his day I chose you to be mine, / Without any regrets, my own sweetheart!" (*Legend of Good Women*, 145–47).

See also Religion

FURTHER READING

Paola, Suzanne. *The Lives of the Saints*. Seattle: University of Washington Press, 2002.

Riches, Samantha J. E., and Sarah Salih, eds. *Gender and Holiness: Men, Women, and Saints in Late Medieval Europe*. New York: Routledge, 2002.

Slavitt, David R. *Lives of the Saints*. New York: Atheneum, 1989.

Whatley, E. Gordon, Anne B. Thompson, and Robert K. Upchurch, eds. *Saints' Lives in Middle English Collections*. Kalamazoo: Medieval Institute Publications, Western Michigan University, 2004.

Stratford-at-Bow

And Frenssh she spak ful faire and fetisly,
After the scole of Stratford atte Bowe,
For Frenssh of Parys was to hire unknowe.

And she spoke French equally well and learnedly
In the style of the school at Stratford-at-Bow
For the French of Paris was unknown to her.

(*Canterbury Tales*,
General Prologue, I (A), 124–26)

Located at the east end of London, near Bethnal Green, Stratford-at-Bow housed the Benedictine priory of nuns that trained the Prioress. The Priory of St. Leonard was first mentioned in 1122 and appears to have been founded by a Bishop of London in the early twelfth century. The inside joke here is that the Prioress, for all of her airs and courtly notions actually speaks French with the medieval equivalent of a cockney accent, marking her forever as lower on the social scale. Had she really been as refined as she pretends, she would have learned her French in the precise Parisian style.

See also London; Prioress; Southwark

FURTHER READING

Archer, Lucy. *Architecture in Britain and Ireland, 600–1500*. London: Harvill Press, 1999.

Brewer, Derek. *Chaucer and His World*. Cambridge, England: D. S. Brewer, 1978; reprinted 1992.

Hanawalt, Barbara A., ed. *Chaucer's England: Literature in Historical Context.* Minneapolis: University of Minnesota Press, 1992.

Lambdin, Laura C., and Robert T. Lambdin, eds. *Chaucer's Pilgrims.* Westport, CT: Praeger, 1999.

Webb, Diana. *Medieval European Pilgrimage, c. 700–c. 1500.* New York: Palgrave, 2002.

———. *Pilgrimage in Medieval England.* New York: Hambledon and London, 2000.

———. *Pilgrims and Pilgrimage in the Medieval West.* New York: I. B. Tauris, 2001.

Summoner

And whan that he wel dronken hadde the wyn,
Thanne wolde he speke no word but Latyn.
A fewe termes hadde he, two or thre,
That he had lerned out of som decree—
No wonder is, he herde it al the day;
And eek ye knowen wel how that a jay
Kan clepen "Watte" as wel as kan the pope.
But whoso koude in oother thyng hym grope,
Thanne hadde he spent al his philosophie;
Ay "*Questio quid iuris*" wolde he crie.

And whenever he had drunk a lot of wine,
Then he would speak nothing but Latin.
He had a few terms, two or three,
That he had learned from some decree—
No wonder that he did, since he heard them all day long;
And you well know that a blue jay
Can say "what?" as well as the pope can.
But whoever tried to press him further,
Then would find that he'd used up all of his learning;
To any question "What is the law on this point?" he would cry.

(*Canterbury Tales,*
General Prologue, I (A), 637–46)

Like millers, summoners labored under a general attitude of suspicion and dislike on the part of their clientele. A summoner was responsible for bringing to court those who were accused of violating Church law, much in the manner of a bailiff in secular courts.

The opportunities for abuse were great, and, while there are not many accounts of extortionate summoners in the legal record, it is safe to assume that there were enough to warrant Chaucer's negative portrayal as well as the popular assumptions of the bad character of summoners in general.

Particularly with a Church-related office, the greed and corruption of a few poisons the perception of the many.

Summoners were known to issue false citations and take bribes to cancel them. Because the Church could levy punishments against the accused that ranged anywhere from public humiliation to physical pain to loss of property, many people were eager to avoid the possibility of court altogether, leaving the summoner in a potentially lucrative position.

On the other hand, the job of the summoner was far from pleasant and sometimes was dangerous. Some were beaten or kidnapped, and many stories survive of summoners being forced to eat their citations, seal and all.

Chaucer's Summoner is an unattractive character. Physically, his face is covered by boils and pimples, which scares little children. Hard-drinking and lecherous, he is quick to anger and aggressively tries to appear more educated than he is (much like the Manciple) by larding his speech with the few words of Latin that knows (*Canterbury Tales,* General Prologue, I (A), 637–46). His mutual feud with the Friar underlines the problems with worldliness that the Church was facing during Chaucer's time.

See also Friar; Miller; Monk; Pardoner; Religion

FURTHER READING

Benson, C. David, and Elizabeth Robertson, eds. *Chaucer's Religious Tales.* Rochester, NY: D. S. Brewer, 1990.

DeWindt, Edwin Brezette, ed. *The Salt of Common Life: Individuality and Choice in the Medieval Town, Countryside, and Church: Essays Presented to J. Ambrose Raftis.* Kalamazoo: Medieval Institute Publications, Western Michigan University, 1995.

Duby, Georges. *The Three Orders: Feudal Society Imagined.* Translated by Arthur Goldhammer. Chicago: University of Chicago Press, 1980; reprinted 1982.

Farmer, Sharon, and Barbara H. Rosenwein, eds. *Monks and Nuns, Saints and Outcasts: Religion in Medieval Society: Essays in Honor of Lester K. Little.* Ithaca, NY: Cornell University Press, 2000.

Foster, Edward E., and David H. Carey, eds. *Chaucer's Church: A Dictionary of Religious Terms in Chaucer.* Brookfield, VT: Ashgate, 2002.

Hirsh, John C. *The Boundaries of Faith: The Development and Transmission of Medieval Spirituality.* New York: E. J. Brill, 1996.

Needham, Paul. *The Printer & the Pardoner: An Unrecorded Indulgence Printed by William Caxton for the Hospital of St. Mary Rounceval, Charing Cross.* Washington, DC: Library of Congress, 1986.

Slater, T. R., and Gervase Rosser, eds. *The Church in the Medieval Town.* Brookfield, VT: Ashgate, 1998.

Thomson, John A. F. *Popes and Princes, 1417–1517: Politics and Polity in the Late Medieval Church.* Boston: Allen & Unwin, 1980.

Surgery. *See* Medicine

Syria

In 1346, Syria was one of the first places to experience the terrible disease that came to be known as the Black Death. Two years later, Italian trading ships brought the pestilence to Europe's shores. As a religious symbol, Syria was important in the Middle Ages, because it encompassed the lands lying between the Mediterranean Sea and the Jordan River known as Palestine.

Overtaken by Muslims in the twelfth century, the boundaries of each individual kingdom within Palestine were repeatedly redrawn, with Syria comprising five districts in the fourteenth century: Filastin (including Jerusalem), Ramla, Ascalon, Hebron, and Nablus. Jerusalem, as the religious center of three major religions, was an important destination of pilgrimage as well as a bone of contention for crusaders.

"The Man of Law's Tale" takes place in Syria, where the Roman emperor's daughter undertakes a long sojourn connected with her betrothal to a Muslim prince who converts in order to marry her.

See also Knight; Travel

FURTHER READING

Cantor, Norman. *The Civilization of the Middle Ages*. Rev. ed. New York: Harper Collins, 1993.

Jones, Terry. *Chaucer's Knight: The Portrait of a Medieval Mercenary*. Baton Rouge: Louisiana State University Press, 1980.

Kaeuper, Richard W. *Chivalry and Violence in Medieval Europe*. New York: Oxford University Press, 1999.

Labarge, Margaret Wade. *Medieval Travellers*. New York: Norton, 1983.

Le Beau, Bryan F., and Menachem Mor, eds. *Pilgrims and Travelers to the Holy Land*. Omaha, NE: Creighton University Press, 1996.

Tyerman, Christopher. *England and the Crusades, 1095–1588*. Chicago: University of Chicago Press, 1988

Verdon, Jean. *Travel in the Middle Ages*. Notre Dame, IN: University of Notre Dame Press, 2003.

T

Tapestry

The art of tapestry weaving has existed for many centuries, dating back at least to ancient Egypt where tapestries were used decoratively and funererally to wrap the dead. The walls of some public buildings in ancient Greece were decorated with tapestries. However, the Middle Ages essentially became the golden age of tapestry weaving, as tapestries were an integral part of life and comfort for the upper echelons of society.

Tapestries were prized for their beauty and artisanry as well as for their practical uses as insulation and privacy screens. In an age when central heating was still many centuries in the future, holding heat in and damp out were of vital importance to everyday comfort. In much the same way that insulated curtains function today, tapestries were utilized to create a more comfortable and pleasant environment. They were hung against the stone walls of castles and manor houses to decorate and keep out the damp, to cover openings and doorways, and as curtains around beds.

Many nobles traveled with their tapestries between manors; because they were easily transported by rolling and were very costly and time-consuming to make, it was more sensible to take tapestries from castle to castle rather than attempt to have them in every home. Often the designs were favorites, as is the case with any treasured artwork, and thus tapestries also certainly must have provided a sense of continuity and familiarity along with beauty as they were carried from place to place.

A detail of boar and bear hunt from the Devonshire hunting tapestries, ca. 1424–1450. © Victoria & Albert Museum, London / Art Resource, NY.

Tapestry of the Lady and the Unicorn, 1480–1490. © Erich Lessing / Art Resource, NY.

Until the fourteenth-century invention of a new type of loom, most of the work in making a tapestry was completed by hand by court ladies. In fact, part of the education of an aristocratic girl was in tapestry weaving. Even with the new looms, however, it might take up to two months to weave one square foot. Tapestries were woven mainly of silk or wool, and often incorporated gold thread. Colors came from the same natural plant and insect sources as it did for clothing, with red from madder or cochineal and blue from indigo or woad, for instance.

Most tapestries depicted some important event (the Bayeux Tapestry) or a mythological story (the Unicorn Tapestries). During Chaucer's time, the Church began to recognize that tapestries could be used in much the same manner as stained glass to depict biblical lessons and stories. The oldest example of Church tapestry work is from 1379 Paris, in which the Apocalypse of St. John is depicted in six 18-feet hangings.

See also Castles; Fashion; Private Houses

FURTHER READING

Brewer, Derek. *Chaucer and His World.* Cambridge, England: D. S. Brewer, 1978; reprinted 1992.

Britnell, Richard, ed. *Daily Life in the Late Middle Ages.* Stroud, England: Sutton, 1998.

Emery, Anthony. *Greater Medieval Houses of England and Wales, 1300–1500.* New York: Cambridge University Press, 1996.

Heinz, Dora. *Medieval Tapestries.* Translated by J. R. Foster. New York: Crown, 1967.

Hilliam, David. *Castles and Cathedrals: The Great Buildings of Medieval Times.* New York: Rosen, 2004.

Quiney, Anthony. *Town Houses of Medieval Britain.* New Haven, CT: Yale University Press, 2003.

Schofield, John. *Medieval London Houses.* New Haven, CT: Yale University Press, 1994.

Snyder, James. *Medieval Art: Painting-Sculpture-Architecture, 4th–14th Century.* New York: H. N. Abrams, 1989.

Swabey, Ffiona. *Medieval Gentlewoman: Life in a Gentry Household in the Later Middle Ages.* New York: Routledge, 1999.

Wood, Margaret. *The English Mediaeval House.* London: Bracken Books, 1983; reprinted 1985.

Taverns

Bifil that in that seson on a day,
In Southwerk at the Tabard as I lay
Redy to wenden on my pilgrymage
To Caunterbury with ful devout corage,
At nyght was come into that hostelrye
Wel nyne and twenty in a compaignye
Of sondry folk, by aventure yfalle
In felaweshipe, and pilgrimes were they alle.

And in that season on a day
In Southwark at the Tabard Inn as I stayed
Ready to set out on my pilgrimage
To Canterbury with full devotion,
That night were come into the hostelry
A company of twenty nine
Sundry folk who by chance fell
Into fellowship, and Pilgrims were they all
Riding as well toward Canterbury.

(*Canterbury Tales,*
General Prologue, I (A), 19–25)

Taverns and inns were a twelfth-century development in England and Wales. Before this time, those traveling across the country or the continent were forced to rely on the hospitality of individuals and monasteries. However, the rise of mercantilism and the necessary travel that went along with it, meant that it became impractical for the steadily rising numbers of

A tavern scene from "Tractatus de septem vitiis …" a treatise on virtues and vices by Cocharelli, ca. 1375–1400. © HIP / Art Resource, NY.

merchants to rely on informal lodgings. Enterprising types correctly predicted a growth industry and created the commercial hospitality field. Some people who had always opened their homes to individuals now sought to capitalize by turning their homes into inns while others leased or purchased space to start a new inn.

By the fifteenth century inns and taverns had become a common element on the landscape, serving travelers in remote areas and providing food and ale to locals when they were located in towns. Some of the more established or prosperous taverns made their own wine, as well as beer and ale, or acted as agents for local vintners.

Most medieval taverns were built like large houses, with several rooms plus a large cellar for storage. Initially, in order to advertise the structure's intension, tavern owners would hang branches and leaves above their doors to symbolize the presence of wine for purchase or place a broom (ale-stake) outside the door to advertise beer. Later, signs would become popular, many of them quite creative with artwork to accompany the name.

The purpose and level of service varied widely from inn to inn. While some taverns only served wine, some served beer as well, and others served food that was either prepared on the premises or brought in from a neighboring cook-shop. Although many confined their business to the serving of food or drink, some had rooms that travelers could rent. The rooms were meant to hold three to four beds and each bed two to three guests. Some people, such as students, rented rooms in inns on a permanent basis.

While many individuals brewed their own beer as a matter of course, there were some (many of whom were women) who excelled at it and became famous for the quality of their brew. Some of these local culinary celebrities used the popularity of their beer as a source of additional income, turning their homes into temporary taverns after brewing a batch. Although there were equipment requirements for making beer, they were not cost prohibitive, allowing even poor women to brew.

The added income was often helpful and could move the craftsman or -woman into a more comfortable economic position. Margery Kempe, the famous fourteenth-century mystic, was a brewer and, with her husband, made enough money to be able to afford pilgrimages to exotic locations.

Many taverns were meant to provide food and rest in an atmosphere that might be described today as "family friendly." However, it did not take long for a baser element to seek out inns as an outlet for other less wholesome activities, and many became known for providing various kinds of gambling and prostitutes. In comportment manuals of the time, girls were cautioned to avoid such places. Chaucer is aware of the low quality of those who hang out in taverns, a point that does escape the Pardoner:

In Flaundres whilom was a compaignye
Of yonge folk that haunteden folye,
As riot, hasard, stywes, and taverns,
Where as with harpes, lutes, and gyternes,
They daunce and pleyen at dees bothe day and nyght,
And eten also and drynken over hir myght
Thurgh which they doon the devel sacrifise
Withinne that develes temple in cursed wise
By superfluytee abhomynable.

In Flanders there was a group
Of young folk who courted folly,
In the form of gambling, dicing, brothels, and taverns,
And they danced and played all day and night
To the sounds of harps, lutes, and citerns,
While they ate and drank with all their might.
They offered the devil their sacrifices
In the devil's cursed temples
With these abominable excesses.

(*Canterbury Tales,*
"The Pardoner's Tale," VI (C), 463–71)

Of course, the most famous example of a tavern in Chaucer is the Tabard Inn, where the Canterbury pilgrims meet before departing on their pilgrimage (*Canterbury Tales,* General Prologue, I (A), 19–25).

See also Entertainment; Food; Music; Pilgrimage

FURTHER READING

Adamson, Melitta Weiss. *Food in Medieval Times.* Westport, CT: Greenwood Press, 2004.

Brewer, Derek. *Chaucer and His World.* Cambridge, England: D. S. Brewer, 1978; reprinted 1992.

Britnell, Richard, ed. *Daily Life in the Late Middle Ages.* Stroud, England: Sutton, 1998.

Carlin, Martha. *Medieval Southwark.* Rio Grande, OH: Hambledon Press, 1996.

Childress, Diana. *Chaucer's England.* North Haven, CT: Linnet Books, 2000.

Clare, John D., ed. *Fourteenth-Century Towns.* San Diego: Harcourt Brace Jovanovich, 1993.

Dyer, Christopher. *Making a Living in the Middle Ages: The People of Britain 850–1520.* New Haven, CT: Yale University Press, 2002.

Labarge, Margaret Wade. *Medieval Travellers.* New York: Norton, 1983.

Wilkins, Nigel E. *Music in the Age of Chaucer.* Totowa, NJ: Rowman and Littlefield, 1979.

Teutonic Knights

The Teutonic Knights were founded in 1190 during the siege of Acre of the Third Crusade. The order was modeled on the Hospitallers and, along with the Knight Templars, they formed the three crusading military orders of the Middle Ages, taking religious vows, but fighting as trained knights. In 1205, Pope Innocent III granted them sole use of their distinctive uniform of the white habit and black cross.

By the Fourth Crusade, the order took a strong political turn, supporting Fredrick II in his opposition to both the papacy and the other two orders, and, by Chaucer's time, it had become a haven for foreign bachelor knights, seeking chances to earn glory and goods through mercenary activities.

During the fourteenth century, the Teutonic Knights were actively involved in aggressive behavior toward Poland and Lithuania, the combined army of which eventually defeated the Order in 1410's Battle of Tannenberg (Grunwald). The Order fell into decline until the ironic turn of 1525, when its Grand Master, Albert of Brandenburg, converted to Lutheranism and used his position in the Order to seize control of Prussia.

See also Knight; Lithuania; Prussia

FURTHER READING

Cantor, Norman. *The Civilization of the Middle Ages.* Rev. ed. New York: Harper Collins, 1993.

Jones, Terry. *Chaucer's Knight: The Portrait of a Medieval Mercenary.* Baton Rouge: Louisiana State University Press, 1980.

Kaeuper, Richard W. *Chivalry and Violence in Medieval Europe*. New York: Oxford University Press, 1999.

Labarge, Margaret Wade. *Medieval Travellers*. New York: Norton, 1983.

Le Beau, Bryan F., and Menachem Mor, eds. *Pilgrims and Travelers to the Holy Land*. Omaha, NE: Creighton University Press, 1996.

Tyerman, Christopher. *England and the Crusades, 1095–1588*. Chicago: University of Chicago Press, 1988.

Verdon, Jean. *Travel in the Middle Ages*. Notre Dame, IN: University of Notre Dame Press, 2003.

Thessaly

O myghty Cesar that in Thessalie
Agayn Pompeus, fader thyn in lawe,
That of the orient hadde al the chivalrie
As fer as that the day bigynneth dawe,
Thou thurgh thy knyghthod hast hem take and slawe,
Save fewe folk that with Pompeus fledde,
Thurgh which thou puttest al th'orient in awe.

O mighty Caesar, who in Thessaly fought
Against Pompey, your father by law,
Who commanded all of the knights in the East
As far as the day's beginning at dawn,
You killed or took them all into captivity
Except for the few who fled with Pompey
And you put the entire east in awe of you.

(*Canterbury Tales,*
"The Monk's Tale," VIII, 2679–85)

Thessaly is located in the northeast part of the Greek peninsula and contains Greece's two largest fertile plains. It figures prominently in Greek mythology, being the home of the centaur and the starting point for Jason and the Argonauts in their search for the Golden Fleece. Thessaly is also the region that Jason was to inherit from his father; however, his brother Pelias usurped Jason's rights.

In the fourth century B.C., Thessaly fell under Macedonian domination when it was conquered by Philip II in 344 B.C. and later, under Roman rule, was officially made a part of Macedonia. It gained independence after the death of Constantine the Great.

In Chaucer's time, Thessaly was a battleground of much contention between the Byzantine Empire and the Turks; under the latter's control, it fell in 1355 and was ceded to Greece in 1881. Thessaly appears in the discussion of Julius Caesar in "The Monk's Tale."

See also Alexandria; Knight; Morocco

FURTHER READING

Cantor, Norman. *The Civilization of the Middle Ages*. Rev. ed. New York: Harper Collins, 1993.

Jones, Terry. *Chaucer's Knight: The Portrait of a Medieval Mercenary*. Baton Rouge: Louisiana State University Press, 1980.

Kaeuper, Richard W. *Chivalry and Violence in Medieval Europe*. New York: Oxford University Press, 1999.

Labarge, Margaret Wade. *Medieval Travellers*. New York: Norton, 1983.

Le Beau, Bryan F., and Menachem Mor, eds. *Pilgrims and Travelers to the Holy Land*. Omaha, NE: Creighton University Press, 1996.

Tyerman, Christopher. *England and the Crusades, 1095–1588*. Chicago: University of Chicago Press, 1988

Verdon, Jean. *Travel in the Middle Ages*. Notre Dame, IN: University of Notre Dame Press, 2003.

Thomas à Becket

The "hooly blissful martir" whose tomb in Canterbury Cathedral was the destination of Chaucer's pilgrims is easily England's most famous saint (*Canterbury Tales,* General Prologue, I (A), 17–18). His solid Saxon heritage, his humble beginnings, and the political overtones of his martyrdom all combined to make Becket a popular figure among the English common people. The Carpenter of "The Miller's Tale" in particular enjoys swearing by "St. Thomas of Kent" as a good all-around saint to rely on while his wife swears to great comic effect that she will find an opportunity to cheat on her husband with Nicholas. Becket also is the saint of choice in *The House of Fame* and "The Wife of Bath's Tale":

And swoor hir ooth, by Seint Thomas of Kent,
That she wol been at his comandement,
Whan that she may hir leyser wel espie.
...

And seyde, "I am adrad, by seint Thomas,
It stondeth nat aright with Nicholas"
...

But yet, by Seint Thomas,
Me reweth soore of hende Nicholas
...

Now wol I seye yow sooth, by Seint Thomas,
Why that I rente out of his book a leef,
For which he smoot me so that I was deef.
...

Thoughte I, "By Seynt Thomas of Kent,
This were a feble fundament
To bilden on a place hye."

And she swore an oath, by Saint Thomas of Kent,
That should be at his command
Whenever she could find a way to come to him.
　...

and he said, "I am afraid, by Saint Thomas,
that things are not well with Nicholas"
...

But yet, by Saint Thomas
I am terribly worried about Nicholas
...

Now listen well to what I say, by Saint Thomas,
When I tore that page out of his book,
He hit me so hard that I went deaf.
...

I thought, "By Saint Thomas of Kent,
This is a weak foundation
To build on a place so high."

(*Canterbury Tales,* "The Miller's Tale," I (A),
3291–93, 3425–26, 3461–62;
Canterbury Tales, "The Wife of Bath's Tale," III,
666–68; *House of Fame,* Book III, 1131–33)

Thomas à Becket (1118–1170) was the son of a London shopkeeper. One of the elder Becket's customers was Theobald, the archbishop of Canterbury and it was through this unlikely connection that Becket attained his meteoric rise to power. Thomas, whose sharp intellect impressed the churchman, was provided with a religious education and made Theobald's protégé, although Becket's worldly personality did not necessarily suit him to Church life. Thomas soon came to the attention of Henry II, and the two men became fast friends. Henry appointed Becket as his chancellor in 1155 and, upon Theobald's death (and against Becket's own wishes), had him consecrated as archbishop of Canterbury in 1162.

Whether it was in response to his critics, who believed Becket to be unsuitable for the highest church office in England, or a genuine dedication to his post, Thomas became a model archbishop. Much to Henry's chagrin, instead of back-

Soldiers attack the archbishop of Canterbury, Thomas à Becket, while he kneels at the altar; from a sixteenth-century publication. © Erich Lessing / Art Resource, NY.

ing the crown, Becket became an unbending adversary in matters of Church policy.

Becket soon found himself at loggerheads with the king over the appropriate punishment for criminous clerks, churchmen who have committed crimes against the king's peace and have been tried and convicted. Henry maintained that they should be punished by the secular court. Becket countered that they, as churchmen, should be punished by the Church instead. The conflict, so common in its broader sense in Europe at the time, was unnegotiable. Each man stubbornly upheld his side of the argument with no chance of compromise. As the argument escalated, Becket resigned as chancellor. A furious Henry retaliated swiftly and with secular legal retribution.

In 1164, Becket was forced to flee England when Henry attempted to have him jailed for trumped up charges of feudal disobedience. Becket lived at the French court under the joint protection of the pope and the French king for the next six years. As Henry had in effect stolen the French king's wife, Eleanor of Aquitaine, Louis was more than willing to support Becket if it meant Henry's discomfort or embarrassment.

In 1170, Becket and Henry effected an uneasy reconciliation. It was to be short-lived, however, as Becket almost immediately set about asserting Church privileges against those of the crown. On December 29, 1170, Henry's famous Angevin temper prompted him to exclaim, "Will nobody rid me of this turbulent priest?" Four knights, eager to curry favor with their monarch, took him at his word, immediately rode to Canterbury, and murdered the archbishop in the cathedral. The source of much controversy in his lifetime, Becket died a martyr to the political struggle between king and Church.

Becket was quickly canonized, and a remorseful Henry had an elaborate tomb commissioned for his long-time adversary and friend. Becket's later shrine, completed in 1120 and placed behind the high altar of the cathedral, became England's most popular pilgrimage destination; belief in the miracle cures he performed was a primary motivating force. By Chaucer's time, Becket's reputation as a miracle worker had declined but visits to his tomb remained fashionable, especially for those who could not afford a more exotic pilgrimage destination. Among Londoners, Becket also remained popular as one of their own, and the sheer beauty of the shrine made it worth a visit. According to one visitor:

> The magnificence of the tomb of St. Thomas … is that which surpasses all belief. This, notwithstanding its great size, is entirely covered over with plates of pure gold; but the gold is scarcely visible from the variety of precious stones with which it is studded, such as sapphires, diamonds, rubies, balasrubies, and emeralds; and on every side that the eye turns something more beautiful than the other appears. And these beauties of nature are enhanced by human skill, for the gold is carved and engraved in beautiful designs, both large and small, and agates, jaspers, and carnelians set in relieve, some of the cameos being of such a size that I do not dare to mention it; but everything is left far behind by a ruby, not larger than a man's

thumbnail, which is set to the right of the altar. The church is rather dark, and particularly so where the shrine is placed, and when we went to see it the sun was nearly gone down, and the weather was cloudy; yet I saw that ruby as well as if I had it in my hand; they say that it was the gift of a king of France. (Rickert, 370)

Some 300 years later, with Henry VIII's dissolution of the monasteries, Becket's shrine was ordered to be destroyed, bones and all. The tomb was disassembled, the gold and jewels carted away to Henry's coffers, and Becket's bones lost. The mystery of what happened to his remains lingers to this day.

See also Canterbury; Pilgrimage

FURTHER READING

Butler, John R. *The Quest for Becket's Bones: The Mystery of the Relics of St Thomas Becket of Canterbury.* New Haven, CT: Yale University Press, 1995.

Collinson, Patrick, Nigel Ramsay, and Margaret Sparks, eds. *A History of Canterbury Cathedral.* New York: Oxford University Press, 1995.

Lyle, Marjorie. *Canterbury: 2000 Years of History.* Rev. ed. Stroud, England: Tempus, 2002.

Michael, M. A. *Stained Glass of Canterbury Cathedral.* London: Scala, 2004.

Paola, Suzanne. *The Lives of the Saints.* Seattle: University of Washington Press, 2002.

Riches, Samantha J. E., and Sarah Salih, eds. *Gender and Holiness: Men, Women, and Saints in Late Medieval Europe.* New York: Routledge, 2002.

Rickert, Edith. *Chaucer's World*, ed. Clair C. Olson and Martin M. Crow. New York: Columbia University Press, 1948; reprint 1968.

Slavitt, David R. *Lives of the Saints.* New York: Atheneum, 1989.

Whatley, E. Gordon, Anne B. Thompson, and Robert K. Upchurch, eds. *Saints' Lives in Middle English Collections.* Kalamazoo: Medieval Institute Publications, Western Michigan University, 2004.

Tournaments

The image of the knight jousting at a tournament is one of the most enduring and pervasive symbol of the Middle Ages. In its conception of good sportsmanship and practicing knightly virtues and skills, not to mention the later ceremonial developments that combined the tournament with courtly love—the choosing of a queen of the tournament and awarding the winning knight her favor—the tournament is the embodiment of the chivalric ideal.

Although it is not clear where and why precisely the tournament developed, it is believed that the first one was held in France. Tournaments most likely were introduced as a safer means for knights to practice charging and fighting one-on-one in a relatively safe environment. Certainly knights were maimed and died as a result of tournaments, but over time, as the Church stepped in to regulate behavior, tournaments became safer, although less useful as training ground.

A fifteenth-century tournament scene. © Bibliothèque nationale de France.

Late in the eleventh century, a new battle tactic was developed, one that had to be practiced to perfection in order to be successful in battle. This new technique involved entire units charging with couched lances. Not only did the unit have to stay together for as long as possible to present an impenetrable wall of lances, but each individual knight had to be able to sustain the shock of striking his opponent and remain seated.

The tournament fulfilled a social and martial need by providing the opportunity to practice this skill and provide some entertainment for the court and masses. In the early tournaments, there was not a lot of difference between the melée and an actual battle. There were no clear boundaries, nor were there rules on carrying only blunt weapons. While the object was to capture and ransom opponents—an important source of revenue for cash-strapped lesser knights—many were killed or hurt during the battle frenzy. Years of training prevailed against keeping a cool head, and knights fought with all of the ferocity of real battle. While "take no prisoners" might not have been the intent, it sometimes was the outcome.

In order to stop, or at least slow, these unnecessary and expensive fatalities, the Church stepped in to regulate tournaments and knightly behavior. The Council of Clermont was called in 1130 to precisely this end and not surprisingly banned all tournaments. Secular authorities complained, realizing that tournaments not only provided useful training, but they also allowed knights—trained since boyhood to kill and fight—who might be restive with inactivity to channel their energies into a positive activity, rather than rebelling.

Despite the Church's prohibitions, the tournament survived and thrived. However, to instill a certain amount of restraint into knights, who were little better than well-dressed thugs for many centuries, the Church created the notion of a ceremonial entry into knighthood, complete with a set of values to uphold.

Around the thirteenth century, tournaments became increasingly ceremonial and heavily regulated, reflecting the desire to curb knightly behavior into socially acceptable channels. The tournament grew to emphasize spectator sport over practical training vehicle. Weapons were blunted to prevent unnecessary bloodshed and to protect the delicate sensibilities of the ladies in the stands.

Heraldry also grew in importance to identify the participants to the spectators much the same way uniforms in sports function today. Theatricality rather than realism became the order of the day. For instance, in 1279, a group of participants in a tournament in Hem acted the parts of the members of the Round Table. In Chaucer's day, in Cheapside, seven knights represented themselves as the Seven Deadly Sins and jousted against any and all comers.

Increasingly during the fourteenth century, in fact, tournaments were staged, complete with a plot and acted parts. They were used to celebrate occasions such as weddings, christenings, and coronations, to name a few. In order to fulfill the demands of this new focus on entertainment, ceremonial armor—heavier and beautifully appointed—developed.

Like the usefulness of the knight himself, the tournament began to fade in popularity as the nature of warfare and the weaponry used changed as well. By the seventeenth century, tournaments had become a distant memory but would be revived with great enthusiasm in the nineteenth century as part of the culturally pervasive Gothic Revival.

See also Chivalry; Courtly Love; Games; Weapons

FURTHER READING

Ainsworth, Peter F. *Jean Froissart and the Fabric of History: Truth, Myth, and Fiction in the* "Chroniques." New York: Oxford University Press, 1990.

Alexander, Jonathan, and Paul Binski, eds. *Age of Chivalry: Art in Plantagenet England, 1200–1400.* London: Royal Academy of Arts in association with Weidenfeld and Nicholson, 1987.

Barber, Richard. *The Reign of Chivalry.* Rochester, NY: Boydell Press, 2005.

Barker, Juliet R. V. *The Tournament in England, 1100–1400.* Wolfeboro, NH: Boydell Press, 1986.

Broughton, Bradford B. *Dictionary of Medieval Knighthood and Chivalry. Concepts and Terms.* Westport, CT: Greenwood Press, 1986.

Bumke, Joachim. *Courtly Culture.* New York: Overlook Press, 2000.

Chickering, Howell, and Thomas H. Seiler, eds. *The Study of Chivalry: Resources and Approaches.* Kalamazoo: Medieval Institute Publications, Western Michigan University, 1988.

De Pisan, Christine. *The Book of Deeds of Arms and of Chivalry.* Translated by Sumner Willard. Edited by Charity Cannon Willard. University Park: Pennsylvania State University Press, 1999.

Jones, Terry. *Chaucer's Knight: The Portrait of a Medieval Mercenary.* Baton Rouge: Louisiana State University Press, 1980.

Kaeuper, Richard W. *Chivalry and Violence in Medieval Europe.* New York: Oxford University Press, 1999.

Laing, Lloyd Robert. *Medieval Britain: The Age of Chivalry.* New York: St. Martin's Press, 1996.

Trim, D.J.B., ed. *The Chivalric Ethos and the Development of Military Professionalism.* Boston: Brill, 2003.

Travel

Bifil that in that seson on a day,
In Southwerk at the Tabard as I lay
Redy to wenden on my pilgrymage
To Caunterbury with ful devout corage,
At nyght was come into that hostelrye
Wel nyne and twenty in a compaignye
Of sondry folk, by aventure yfalle
In felaweshipe, and pilgrimes were they alle.

And in that season on a day
In Southwark at the Tabard Inn as I stayed
Ready to set out on my pilgrimage
To Canterbury with full devotion,
That night were come into the hostelry
A company of twenty nine
Sundry folk who by chance fell
Into fellowship, and Pilgrims were they all
Riding as well toward Canterbury.

(*Canterbury Tales,*
General Prologue, I (A), 19–25)

The framework of *The Canterbury Tales* is built around the idea of travel, from London to Canterbury for the purpose of making a pilgrimage to the tomb of Thomas à Becket, the twelfth-century martyred archbishop of Canterbury. The pilgrims plan to entertain themselves on the trip—which will be made on horseback—by telling stories to pass the time.

The plan is for each pilgrim to tell two tales, and the one who is judged the best will win a free meal. The mood of the company is light-hearted overall, although there is a certain degree of friction and belligerence on the part of some members of the party, reflecting the excitement that was present in planning and undertaking a trip outside of one's constrained everyday environment.

Most medieval people, unless they were involved in trade, politics, or religion, did not travel frequently. When they did, it was a great event. Kings, of course, traveled nearly constantly, going on progress to make their presence known, to reinforce their authority, and to conduct courts in far-flung areas. They needed to visit individual nobles to remind them of feudal duties and loyalties and to present themselves to other subjects to make the notion of a king a reality.

This was especially important in the early centuries of the Middle Ages, when the centralized authority was at its weakest and the chance of rebellion was high. Nobles left to their own devices in their own lands, where loyalty was more freely given to the lord one saw rather than a faceless king, could be inspired to stage a coup. To keep his position intact, the king packed up the entire royal court and took it to where the nobles lived.

Other members of the aristocracy traveled on court business, knights traveled to fight, priests and friars traveled for various reasons on church business, including purposes of underlining authority that were similar to a king's progress. Merchants traveled in their line of work, often going to exotic locales to purchase luxury goods such as spices and silks.

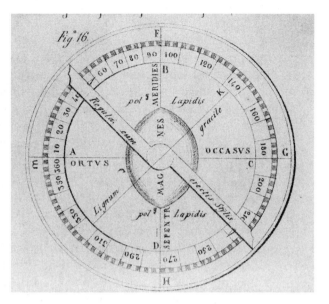

A thirteenth-century engraving of a mariner's compass. Courtesy of the Library of Congress.

For peasants, however, travel was only undertaken for family emergencies or pilgrimages. It is, therefore, no real surprise that pilgrimages were such a popular form of religious devotion during the Middle Ages.

Earlier in the period, until the tenth century, travel was quite dangerous. Robbers and kidnappers prowled the roads, and no strong centralized authority existed to police them. The king was usually too busy with other more pressing issues to worry too much about threats to peace that occurred in distant rural areas.

However, around the tenth century, when trade improved and Europe enjoyed a turning point in fortunes, the safety and enjoyableness of travel improved dramatically. Peasants could now safely move about the country and even the continent, seeking remittance from sins through the act of pilgrimage. For the times, the roads became what must have seemed quite busy. A network of fairs was created whereby merchants could buy from and sell to one another and to other customers in centralized locations. Many merchants employed men to carry their goods to market, enabling them to participate in several fairs at once. The local lords, who found a source of revenue in renting the space for fair participants, found it behooved them to make the roads safer for passage.

Along pilgrimage routes as well, innkeepers and nobles all found sound financial reasons to make travel safe and enjoyable. In fact, when a particular church was running short on funds, it would institute a sort of reverse pilgrimage, putting its relics on tour and charging admission for the faithful to see them.

Although horseback was the quickest and easiest means of transportation, an individual could cover a fair amount of ground on foot. Medieval people were used to walking distances, just in traversing their villages or, for peasants, walking around the fields and accomplishing daily tasks. The average individual could walk a mile in 20 to 30 minutes, depending on the season, and 10 to 20 miles per day. This was only slightly below the amount of ground that could be covered by a merchant train, which would ordinarily move 15 to 18 miles per day, and well above the movement of an army or royal household, which could only cover 10 to 12 miles per day. A mounted individual could ride 40 miles per day, while a courier could travel 60. In the need of haste over long distances, a relay system of horses could be arranged allowing a rider to travel up to 120 miles per day.

Water routes played an important role in medieval travel. Depending on placement and infrastructure of roads and bridges, water could either slow or speed travel. For overland travel, a river or stream could require one to travel miles out of the way to find a bridge or ferry. On the other hand, a well-placed ferry could speed one's travel along considerably along a canal or river. For travel to the continent, taking ship was necessary, and ship speeds depended almost entirely on the weather. In favorable conditions, a ship could sail 75 to 100 miles per day, or 5 to 6 knots. A strong headwind moving against the ship or no wind at all would result in a very slow trip, making accurate predictions for the duration of a sea trip nearly impossible. For instance, a trip from London to Bordeaux might take anywhere from 10 days to one month.

In *The Canterbury Tales,* we do not get a moment-to-moment idea of what travel is like. The pilgrimage is mainly the plot device that enables Chaucer to tie his stories together. However, from time to time, the group's arrival at a particular location is mentioned, giving us a sense of some movement. For instance, at the end of "The Summoner's Tale," the pilgrims have arrived in Sittingbourne:

My tale is doon; we been almost at towne.

My tale is done; and we are almost at Sittingbourne town.

(*Canterbury Tales,*
"The Summoner's Tale," III (D), 2294)

See also Animals; Pilgrimage; Taverns

FURTHER READING

Archer, Lucy. *Architecture in Britain and Ireland, 600–1500.* London: Harvill Press, 1999.

Brewer, Derek. *Chaucer and His World.* Cambridge, England: D. S. Brewer, 1978; reprinted 1992.

Hanawalt, Barbara A., ed. *Chaucer's England: Literature in Historical Context.* Minneapolis: University of Minnesota Press, 1992.

Lambdin, Laura C., and Robert T. Lambdin, eds. *Chaucer's Pilgrims.* Westport, CT: Praeger, 1999.

Webb, Diana. *Medieval European Pilgrimage, c. 700–c. 1500.* New York: Palgrave, 2002.

———. *Pilgrimage in Medieval England.* New York: Hambledon and London, 2000.

———. *Pilgrims and Pilgrimage in the Medieval West.* New York: I. B. Tauris, 2001.

Trojan War

For which he for Sibille his suster sente,
That called was Cassandre ek al aboute,
And al his drem he tolde hire er he stente,
And hire bisoughte assoilen hym the doute
Of the stronge boor with tuskes stoute;
And fynaly, withinne a litel stounde,
Cassandre hym gan right thus his drem expounde.
…
Unwar of this, Achilles thorugh the maille
And thorugh the body gan hym for to ryve;
And thus this worthi knight was brought of lyve
…
Despitously hym slough the fierse Achille.

For which he sent for his sister Cassandra
Who was a Sybil,
And he told her his dream before he lost his nerve,
And asked her to explain to him the meaning
Of the ferocious boor with huge tusks;
And finally, after a little while to think,
Cassandra became to tell him what his dream meant.
…
Unaware of this, Achilles ran him through his mail
and through his body
And thus this worthy knight was killed
…
The fierce Achilles slew him without pity.

(*Troilus and Criseyde,*
Book V, 1450–1540, 1559–61, 1806)

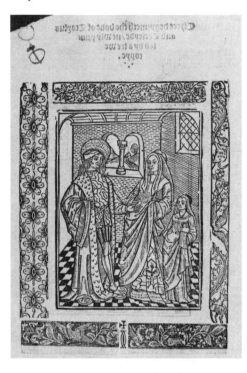

Woodcut at the beginning of *Troilus and Criseyde* from Geoffrey Chaucer's *The Boke of Caunterbury Tales with The Boke of Fame and The Boke of Troylus and Creseyde*, 1526. Courtesy of the Glasgow University Library.

The legendary war between Troy and Sparta is the backdrop to Chaucer's *Troilus and Criseyde*. Described by Homer in the *Iliad*, the Trojan War culminated in the sack of Troy in modern-day western Anatolia by the Mycenaeans in the twelfth century B.C. Mycenaean Greece was named by the nineteenth-century amateur archaeologist Heinrich Schliemann, who excavated the fortified site of the city of Mycenae and discovered the "mask of Agamemnon," a relic of much contention. Schliemann maintained that the golden funeral mask belonged to Agamemnon, the conquering king of the *Iliad*.

In the traditional accounts, Paris, son of the Trojan king Priam, ran off with Helen, the wife of Menelaus of Sparta, whose brother Agamemnon then led a Greek expedition against Troy. The ensuing war lasted 10 years, finally ending when the Greeks pretended to withdraw, leaving behind them a large wooden horse with a raiding party concealed inside. When the Trojans brought the horse into their city, the hidden Greeks opened the gates to their comrades, who then sacked Troy, massacred its men, and carried off its women.

The hero of the Trojan War was Achilles, without whom it had been prophesied that Troy could not be conquered. Despite his mother's serious qualms, Achilles accompanied Odysseus to Troy, leading a company of Myrmidons that included his friend Patroclus. During the war, Achilles was undefeatable, but petty jealousy soon undermined his role in Agamemnon's army: when Apollo forced the king to give up his war-prize, the woman Chyseis, Agamemnon retaliated by forcing Achilles to give up his own prize, Briseis.

Infuriated, Achilles refused to fight further for the Greeks, for whom the war began to go badly. Finally, in response to prolonged negotiations and promises of large rewards, the warrior agreed to let Patroclus fight in his place, wearing his armor. Mistaken for Achilles, Patroclus was killed the next day by Hector, the Trojan hero and prince. In a fury of rage and grief, Achilles returned to battle, killing Hector and dragging his body behind a chariot. The desecration of the corpse was insult enough, but Achilles also refused to grant funeral rites, which would deny Hector entry into Hades, condemning his soul to restlessly wander the earth for eternity.

Priam entered the Trojan camp in secret, begging for his son's release and, moved by the father's pleas, Achilles agreed to let Priam take the body. Achilles returned to battle and fought nobly, but ultimately was fatally wounded in the heel by an arrow fired by Paris. Agamemnon did not live to enjoy the spoils of war; his wife Clytemnestra, who had taken another lover, murdered him upon his return. Her son Orestes, in turn, killed her.

See also Achates; Achilles; Aeneas; Cassandra; Chivalry

FURTHER READING

Brown, Peter, ed. *A Companion to Chaucer.* Malden, MA: Blackwell, 2002.

Frye, Northrop. *Biblical and Classical Myths: The Mythological Framework of Western Culture.* Buffalo: University of Toronto Press, 2004.

Hansen, William F. *Classical Mythology: A Guide to the Mythical World of the Greeks and Romans.* New York: Oxford University Press, 2005.

Manser, Martin H. *The Facts On File Dictionary of Classical and Biblical Allusions.* New York: Facts On File, 2003.

Morford, Mark P. O. *Classical Mythology.* 7th ed. New York: Oxford University Press, 2003.

Nolan, Barbara. *Chaucer and the Tradition of the Roman Antique.* New York: Cambridge University Press, 1992.

Powell, Barry B. *Classical Myth.* Translated by Herbert M. Howe. 4th ed. Upper Saddle River, NJ: Pearson/Prentice Hall, 2004.

Price, Simon, and Emily Kearns, eds. *The Oxford Dictionary of Classical Myth and Religion.* New York: Oxford University Press, 2003.

Scenes from the Battle of Troy: disembarkation of the Greeks into Troy, the siege of Troy, the crowning of a king, and a battle. © Bibliothèque nationale de France.

U
W

Universities. *See* Education

Wat Tyler's Rebellion. *See* Peasant Revolt

Weapons

Som wol ben armed in an haubergeoun,
And in a brestplate and a light gypoun;
And som wol have a paire plates large;
And som wol have a Pruce shield or a targe;
Som wol ben armed on his legges weel,
And have an ax, and som a mace of steel—
Ther is no newe gyse that it nas old.

Some were armed in a coat of mail,
Along with a breastplate and a lightweight tunic,
While some others would have a set of heavy plate mail;
And some would have a Prussian shield or a targe;
Some of them would cover their legs well with armor,
And carry an ax, while others would carry a steel mace—
For there is no new fashion that hasn't been old.

(*Canterbury Tales,*
"The Knight's Tales," I (A) 2119–25)

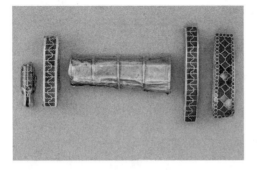

Various items from the tomb of Childéric: Parts of the spatha (sword) from left to right: pommel, lower guard, handle, upper guard. © Bibliothèque nationale de France.

The face of warfare evolved greatly during the course of the Middle Ages, changing the shape of armor, weaponry, and even battle tactics—the last of which effected long-term changes to the feudal system and notions of one's place and role in society. Much of warfare changed during Chaucer's day because of new technological innovations in weaponry that rendered obsolete old fighting techniques and pieces of equipment. People simply got better at killing one another en masse.

The use of crossbows, longbows, and especially cannon meant that armor had to evolve to prevent unnecessarily high injury, maiming, and death rates on the field. It quickly became apparent that the mounted knight was no longer the premier fighting machine of the day. He had been superseded by larger, stronger engines of war.

Although the time of the knight was passing, it would be a gradual obsolescence, and many of the older weapons, such as the sword and lance, continued to be used for some time, while newer weapons, such as cannon and crossbows, would be phased in. The use of a particular weapon depended greatly on whether one was fighting from a mounted position or on foot and on one's social class. Only those who were born into the nobility could become knights, and, as the cost of equipment rose, only those who were from wealthy noble families could hope to attain full status as a knight as opposed to remaining a bachelor foreign mercenary.

Pointed Sticks

Even in Chaucer's day, the knight on horseback was still the grandest and dominant member of the army. The primary weapon of a mounted knight was the sword. Swords were very expensive, because they were difficult to make and were usually constructed specifically for an individual to fit handgrip and to weight it properly. To make a sword, a smith hammered thin strips of steel and welded a core of iron between them. Once sealed, the edges were heated and hammered down to make razor sharp edges.

A sword could be made with a double edge, which made it especially efficient for slashing. This design was popular from the eleventh to the thirteenth centuries, as the construction of armor at that time left knights vulnerable to a slashing motion on the limbs. From the fourteenth to sixteenth centuries, a sharp point was added in response to the increased use of plate mail. The point made it easier to penetrate the new type of mail but had not been necessary with the older style of chain mail.

The lance was another important weapon of the mounted knight. Again, the changes in design were in response to changes in armor. The lance of the High Middle Ages was made of wood, was 10 to 12 feet long and had a sharpened steel point. By the end of the fourteenth century, it had become heavier and thicker in order to pierce heavier armor. Fifteenth-century armor adjusted to accommodate the lance from an offensive position, including a resting place in the armor to couch the heavy pole more comfortably. Infantry also used the lance or a shorter modified version that more resembled a spear. Knights would plant them into the ground, forming a prickly hedge in order to stop cavalry charges. There were also pikemen who used very long, 12- to 15-foot wooden pikes in much the same way as one would use a spear.

When fighting on foot, whether it was infantry or dismounted knights, a different set of weapons came into play. The sword remained important, but the smaller dagger also worked well in face-to-face combat. A dagger could slip between chinks in a man's armor, stabbing vulnerable parts. The dagger could also be used for mercy killings of the wounded. Small axes also were important tools of the infantry and could be thrown or used to chop at an opponent. More exotic weapons included the halberd, which was an ax on one side and a hammer or spike on the other. A soldier could hack his opponent or use the spike to impale him in a vulnerable spot, such as the head. The flail was adopted from a thresher, and was made into a formidable weapon with the addition of spiked balls.

Projectiles

Projectile weapons became increasingly popular from the fourteenth century forward. In prior centuries, they had been frowned upon by those who saw real hand-to-hand combat as glorious and ennobling. A weapon that would allow one to kill from a distance was almost considered to be dishonorable. The Welsh were continually maligned by the English as cowardly for their adept use of the longbow, for instance. However, as common soldiers became a more regular and necessary part of a fighting force, the romantic ideals of warfare diluted, and the ability to strike down multiple opponents with little to no risk to one's own person became increasingly attractive and desirable.

The lightest of these weapons was the bow and arrow. Historians have hotly debated the use of this particular weapon and when it came into greatest use. It had been popular in some places since the ninth century, but really did not catch on in England until the fourteenth. There were essentially two types of bows, besides the Welsh longbow, that were in use during Chaucer's time. The self-bow was made of wood, all one piece, carved for greatest flexibility and power. The longer the bow, the more power it had, although accuracy was then an issue for all but the very well trained. Arrowhead shapes and sizes varied by use. Broader ones were fired at horses and unarmored men, while narrow, square-head arrows achieved greatest penetration of armor.

Crossbows, however, were key to penetrating armor effectively. The development of the crossbow has been called the most important event in medieval Western warfare. The crossbow had been around since antiquity, but only came into general use again during the eleventh century. Its design, which made it a very effective killing device, had drawn harsh criticism from the Church, which banned its use against Christians. While a self-bow required great arm strength to hold steady and pull, the crossbow allowed a smaller, weaker man to fire a bolt over a great distance. The bow was set horizontally on a stock and then fired like a rifle. Unlike a self-bow, the crossbow could be preloaded. Its one drawback was that it was difficult and time-consuming to reload.

On a grander scale were the medieval weapons of mass destruction: artillery. Even before the fourteenth-century use of gunpowder, artillery was a devastating part of any besieging army. Early artillery was used to breach castle walls and crush whomever got in the way of the projectile, and most of it was adapted from weapons that had been used, like the bow and arrow, since antiquity. The ballista was adapted from the Romans and was essentially a giant crossbow that fired missiles using torsion, or twisting. The ballista was used to great success by the Vikings during the siege of Paris in 885.

The mangonel was another torsion-based weapon. First developed during the Middle Ages, the mangonel could fling a projectile with limited accuracy to a range up to 200 yards. This limited range, of course, made it risky to use, as those manning the mangonel were in danger themselves from arrow fire from the walls of the besieged castle. The mangonel was also finicky about weather conditions—humidity changed the response of the rope—and heavy use would wear the spring, lessening the torsion effect.

Therefore, when the trebuchet was introduced in the twelfth century, it sparked a revolution in warfare. The trebuchet operated on a concept like a seesaw. It consisted of two ends, one short with a heavy weight and one long end that carried the projectile. To fire, the long end was compressed and then released. The short end was pulled down by its weight and the projectile was flung at the target. The trebuchet's range was up to 400 yards, which enabled its crew to remain safely out of range of any fire from the enemy. The trebuchet enjoyed a long and successful career until it was superseded by gunpowder, being the most reliable artillery device ever invented up to that point. It was, in fact, used successfully by the crusaders in the siege at Acre in 1191.

The invention of gunpowder by the Chinese was probably the single most important development in warfare for ushering in the modern period. It was brought to Europe by Muslim merchants and was first used to sap castle walls. In sapping, a hole was dug under the wall, gunpowder was poured into the hole and lit. The resulting explosion weakened the foundation, bringing the wall to the ground. When cannons were invented, the potential uses of gunpowder exploded with possibility. The fourteenth century saw the first use in Europe of cannons, with the first being produced in 1320. The first recorded use of a cannon was in France in 1324.

The first cannons were, as might be expected, rather unreliable and crudely built. The simplest were merely cylinders into which gunpowder was poured. Any projectile that was placed in the barrel was hurled with the explosion. The main problem was that the barrels often exploded too, killing or maiming the crew. Bigger cannons solved some of the problem because they allowed for thicker barrels. However, they carried a dangerous recoil and could easily crush a man who failed to get out of the way after lighting the fuse.

Although artillery would be used during the Hundred Years War, the major battles were not decided by its use. It would not be until the fifteenth century that cannons really came into their own as a killing device, and even then the process of integration was slow. The potential was there and military commanders longed to make use of them. But until cannons could become reliable and safe, their practicality was limited. Throughout the late fourteenth and fifteenth centuries, innovations helped to make cannons more useful. Wheels added to the cannon made it easier to transport and reduced recoil. Heavier carts were developed to transport the cannons, making them more practical to take to war.

While they might have been slow to come into widespread use, the very presence of cannons, and the threat of what they were capable of doing, changed the way that battles were fought. Castle sieges became irrelevant as gunpowder could knock the walls down more quickly than starving the inhabitants out. Therefore, expensive stone fortifications were no longer practical or necessary. Pitched battles became more common.

See also Armor; Estates; Hundred Years War; Knight

FURTHER READING

Barker, Juliet R. V. *The Tournament in England, 1100–1400.* Wolfeboro, NH: Boydell Press, 1986.

Bell, Adrian R. *War and the Soldier in the Fourteenth Century.* Rochester, NY: Boydell Press, 2004.

De Pisan, Christine. *The Book of Deeds of Arms and of Chivalry.* Translated by Sumner Willard. Edited by Charity Cannon Willard. University Park: Pennsylvania State University Press, 1999.

Dressler, Rachel Ann. *Of Armor and Men in Medieval England: The Chivalric Rhetoric of Three English Knights' Effigies.* Burlington, VT: Ashgate, 2004.

Hilliam, David. *Medieval Weapons and Warfare: Armies and Combat in Medieval Times.* New York: Rosen, 2004.

Jones, Terry. *Chaucer's Knight: The Portrait of a Medieval Mercenary.* Baton Rouge: Louisiana State University Press, 1980.

Nicolle, David, ed. *A Companion to Medieval Arms and Armour*. Rochester, NY: Boydell Press, 2002.

Oakeshott, R. Ewart. *The Archaeology of Weapons: Arms and Armour from Prehistory to the Age of Chivalry*. Rochester, NY: Boydell Press, 1994.

———. *A Knight and His Armor*. 2nd ed. Chester Springs, PA: Dufour Editions, 1999.

Thordeman, Bengt. *Armour from the Battle of Wisby, 1361*. In collaboration with Poul Nörlund and Bo E. Ingelmark. New ed. Union City, CA: Chivalry Bookshelf, 2002.

Westminster Abbey

Westminster Abbey is one of London's most recognizable landmarks and is the center for much of Britain's ceremonial history. Located across from the Houses of Parliament, the present Abbey stands on the site of a tenth-century Benedictine monastery that was co-founded by King Edgar and St. Dunstan in 960. It has been the site of every monarch's coronation since William the Conqueror and is the burial place of many other monarchs. It is also the final resting place for many of England's most treasured literary figures, including Chaucer, in the famous Poet's Corner.

Edward the Confessor was the first to add to the monastery, building a large stone church beginning in the early 1040s. Sadly, the project took so long that Edward was too old and ill to attend the December 1065 consecration ceremony. When he died in 1066, he was buried in front of the high altar, starting a centuries-long tradition for many of England's future kings.

Poet's Corner is located in the south transept of the Abbey and was originally not intended to function as the final resting place of British authors. Chaucer, the first poet to be buried there, was only allowed to be buried in the Abbey because of his position as Clerk of Works.

Westminster Abbey. Courtesy of Lisa Kirchner.

However, it was as the author of *The Canterbury Tales* on which his fame rested and spread. When Edmund Spenser, the Elizabethan author of *The Faerie Queene,* was buried near Chaucer in 1599, the tradition of Poet's Corner began.

Chaucer's monument is made of grey Purbeck marble and was erected by fellow poet Nicholas Brigham in 1556. According to William Camden, Chaucer's bones were transferred to this tomb, although there remain some questions as to whether they are really his. The inscription on the tomb reads, in translation:

Of old the bard who struck the noblest strains
Great Geoffrey Chaucer, now this tomb retains.
If for the period of his life you call,
the signs are under that will note you all.
In the year of our Lord 1400, on the 25th day of October. Death is the repose of cares.
N. Brigham charged himself with these in the name of the Muses 1556

Westminster Abbey. Courtesy of Lisa Kirchner.

In 1868, a stained glass window illustrating scenes from *The Canterbury Tales* was erected above Chaucer's tomb but was destroyed during World War II.

See also London

A close look at the door figurines at Westminster Abbey. Courtesy of Lisa Kirchner.

A view of Westminster Abbey. Courtesy of Lisa Kirchner.

FURTHER READING

Archer, Lucy. *Architecture in Britain and Ireland, 600–1500.* London: Harvill Press, 1999.

Brewer, Derek. *Chaucer and His World.* Cambridge, England: D. S. Brewer, 1978; reprinted 1992.

———. *Growing Up in Medieval London: The Experience of Childhood in History.* New York: Oxford University Press, 1993.

Wheel of Fortune. *See* Fortune

Wolf

Unlike the skittish hare, the ferocious wolf represents strength and un-flinching aggression, even rapacity, in battle as well as life. Interestingly, this rapaciousness also takes on a sexual overtone. While the rabbit appears to represent a shameful lechery, the wolf symbolizes an open and nearly violent lust. Chaucer employs the image of the wolf sparingly, but his meaning is clear. In "The Manciple's Tale," Phebus's wife is compared to the she-wolf, who "hath also a vileyns kynde. / The lewedeste wolf that she may fynde, / Or leest of reputacioun, wol she take, / In time whan hir lust to han a make" (*her nature is of the lowest kind / She'll take the lustiest world that she can find / or the one of the lowest reputation, / Whenever she's in heat and needs a mate*) (*Canterbury Tales,* "The Manciple's Tale," IX (H), 183–86).

The image of the wolf also has direct correlation to the Church, as the priest was considered to be the shepherd of his flock and sheep are common victims of the hungry wolf. Of the good Parson of *The Canterbury Tales,* Chaucer writes that:

A fifteenth-century depiction of a wolf hunt. © Bibliothèque nationale de France.

> He sette nat his benefice to hyre
> And leet his sheep encombred in the myre
> And ran to Londoun unto Seinte Poules
> To seken hym a chaunterie for soules,
> Or with a bretherhed to been witholde;
> But dwelte at hoom, and kepte wel his folde,
> So that the wolf ne made it nat myscarie;
> He was a shepherde and noght a mercenarie.
>
> *He would not hire out his benefice to others*
> *Or allow his "sheep" to wander freely in the muck*
> *In order to run to Saint Paul's in London*
> *To seek a chantry for other souls,*
> *Or to enter a brotherhood.*
> *Instead he stayed at home and kept watch over his fold*
> *So that the wolf would not prey upon it;*
> *He was a shepherd, not a mercenary.*

(*Canterbury Tales,*
General Prologue, I (A), 507–14)

As is the case throughout *The Canterbury Tales,* this passage underlines Chaucer's critique of the church and its representatives. The shepherds have turned into wolves who spend more time fleecing and even preying upon their flocks than administering spiritual guidance.

FURTHER READING

Rowland, Beryl. *Blind Beasts: Chaucer's Animal World.* Kent, OH: Kent State University Press, 1971.

Salisbury, Joyce E., ed. *The Medieval World of Nature: A Book of Essays.* New York: Garland, 1993.

Strickland, Debra Higgs. *Medieval Bestiaries: Text, Image, Ideology.* New York: Cambridge University Press, 1995.

Telesko, Werner. *The Wisdom of Nature: The Healing Powers and Symbolism of Plants and Animals in the Middle Ages.* New York: Prestel, 2001.

Wood

A YEMAN hadde he and servantz namo
At that tyme, for hym liste ride so,
And he was clad in cote and hood of grene.
A sheef of pecok arwes, bright and kene,
Under his belt he bar ful thriftily
(Wel koude he dresse his takel yemanly;
His arwes drouped noght with fetheres lowe),
And in his hand he baar a myghty bowe.
A not heed hadde he, with a broun visage.
Of wodecraft wel koude he al the usage.
Upon his arm he baar a gay bracer,
And by his syde a swerd and a bokeler,
And on that oother syde a gay daggere
Harneised wel and sharp as point of spere;
A Cristopher on his brest of silver sheene.
An horn he bar, the bawdryk was of grene;
A forster was he, soothly, as I gesse.

A Yeoman he had, his only servant
At that time, for that's the way he wished to ride,
And he was dressed in a green hood and coat.
A sheaf of peacock arrows, bright and sharp,
Under his belt he carried handily
(He could well dress his tackle in yeoman fashion;
His arrows never dropped low from bad feathering),
And in his hand he carried a mighty bow.
He had a cropped head, like a nut, with a brown tanned face.
He knew everything to know about woodcraft.
He wore a fancy bracer on his arm,
And on his side he carried a sword and a buckler,
And on the other he had a dagger
Well-mounted and sharp as the point of a spear;
He wore a shiny silver St. Christopher medal on his breast.
He carried a horn that was hung from a green cord;
A forester he was, I guess.

(*Canterbury Tales,*
General Prologue, I (A), 101–17)

Because of its usefulness for cooking and heating, wood might have been the most important natural resource to the Middle Ages. Although coal was used more by Londoners, firewood was the sole source of heat and flame for those outside the city. However, because of forestry laws, not everyone had unrestricted access to wood, and, because it was also vastly important in building houses and ships as well as furniture and other necessary trappings of daily life, it was a resource that could easily be depleted, taking many years to regrow and leaving Europeans in a difficult spot.

Forest laws were designed to protect the privileges of the nobility to the detriment of the peasantry, who perhaps found the situation to be exploitive. The laws had their roots in the early Germanic kingdoms, when there was no official restriction on who could hunt or cut. Many trees were left untouched, in fact, and the minimum of land was cleared because the Germans believed trees to be sacred.

However, in the seventh century, with the ascension of the Merovingians, forestry laws began to be enacted to exert centralized control and authority over lands important to the king. The successors to the Merovingians, the Carolingians, made the laws more inclusive and strict. Some of these laws, in fact, gave exclusive rights to the king for hunting, creating royal forests. For the peasants living at subsistence, the inability to supplement their diet with fresh meat was a dangerous blow.

After the collapse of the Carolingian empire and the rise of separate German and French kingdoms, the tradition of royal forests continued, with each monarchy maintaining and expanding forest laws and allowing the local nobilities to enact their own as well. Forestry laws would make their way to England with the Norman Conquest.

Prior to 1066 there is little evidence of Anglo-Saxon kings delineating royal forests from others. William the Conqueror passed laws to protect "those beasts of the forests" that he liked to hunt, forbidding others to do so without his express permission. The laws he began were perpetuated under successive reigns, becoming increasingly complex. For instance, the idea of a chase was established whereby the nobility could hunt wild game, and warrens were defined where they could hunt other animals than "beasts of the fields."

These areas expanded to such a degree that, by the thirteenth century, nearly one quarter of England's lands were protected. Ironically, protection was extended beyond woodlands to also include towns and villages. This severely limited peasants' ability to heat their homes, cook their food, and hunt or fish for important animal-based protein sources. For those who could not afford to keep livestock, their main source of meat was forbidden.

Some peasants risked being punished in order to continue hunting, and enforcement varied widely. Although a judicial system and even a police force of sorts was created to protect royal lands, national laws did not equate to a standardized national system of justice. Punishment was usually severe, because the underlying principal behind restricted access was the right of the king to assert his authority. However, physical punishment was rare. Fines were more common for first and second offenses. For the third offense, mutilation or death was possible. However, even for a third offense, judges were more likely to impose a cripplingly stiff fine because they were an important source of revenue for the crown.

Chaucer does not talk about forestry laws much; however, he does include some allusions to hunting that demonstrates what a pervasively important cultural activity it was. His allusions mainly refer to the hunt in its allegorical sense—the woman as prey and the man as hunter in the sport of love. In this context, Diana is invoked to protect the woman from the threat to her chastity.

In Chaucer's description of the Yeoman, however, readers get an indication of what someone who hunted and worked in the forest would have been like (*Canterbury Tales,* General Prologue, I (A), 101–17). Although the Yeoman is the Knight's servant, he is attired to move silently and invisibly through the forest, indicating that his role is perhaps to provide the Knight with fresh meat or to assist him in finding good sport.

See also Daily Life; Hunting

FURTHER READING

Bowden, Muriel. *A Reader's Guide to Geoffrey Chaucer.* Syracuse, NY: Syracuse University Press, 2001.

Brewer, Derek. *Chaucer and His World.* Cambridge, England: D. S. Brewer, 1978; reprinted 1992.

Britnell, Richard, ed. *Daily Life in the Late Middle Ages.* Stroud, England: Sutton, 1998.

DeWindt, Edwin Brezette, ed. *The Salt of Common Life: Individuality and Choice in the Medieval Town, Countryside, and Church: Essays Presented to J. Ambrose Raftis.* Kalamazoo: Medieval Institute Publications, Western Michigan University, 1995.

Duby, Georges. *The Three Orders: Feudal Society Imagined.* Translated by Arthur Goldhammer. Chicago: University of Chicago Press, 1980; reprinted 1982.

Dyer, Christopher. *Making a Living in the Middle Ages: The People of Britain 850–1520.* New Haven, CT: Yale University Press, 2002.

French, Katherine L. *The People of the Parish: Community Life in a Late Medieval English Diocese.* Philadelphia: University of Pennsylvania Press, 2001.

Masschaele, James. *Peasants, Merchants, and Markets: Inland Trade in Medieval England, 1150–1350.* New York: St. Martin's Press, 1997.

Morgan, Gwyneth. *Life in a Medieval Village.* New York: Cambridge University Press, 1975.

Power, Eileen. *Medieval People.* New York: Barnes and Noble, 1924; reprinted 1968.

Singman, Jeffrey L., and Will McLean. *Daily Life in Chaucer's England*. Westport, CT: Greenwood Press, 1995.

Wool

Ful thredbare was his overeste courtepy,
For he hadde geten hym yet no benefice.

His overcoat was threadbare
Because he had not yet gotten himself an income.

(*Canterbury Tales*,
General Prologue, I (A), 285–86)

During the Middle Ages, England experienced an economic boom thanks to the chief product of the largest group in their population: sheep. Because of an ideal climate that combined coolness with damp, English sheep produced an extremely thick soft coat that was not only abundant but also perfect for cloth-making. East Anglia and the Cotswolds, especially, produced top quality wool. While Germany, Flanders, and Spain also exported their wool, it was all of noticeably lower quality. Thus, English wool dominated the cloth market from the twelfth century forward.

Initially, England provided raw, uncleaned wool to other countries, such as France and Italy, which were known for their fine woolen cloth. Italian merchants, in fact, had a distinct advantage because papal tax collectors there were given first pick of the highest quality wool. Over time, however, the English began to participate in more of the process that went into turning wool into woolens. A cottage industry developed that took the raw wool through its various steps. It was first combed out, which could be accomplished by cottagers and housewives who remained home with their children. It was then cleaned of lanolin and dirt, another task that was contracted out to cottagers.

Weaving was the next step in the process, and the English had typically allowed

An illumination of a medieval wool merchant. © Bibliothèque nationale de France.

the French and Italians to take over from this stage. However, the price fetched by finished cloth was many times more than that of the raw materials, and it quickly became obvious that English woolen merchants could make greater fortunes if they diversified and expanded their production. Revolutionary changes in the spinning wheel and the developments in fulling mills completely changed the English woolen industry, and the country was blessed by natural conditions that made its success all but guaranteed.

Fulling mills were developed from adjustments to grain mills. The hammers that mashed grain into flour, it was discovered, could be altered to pound the wool into a softer product, and, instead of the tortuous process of fulling by hand—with the aid of a horse that powered a small fuller—now it could be accomplished on a much grander scale. The secret was the same as for grain mills: running water. And England had sufficient running waterways to convert to cloth production, thereby eliminating the sale to foreign intermediaries.

The final steps in cloth production were weaving, which was accomplished by home wheels and water-powered wheels, and dying. People of the Middle Ages loved bright colors, which were sometimes difficult to achieve with the native plants that provided most of the dyes through the early part of the medieval period. Blues were fairly easy and were derived from woad and indigo. However, the growth of trade and exploration into more exotic locations greatly expanded the possibilities in cloth dyeing. Scarlet red, in particular, was produced from kermes, an insect found in the Mediterranean. It was very rare and thus only royalty and the upper nobility were able to afford scarlet garments. Black was especially hard to achieve—even with imported plants, it often came out looking rusty—and thus it was rare to even see a king wearing black.

See also Business and Commerce; Fashion; Tapestry

FURTHER READING

Brewer, Derek. *Chaucer and His World.* Cambridge, England: D. S. Brewer, 1978; reprinted 1992.

Britnell, Richard, ed. *Daily Life in the Late Middle Ages.* Stroud, England: Sutton, 1998.

Burns, E. Jane, ed. *Medieval Fabrications: Dress, Textiles, Clothwork, and Other Cultural Imaginings.* New York: Palgrave Macmillan, 2004.

Hodges, Laura F. *Chaucer and Clothing: Clerical and Academic Costume in the Prologue to the "Canterbury Tales."* Rochester, NY: D. S. Brewer, 2005.

———. *Chaucer and Costume.* Cambridge, England: D. S. Brewer, 2005.

Koslin, Désirée G., and Janet E. Snyder. *Encountering Medieval Textiles and Dress: Objects, Texts, Images.* New York: Palgrave Macmillan, 2002.

Netherton, Robin, and Gale R. Owen-Crocker, eds. *Medieval Clothing and Textiles.* Woodbridge, Suffolk, England: Boydell Press, 2005.

Richardson, Catherine, ed. *Clothing Culture, 1350–1650.* Burlington, VT: Ashgate, 2004.

Scott, Margaret. *Medieval Clothing and Costumes: Displaying Wealth and Class in Medieval Times.* New York: Rosen, 2004.

Wycliffe, John. *See* Lollardy

Y
Z

Yeoman

A YEMAN hadde he and servantz namo
At that tyme, for hym liste ride so,
And he was clad in cote and hood of grene.
A sheef of pecok arwes, bright and kene,
Under his belt he bar ful thriftily
(Wel koude he dresse his takel yemanly;
His arwes drouped noght with fetheres lowe),
And in his hand he baar a myghty bowe.
A not heed hadde he, with a broun visage.
Of wodecraft wel koude he al the usage.
Upon his arm he baar a gay bracer,
And by his side a swerd and a bokeler,
And on that oother side a gay daggere
Harneised wel and sharp as point of spere;
A Cristopher on his brest of silver sheene.
An horn he bar, the bawdryk was of grene;
A forster was he, soothly, as I gesse.

A Yeoman he had, his only servant
At that time, for that's the way he wished to ride,
And he was dressed in a green hood and coat.

A sheaf of peacock arrows, bright and sharp,
Under his belt he carried handily
(He could well dress his tackle in yeoman fashion;
His arrows never dropped low from bad feathering),
And in his hand he carried a mighty bow.
He had a cropped head, like a nut, with a brown tanned face.
He knew everything to know about woodcraft.
He wore a fancy bracer on his arm,
And on his side he carried a sword and a buckler,
And on the other he had a dagger
Well-mounted and sharp as the point of a spear;
He wore a shiny silver St. Christopher medal on his breast.
He carried a horn that was hung from a green cord;
A forester he was, I guess.

(*Canterbury Tales,*
General Prologue, I (A), 101–17)

A yeoman (from the Old English *gaman,* Middle English *yeman*) was a freeborn servant or attendant to a noble. As the feudal system declined, the term eventually came to represent a particular class of freeholding farmers who cultivated their own land, forming a rural middle class. A yeoman farmed his own land, as opposed to the gentry who hired tenant farmers.

Chaucer's Yeoman is an undeveloped figure, although his lively description implies that there were plans to provide him with a tale. He is the Knight's only servant, clad in green, with close-cropped hair and an array of weaponry. It is unclear whether his position is consonant with the above definition entirely or might encompass the earlier definition of an archer who used the longbow of the kind popular in the Hundred Years War. The fact that he is accompanying the Knight indicates that this latter interpretation is the more correct one.

Further on in *The Canterbury Tales,* we are introduced to the Canon's Yeoman, another character who complicates the definition of a yeoman. He provides the lengthy description of alchemy that earned Chaucer the dubious reputation of devoted alchemist. Similar to the Yeoman, the Canon's Yeoman seems to be simply an assistant or servant. Neither man could have managed his lands while working and traveling with his master.

See also Estates; Knight; Wood

FURTHER READING

Bisson, Lillian M. *Chaucer and the Late Medieval World.* New York: St. Martin's Press, 1998.

Bloch, Marc. *Feudal Society.* Translated by L. A. Manyon. New York: Routledge, 1961; 1989.

Cantor, Norman. *The Civilization of the Middle Ages.* Rev. ed. New York: Harper Collins, 1993.

DeWindt, Edwin Brezette, ed. *The Salt of Common Life: Individuality and Choice in the Medieval Town, Countryside, and Church: Essays Presented to J. Ambrose Raftis.* Kalamazoo: Medieval Institute Publications, Western Michigan University, 1995.

Duby, Georges. *The Three Orders: Feudal Society Imagined.* Translated by Arthur Goldhammer. Chicago: University of Chicago Press, 1980; reprinted 1982.

Dyer, Christopher. *Making a Living in the Middle Ages: The People of Britain 850–1520.* New Haven, CT: Yale University Press, 2002.

Goldberg, P.J.P. *Medieval England: A Social History, 1250–1550.* New York: Oxford University Press, 2004.

Hindley, Geoffrey. *The Medieval Establishment, 1200–1500.* New York: Putnam, 1970.

Knapp, Peggy. *Chaucer and the Social Contest.* New York: Routledge, 1990.

Lambdin, Laura C., and Robert T. Lambdin, eds. *Chaucer's Pilgrims.* Westport, CT: Praeger, 1999.

Strohm, Paul. *Social Chaucer.* Cambridge, MA: Harvard University Press, 1989.

Ypres

A good WIF was ther OF biside BATHE,
But she was somdel deef, and that was scathe.
Of clooth-makyng she hadde swich an haunt
She passed hem of Ypres and of Gaunt.

A good Wife there was from near Bath,
But she was a bit deaf, which was a shame.
She had such a talent at cloth making that
She surpassed the skills of the men of Ypres and Ghent

(*Canterbury Tales,*
General Prologue, I (A), 445–48)

Located in Flanders, Ypres was conveniently located on the trade route between Bruges and Lille, helping it to rise during the twelfth century to a city of great importance in the Flemish cloth industry. Ypres was perhaps the most important producer of linen, because the flax needed for the fabric was grown in great quantities around the city. It reached its zenith of economic power in the late thirteenth century, when its merchants joined forces with English wool producers to dominate the woolen cloth market.

During this time, Ypres would be the third most important city in Flanders, after Ghent and Bruges, its population numbering 40,000. Unfortunately, internal political and social unrest initiated the undoing of Ypres as a world economic power, a decline exacerbated by the growth of England's burgeoning cloth production and, eventually, the destruction of Ypres's surrounding countryside by an English army in 1383.

In *The Canterbury Tales,* it is said that the Wife of Bath's skill at weaving is so high that she "passed hem of Ypres and of Gaunt," a comparison that might be ironic, as weavers from the area around Bath were not well respected.

See also Bath; Bruges; Fashion

FURTHER READING

Attreed, Lorraine Christine. *The King's Towns: Identity and Survival in Late Medieval English Boroughs.* New York: P. Lang, 2001.

Britnell, R. H. *The Commercialisation of English Society, 1000–1500.* 2nd ed. New York: Manchester University Press, 1996.

Clare, John D., ed. *Fourteenth-Century Towns.* San Diego: Harcourt Brace Jovanovich, 1993.

Zodiac. *See* Astrology and Astronomy

Appendices

Genealogy of Edward III

An abbreviated lineage for Edward III as it applies to Chaucer and his works.

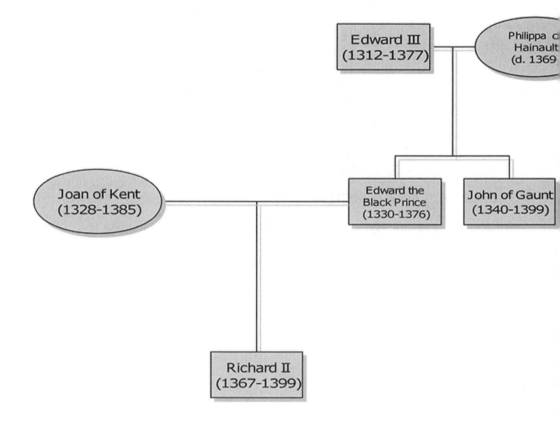

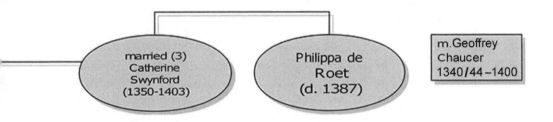

married (3)
Catherine
Swynford
(1350-1403)

Philippa de
Roet
(d. 1387)

m.Geoffrey
Chaucer
1340/44 –1400

Map of Route to Canterbury

In Southwerk at the Tabard as I lay
Redy to wenden on my pilgrymage....

London

And forth we riden a litel moore than paas
Unto the Wateryng of Seint Thomas

Southwark

Deptford

Greenwich

St. Thomas Watering

Lo Depeford! and it is half-wey pryme
Lo Grenewych, ther many a shrewe is inne!

Dartford

N
W E
S

0   5   10
Scale of Miles

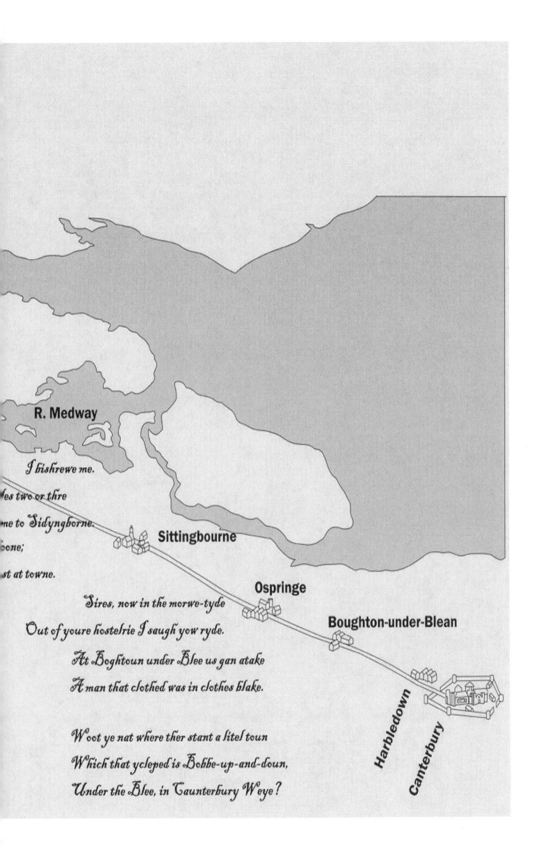

R. Medway

I bishrewe me.

...es two or thre

...me to Sidyngborne.

...bone;

...st at towne.

Sittingbourne

Ospringe

Sires, now in the morwe-tyde

Out of youre hostelrie I saugh yow ryde.

Boughton-under-Blean

At Boghtoun under Blee us gan atake

A man that clothed was in clothes blake.

Woot ye nat where ther stant a litel toun

Which that ycleped is Bobbe-up-and-doun,

Under the Blee, in Caunterbury Weye?

Harbledown

Canterbury

Bibliography

Aberth, John. *From the Brink of the Apocalyspe.* New York: Routledge, 2001.

Abou-El-Haj, Barbara Fay. *The Medieval Cult of Saints: Formations and Transformations.* New York: Cambridge University Press, 1997.

Abulafia, David, Michael Franklin, and Miri Rubin, eds. *Church and City, 1000–1500: Essays in Honour of Christopher Brooke.* New York: Cambridge University Press, 1992.

Adamson, Melitta Weiss. *Food in Medieval Times.* Westport, CT: Greenwood Press, 2004.

Ainsworth, Peter F. *Jean Froissart and the Fabric of History: Truth, Myth, and Fiction in the* "Chroniques." New York: Oxford University Press, 1990.

Alexander, Jonathan, and Paul Binski, eds. *Age of Chivalry: Art in Plantagenet England, 1200–1400.* London: Royal Academy of Arts in association with Weidenfeld and Nicholson, 1987.

Alfred the Great: Asser's Life of King Alfred *and Other Contemporary Sources.* Trans. and Introd. Simon Keynes and Michael Lapidge. New York: Penguin, 1983.

Allen, Peter L. *The Art of Love: Amatory Fiction from Ovid to the* "Romance of the Rose." Philadelphia: University of Pennsylvania Press, 1992.

Archer, Lucy. *Architecture in Britain and Ireland, 600–1500.* London: Harvill Press, 1999.

Arnold, Morris, et al. *On the Laws and Customs of England: Essays in Honor of Samuel E. Thorne.* Chapel Hill: University of North Carolina Press, 1981.

Astell, Ann W. *Chaucer and the Universe of Learning.* Ithaca, NY: Cornell University Press, 1996.

Aston, Margaret, and Colin Richmond, eds. *Lollardy and the Gentry in the Later Middle Ages.* New York: St. Martin's Press, 1997.

Attreed, Lorraine Christine. *The King's Towns: Identity and Survival in Late Medieval English Boroughs.* New York: P. Lang, 2001.

Backhouse, Janet, ed. *The Medieval English Cathedral: Papers in Honour of Pamela Tudor-Craig: Proceedings of the 1998 Harlaxton Symposium.* Donington, Lincolnshire, England: Shaun Tyas, 2003.

Backman, Clifford R. *The Worlds of Medieval Europe.* New York: Oxford University Press, 2003.

Barber, Richard. *Edward Prince of Wales and Aquitaine*. Woodbridge, Suffolk, England: Boydell and Brewer, 1996.

———. *The Reign of Chivalry*. Rochester, NY: Boydell Press, 2005.

Barker, Juliet R. V. *The Tournament in England, 1100–1400*. Wolfeboro, NH: Boydell Press, 1986.

Barnie, John. *War in Medieval English Society: Social Values in the Hundred Years War 1337–99*. Ithaca, NY: Cornell University Press, 1974.

Bean, J.M.W. *From Lord to Patron: Lordship in Late Medieval England*. Manchester, England: Manchester University Press, 1989

Bell, Adrian R. *War and the Soldier in the Fourteenth Century*. Rochester, NY: Boydell Press, 2004.

Bellamy, John G. *Bastard Feudalism and the Law*. Portland, OR: Areopagitica Press, 1989.

Bennett, Michael. *Richard II and the Revolution of 1399*. Gloucestershire, England: Sutton, 1999.

Benson, C. David, and Elizabeth Robertson, eds. *Chaucer's Religious Tales*. Rochester, NY: D. S. Brewer, 1990.

Bentley, James. *A Calendar of Saints: The Lives of the Principal Saints of the Christian Year*. New York: Facts On File, 1986.

Besserman, Lawrence. *Chaucer's Biblical Poetics*. Norman: University of Oklahoma Press, 1998.

Bevan, Bryan. *Edward III: Monarch of Chivalry*. London: Rubicon Press, 1992.

Biller, Peter, and Barrie Dobson, eds. *The Medieval Church: Universities, Heresy, and the Religious Life: Essays in Honour of Gordon Leff*. Rochester, NY: Boydell Press, 1999.

Binding, Günther. *Medieval Building Techniques*. Stroud, England: Tempus, 2004.

Biscoglio, Frances Minetti. *The Wives of "The Canterbury Tales" and the Tradition of the Valiant Woman of Proverbs 31: 10–31*. San Francisco: Mellen Research University Press, 1993.

Bisson, Lillian M. *Chaucer and the Late Medieval World*. New York: St. Martin's Press, 1998.

Blick, Sarah, and Rita Tekippe, eds. *Art and Architecture of Late Medieval Pilgrimage in Northern Europe and the British Isles*. Boston: Brill, 2005.

Bloch, Marc. *Feudal Society*. Translated by L. A. Manyon. New York: Routledge, 1961; 1989.

Blumenfeld-Kosinski, Renate. *Poets, Saints, and Visionaries of the Great Schism, 1378–1417*. University Park: Pennsylvania State University Press, 2006.

Boenig, Robert. *Chaucer and the Mystics: "The Canterbury Tales" and the Genre of Devotional Prose*. Lewisburg, PA: Bucknell University Press, 1995.

Boitani, Piero, and Jill Mann. *The Cambridge Chaucer Companion*. New York: Cambridge University Press, 1986.

Boulton, D'Arcy Jonathan Dacre. *The Knights of the Crown: The Monarchical Orders of Knighthood in Later Medieval Europe, 1325–1520*. New York: St. Martin's Press, 1986.

Bowden, Muriel. *A Reader's Guide to Geoffrey Chaucer*. Syracuse, NY: Syracuse University Press, 2001.

Brewer, Derek. *Chaucer and His World*. Cambridge, England: D. S. Brewer, 1978; reprinted 1992.

Britnell, R. H. *The Commercialisation of English Society, 1000–1500*. 2nd ed. New York: Manchester University Press, 1996.

Britnell, Richard, ed. *Daily Life in the Late Middle Ages*. Stroud, England: Sutton, 1998.

Broughton, Bradford B. *Dictionary of Medieval Knighthood and Chivalry. Concepts and Terms*. Westport, CT: Greenwood Press, 1986.

Brown, Peter, ed. *A Companion to Chaucer*. Malden, MA: Blackwell, 2002.

Bulfinch, Thomas. *Bulfinch's Mythology*. New York: Modern Library, 1998.

Bullough, Vern L. *Sexual Practices and the Medieval Church.* Buffalo, NY: Prometheus Books, 1982.

Bumke, Joachim. *Courtly Culture.* New York: Overlook Press, 2000.

Burnley, J. D. *Courtliness and Literature in Medieval England.* New York: Longman, 1998.

Burns, E. Jane, ed. *Medieval Fabrications: Dress, Textiles, Clothwork, and Other Cultural Imaginings.* New York: Palgrave Macmillan, 2004.

Butler, John R. *The Quest for Becket's Bones: The Mystery of the Relics of St Thomas Becket of Canterbury.* New Haven, CT: Yale University Press, 1995.

Calkins, Robert G. *Medieval Architecture in Western Europe: from A.D. 300 to 1500.* New York: Oxford University Press, 1998.

Camden, William. *Remains Concerning Britain.* Edited by R. D. Dunn. Toronto: University of Toronto Press, 1984.

Campbell, Bruce M. S., ed. *Before the Black Death: Studies in the "Crisis" of the Early Fourteenth Century.* New York: Manchester University Press, 1991.

Cantor, Norman. *The Civilization of the Middle Ages.* Rev. ed. New York: Harper Collins, 1993.

———. *The Encyclopedia of the Middle Ages.* New York: Viking Press, 1999.

———. *In the Wake of the Plague.* New York: Free Press, 2001.

Carlin, Martha. *Medieval Southwark.* Rio Grande, OH: Hambledon Press, 1996.

Carlson, David R. *Chaucer's Jobs.* New York: Palgrave, 2004.

Carroll, Jane L., and Alison G. Stewart, eds. *Saints, Sinners, and Sisters: Gender and Northern Art in Medieval and Early Modern Europe.* Burlington, VT: Ashgate, 2003.

Carter, John Marshall. *Medieval Games: Sports and Recreations in Feudal Society.* New York: Greenwood Press, 1992.

Chaucer, Geoffrey. *The Canterbury Tales.* Translated by David Wright. New York: Oxford University Press, 1985.

———. *The Riverside Chaucer.* Edited by Larry D. Benson. Boston: Houghton Mifflin, 1987.

———. *Troilus and Criseyde.* Translated by Nevill Coghill. New York: Penguin Putnam, 1971.

Chickering, Howell, and Thomas H. Seiler, eds. *The Study of Chivalry: Resources and Approaches.* Kalamazoo: Medieval Institute Publications, Western Michigan University, 1988.

Childress, Diana. *Chaucer's England.* North Haven, CT: Linnet Books, 2000.

Clare, John D., ed. *Fourteenth-Century Towns.* San Diego: Harcourt Brace Jovanovich, 1993.

Coldstream, Nicola. *Medieval Architecture.* New York: Oxford University Press, 2002.

Collins, Hugh E. L. *The Order of the Garter, 1348–1461: Chivalry and Politics in Late Medieval England.* New York: Oxford University Press, 2000.

Collinson, Patrick, Nigel Ramsay, and Margaret Sparks, eds. *A History of Canterbury Cathedral.* New York: Oxford University Press, 1995.

Copeland, Rita. *Pedagogy, Intellectuals, and Dissent in the Later Middle Ages: Lollardy and Ideas of Learning.* New York: Cambridge University Press, 2001.

Corfis, Ivy A., and Michael Wolfe, eds. *The Medieval City Under Siege.* Rochester, NY: Boydell Press, 1995.

Cosman, Madeleine Pelner. *Fabulous Feasts: Medieval Cookery and Ceremony.* New York: George Braziller, 1976.

Coss, Peter, and Maurice Keen, eds. *Heraldry, Pageantry, and Social Display in Medieval England.* Rochester, NY: Boydell Press, 2002.

Coulton, G. G. *Chaucer and His England.* London: Methuen, 1908; reprinted 1968.

Curry, Anne, and Elizabeth Matthew, eds. *Concepts and Patterns of Service in the Later Middle Ages.* Rochester, NY: Boydell Press, 2000.

Curry, Patrick, ed. *Astrology, Science, and Society: Historical Essays.* Wolfeboro, NH: Boydell Press, 1987.

Davies, R. Trevor. *Documents Illustrating the History of Civilization in Medieval England, 1066–1500.* New York: Barnes & Noble, 1969.

Delany, Sheila, ed. *Chaucer and the Jews : Sources, Contexts, Meanings.* New York: Routledge, 2002.

Denton, Jeffrey, ed. *Orders and Hierarchies in Late Medieval and Renaissance Europe.* Buffalo, NY: University of Toronto Press, 1999.

De Pisan, Christine. *The Book of Deeds of Arms and of Chivalry.* Translated by Sumner Willard. Edited by Charity Cannon Willard. University Park: Pennsylvania State University Press, 1999.

De Rola, Stanislas Klossowski. *Alchemy: The Secret Art.* New York: Bounty Books, 1973.

DeWindt, Edwin Brezette, ed. *The Salt of Common Life: Individuality and Choice in the Medieval Town, Countryside, and Church: Essays Presented to J. Ambrose Raftis.* Kalamazoo: Medieval Institute Publications, Western Michigan University, 1995.

Dickson, Gary. *Religious Enthusiasm in the Medieval West: Revivals, Crusades, Saints.* Burlington, VT: Ashgate, 2000.

Dressler, Rachel Ann. *Of Armor and Men in Medieval England: The Chivalric Rhetoric of Three English Knights' Effigies.* Burlington, VT: Ashgate, 2004.

Duby, Georges. *Love and Marriage in the Middle Ages.* Translated by Jane Dunnett. Chicago: Univesrity of Chicago Press, 1988; reprinted in translation 1994.

———. *The Three Orders: Feudal Society Imagined.* Translated by Arthur Goldhammer. Chicago: University of Chicago Press, 1980; reprinted 1982.

Dunn, Alastair. *The Peasant's Revolt: England's Failed Revolution of 1381.* Stroud, England: Tempus, 2004.

Dunn, Diana, ed. *War and Society in Medieval and Early Modern Britain.* Liverpool, England: Liverpool University Press, 2000.

Dyas, Dee. *Pilgrimage in Medieval English Literature, 700–1500.* Rochester, NY: D. S. Brewer, 2001.

Dyer, Christopher. *Making a Living in the Middle Ages: The People of Britain 850–1520.* New Haven, CT: Yale University Press, 2002.

Edwards, Robert. *Chaucer and Boccaccio: Antiquity and Modernity.* New York: Palgrave, 2002.

Ellis, Steve, ed. *Chaucer: An Oxford Guide.* New York: Oxford University Press, 2005.

Emery, Anthony. *Greater Medieval Houses of England and Wales, 1300–1500.* New York: Cambridge University Press, 1996.

Erlande-Brandenburg, Alain. *The Cathedral Builders of the Middle Ages.* Translated by Rosemary Stonehewer. London: Thames and Hudson, 1995.

Farmer, Sharon, and Barbara H. Rosenwein, eds. *Monks and Nuns, Saints and Outcasts: Religion in Medieval Society: Essays in Honor of Lester K. Little.* Ithaca, NY: Cornell University Press, 2000.

Finucane, Ronald C. *Miracles and Pilgrims: Popular Beliefs in Medieval England.* New York: St. Martin's Press, 1995.

Fisher, John H. *The Importance of Chaucer.* Carbondale: Southern Illinois University Press, 1992.

Foster, Edward E., and David H. Carey, eds. *Chaucer's Church: A Dictionary of Religious Terms in Chaucer.* Brookfield, VT: Ashgate, 2002.

Fraser, Antonia, ed. *The Lives of the Kings and Queens of England.* Rev. ed. Berkeley: University of California Press, 1998.

French, Katherine L. *The People of the Parish: Community Life in a Late Medieval English Diocese.* Philadelphia: University of Pennsylvania Press, 2001.

French, Roger. *Canonical Medicine: Gentile da Foligno and Scholasticism.* Boston: Brill, 2001.

French, Roger, Jon Arrizabalaga, Andrew Cunningham, and Luis García-Ballester, eds. *Medicine from the Black Death to the French Disease*. Aldershot, England: Ashgate, 1998.

Frugoni, Chiara. *A Day in a Medieval City*. Introduction by Arsenio Frugoni. Translated by William McCuaig. Chicago: University of Chicago Press, 2005.

Frye, Northrop. *Biblical and Classical Myths: The Mythological Framework of Western Culture*. Buffalo, NY: University of Toronto Press, 2004.

Gardner, Keith. *In Pursuit: Early Iconography of British Sporting Art; Being a Review of the Artistic Portrayal of Hunting with Hawk and Hound from Celtic to Post-Medieval Times*. Newmarket, England: British Sporting Art Trust, 2003.

Gersh, Stephen, and Bert Roest, eds. *Medieval and Renaissance Humanism: Rhetoric, Representation and Reform*. Boston: Brill, 2003.

Getz, Faye Marie, ed. *Healing and Society in Medieval England: A Middle English Translation of the Pharmaceutical Writings of Gilbertus Anglicus*. Madison: University of Wisconsin Press, 1991.

Gies, Frances, and Joseph Gies. *Women in the Middle Ages*. New York: Harper, 1978.

———. *Cathedral, Forge, and Waterwheel*. New York: Harper Collins, 1994.

Gimpel, Jean. *The Cathedral Builders*. Translated by Teresa Waugh. New York: HarperPerennial, 1992.

Ginsberg, Warren. *Chaucer's Italian Tradition*. Ann Arbor: University of Michigan Press, 2002.

Given-Wilson, Chris. *The English Nobility in the Late Middle Ages: The Fourteenth-Century Political Community*. New York: Routledge & Kegan Paul, 1987.

Goldberg, P.J.P. *Medieval England: A Social History, 1250–1550*. New York: Oxford University Press, 2004.

Gottfried, Robert S. *Doctors and Medicine in Medieval England, 1340–1530*. Princeton, NJ: Princeton University Press, 1986.

Grant, Lindy, ed. *Medieval Art, Architecture and Archaeology in London*. London: British Archaeological Association, 1990.

Gray, Douglas, ed. *The Oxford Companion to Chaucer*. New York: Oxford University Press, 2003.

Green, Monica Helen. *Women's Healthcare in the Medieval West: Texts and Contexts*. Burlington, VT: Ashgate/Variorum, 2000.

Hallissy, Margaret. *Clean Maids, True Wives, Steadfast Widows: Chaucer's Women and Medieval Codes of Conduct*. Westport, CT: Greenwood Press, 1993.

———. *A Companion to Chaucer's "Canterbury Tales."* Westport, CT: Greenwood Press, 1995.

Hanawalt, Barbara A., ed. *Chaucer's England: Literature in Historical Context*. Minneapolis: University of Minnesota Press, 1992.

———. *Growing Up in Medieval London: The Experience of Childhood in History*. New York: Oxford University Press, 1993.

Hansen, William F. *Classical Mythology: A Guide to the Mythical World of the Greeks and Romans*. New York: Oxford University Press, 2005.

Hawkes, Gail. *Sex and Pleasure in Western Culture*. Malden, MA: Polity, 2004.

Heinz, Dora. *Medieval Tapestries*. Translated by J. R. Foster. New York: Crown, 1967.

Herlihy, David. *The Black Death and the Transformation of the West*. Introduction by Samuel K. Cohn, Jr. Cambridge, MA: Harvard, 1997.

Heywood, Colin. *A History of Childhood: Children and Childhood in the West from Medieval to Modern Times*. Malden, MA: Blackwell, 2001.

Hicks, M. A. *Bastard Feudalism*. New York: Longman, 1995.

Hildegard of Bingen. *On Natural Philosophy and Medicine: Selections from "Case et Cure."* Translation and introduction by Margret Berger. Cambridge, England: D. S. Brewer, 1999.

Hill, John M. *Chaucerian Belief: The Poetics of Reverence and Delight.* New Haven, CT: Yale University Press, 1991.

Hilliam, David. *Castles and Cathedrals: The Great Buildings of Medieval Times.* New York: Rosen, 2004.

———. *Medieval Weapons and Warfare: Armies and Combat in Medieval Times.* New York: Rosen, 2004.

Hindley, Geoffrey. *The Medieval Establishment, 1200–1500.* New York: Putnam, 1970.

Hirsh, John C. *The Boundaries of Faith: The Development and Transmission of Medieval Spirituality.* New York: E. J. Brill, 1996.

Hodges, Laura F. *Chaucer and Clothing: Clerical and Academic Costume in the Prologue to the* "Canterbury Tales." Rochester, NY: D. S. Brewer, 2005.

———. *Chaucer and Costume.* Cambridge, England: D. S. Brewer, 2005.

Holsinger, Bruce W. *Music, Body, and Desire in Medieval Culture: Hildegard of Bingen to Chaucer.* Stanford, CA: Stanford University Press, 2001.

Hornsby, Joseph Allen. *Chaucer and the Law.* Norman, OK: Pilgrim Books, 1988.

Howes, Laura L. *Chaucer's Gardens and the Language of Convention.* Gainesville: University Press of Florida, 1997.

Huppert, George. *After the Black Death.* Bloomington: Indiana University Press, 1986.

Jacobs, Kathryn Elisabeth. *Marriage Contracts from Chaucer to the Renaissance Stage.* Gainesville: University Press of Florida, 2001.

Jeffery, Paul. *The Collegiate Churches of England and Wales.* London: Robert Hale, 2004.

Jones, Terry. *Chaucer's Knight: The Portrait of a Medieval Mercenary.* Baton Rouge: Louisiana State University Press, 1980.

Kaeuper, Richard W. *Chivalry and Violence in Medieval Europe.* New York: Oxford University Press, 1999.

Kamerick, Kathleen. *Popular Piety and Art in the Late Middle Ages: Image Worship and Idolatry in England 1350–1500.* New York: Palgrave, 2002.

Keen, Maurice Hugh. *Chivalry.* New Haven, CT: Yale University Press, 1984.

Kibre, Pearl. *Studies in Medieval Science: Alchemy, Astrology, Mathematics, and Medicine.* London: Hambledon Press, 1984.

King, Margot H., and Wesley M. Stevens, eds. *Saints, Scholars, and Heroes: Studies in Medieval Culture in Honor of Charles W. Jones.* Collegeville, MN: Hill Monastic Manuscript Library, Saint John's Abbey and University, 1979.

Kircher, Timothy. *The Poet's Wisdom: The Humanists, the Church, and the Formation of Philosophy in the Early Renaissance.* Boston: Brill, 2006.

Knapp, Peggy. *Chaucer and the Social Contest.* New York: Routledge, 1990.

Knowles, David. *Saints and Scholars: Twenty-Five Medieval Portraits.* Cambridge, England: Cambridge University Press, 1962.

Koff, Leonard Michael, and Brenda Deen Schildgen, eds. *The* "Decameron" *and the* "Canterbury Tales"*: New Essays on an Old Question.* Madison, NJ: Fairleigh Dickinson University Press, 2000.

Koslin, Désirée G., and Janet E. Snyder. *Encountering Medieval Textiles and Dress: Objects, Texts, Images.* New York: Palgrave Macmillan, 2002.

Kroesen, J.E.A. *The Interior of the Medieval Village Church.* Dudley, MA: Peeters, 2004.

Krueger, Roberta L. *The Cambridge Companion to Medieval Romance.* New York: Cambridge University Press, 2000.

Labarge, Margaret Wade. *Medieval Travellers.* New York: Norton, 1983.

Lacroix, Paul. *Military and Religious Life in the Middle Ages.* New York: Frederick Ungar, 1874; reprinted 1964.

Laing, Lloyd Robert. *Medieval Britain: The Age of Chivalry.* New York: St. Martin's Press, 1996.

Lambdin, Laura C., and Robert T. Lambdin, eds. *Chaucer's Pilgrims.* Westport, CT: Praeger, 1999.

Lasansky, D. Medina, and Brian McLaren, eds. *Architecture and Tourism: Perception, Performance and Place*. New York: Berg, 2004.

Laule, Ulrike. *Architecture of the Middle Ages*. Berlin: Feierabend, 2004.

Le Beau, Bryan F., and Menachem Mor, eds. *Pilgrims and Travelers to the Holy Land*. Omaha, NE: Creighton University Press, 1996.

Le Goff, Jacques. *Medieval Callings*. Translated by Lydia G. Cochrane. Chicago: University of Chicago Press, 1980.

———. *Time, Work, and Culture in the Middle Ages*. Translated by Arthur Goldhammer. Chicago: University of Chicago Press, 1980.

Lerer, Seth, ed. *The Yale Companion to Chaucer*. New Haven, CT: Yale University Press, 2006.

Lever, Jill, and John Harris. *Illustrated Dictionary of Architecture, 800–1914*. 2nd ed. Boston: Faber and Faber, 1993.

Liddy, Christian D. *War, Politics and Finance in Late Medieval English Towns: Bristol, York and the Crown, 1350–1400*. Woodbridge, VT: Boydell Press, 2005.

Lilley, Keith D. *Urban Life in the Middle Ages, 1000–1450*. New York: Palgrave, 2002.

Lyle, Marjorie. *Canterbury: 2000 Years of History*. Rev. ed. Stroud, England: Tempus, 2002.

Lynch, Kathryn L., ed. *Chaucer's Cultural Geography*. New York: Routledge, 2002.

MacDonald, Alasdair A., and Michael W. Twonmey, eds. *Schooling and Society: The Ordering and Reordering of Knowledge in the Western Middle Ages*. Dudley, MA: Peeters, 2004.

Manser, Martin H. *The Facts On File Dictionary of Classical and Biblical Allusions*. New York: Facts On File, 2003.

Marenbon, John. *Boethius*. New York: Oxford University Press, 2003.

Martin, Priscilla. *Chaucer's Women: Nuns, Wives, and Amazons*. Iowa City: University of Iowa Press, 1990.

Masi, Michael. *Chaucer and Gender*. New York : P. Lang, 2005.

Masschaele, James. *Peasants, Merchants, and Markets: Inland Trade in Medieval England, 1150–1350*. New York: St. Martin's Press, 1997.

McCarthy, Conor. *Marriage in Medieval England: Law, Literature, and Practice*. Woodbridge, VT: Boydell Press, 2004.

Mennell, Stephen. *All Manners of Food: Eating and Taste in England and France from the Middle Ages to the Present*. 2nd ed. Urbana: University of Illinois Press, 1996.

Mertes, Kate. *The English Noble Household, 1250–1600: Good Governance and Politic Rule*. New York: Blackwell, 1988.

Michael, M. A. *Stained Glass of Canterbury Cathedral*. London: Scala, 2004.

Miller, Mark. *Philosophical Chaucer: Love, Sex, and Agency in the* "Canterbury Tales." New York: Cambridge University Press, 2004.

Minnis, A. J. *Chaucer's Boece and the Medieval Tradition of Boethius*. Rochester, NY: D. S. Brewer, 1993.

Mitchell, Linda Elizabeth. *Portraits of Medieval Women: Family, Marriage, and Politics in England, 1255–1350*. New York: Palgrave Macmillan, 2003.

Morford, Mark P. O. *Classical Mythology*. 7th ed. New York: Oxford University Press, 2003.

Morgan, Gwyneth. *Life in a Medieval Village*. New York: Cambridge University Press, 1975.

Myers, A. R. *England in the Late Middle Ages*. 8th ed. Middlesex, England: Penguin, 1985.

Myles, Robert. *Chaucerian Realism*. Rochester, NY: D. S. Brewer, 1994.

Needham, Paul. *The Printer & the Pardoner: An Unrecorded Indulgence Printed by William Caxton for the Hospital of St. Mary Rounceval, Charing Cross*. Washington, DC: Library of Congress, 1986.

Netherton, Robin, and Gale R. Owen-Crocker, eds. *Medieval Clothing and Textiles*. Woodbridge, Suffolk, England: Boydell Press, 2005.

Nicholas, David. *The Growth of the Medieval City: From Late Antiquity to the Early Fourteenth Century.* New York: Longman, 1997.

———. *The Later Medieval City, 1300–1500.* New York: Longman, 1997.

———. *Urban Europe, 1100–1700.* New York: Palgrave Macmillan, 2003.

Nicolle, David, ed. *A Companion to Medieval Arms and Armour.* Rochester, NY: Boydell Press, 2002.

Nolan, Barbara. *Chaucer and the Tradition of the Roman Antique.* New York: Cambridge University Press, 1992.

Oakeshott, R. Ewart. *The Archaeology of Weapons: Arms and Armour from Prehistory to the Age of Chivalry.* Rochester, NY: Boydell Press, 1994.

———. *A Knight and His Armor.* 2nd ed. Chester Springs, PA: Dufour Editions, 1999.

———. *A Knight and His Weapons.* 2nd ed. Chester Springs, PA: Dufour Editions, 1997.

O'Brien, Mark. *When Adam Delved and Eve Span: A History of the Peasants' Revolt of 1381.* Cheltenham, England: New Clarion, 2004.

Ogden, Dunbar H. *The Staging of Drama in the Medieval Church.* Newark: University of Delaware Press, 2002.

Orme, Nicholas. *English Schools in the Middle Ages.* London: Methuen, 1973.

Osborn, Marijane. *Time and the Astrolabe in the* "Canterbury Tales." Norman: University of Oklahoma Press, 2002.

Page, Sophie. *Astrology in Medieval Manuscripts.* London: British Library, 2002.

Palmer, J.J.N. *Froissart: Historian.* Totowa, N J: Rowman & Littlefield, 1981.

Paola, Suzanne. *The Lives of the Saints.* Seattle: University of Washington Press, 2002.

Paolucci, Anne, ed. *Dante: Beyond the Commedia.* Wilmington, DE: Griffon House, 2004.

Parish, Helen L. *Monks, Miracles and Magic: Reformation Representations of the Medieval Church.* New York: Routledge, 2005.

Patterson, Lee. *Chaucer and the Subject of History.* Madison: University of Wisconsin Press, 1991.

Penninger, Frieda Elaine. *Chaucer's* "Troilus and Criseyde" *and the* "Knight's Tale": *Fictions Used.* Lanham, MD: University Press of America, 1993.

Platt, Colin. *The Architecture of Medieval Britain: A Social History.* New Haven, CT: Yale University Press, 1990.

———. *King Death: The Black Death and Its Aftermath in Late-Medieval England.* Toronto: University of Toronto Press, 1996.

Porter, Pamela J. *Courtly Love in Medieval Manuscripts.* Toronto: University of Toronto Press, 2003.

Pounds, Norman John Greville. *The Medieval City.* Westport, CT: Greenwood Press, 2005.

Powell, Barry B. *Classical Myth.* Translated by Herbert M. Howe. 4th ed. Upper Saddle River, NJ: Pearson/Prentice Hall, 2004.

Power, Eileen. *Medieval People.* New York: Barnes & Noble, 1924; reprinted 1968.

———. *The Wool Trade in English Medieval History: Being the Ford Lectures.* New York: Oxford University Press, 1942.

Powicke, F. M. *Medieval England, 1066–1485.* New York: Oxford University Press, 1969.

Prache, Anne. *Cathedrals of Europe.* Ithaca, NY: Cornell University Press, 2000.

Price, Simon, and Emily Kearns, eds. *The Oxford Dictionary of Classical Myth and Religion.* New York: Oxford University Press, 2003.

Purdon, Liam O., and Cindy L. Vitto, eds. *The Rusted Hauberk: Feudal Ideals of Order and Their Decline.* Gainesville: University Press of Florida, 1994.

Quiney, Anthony. *Town Houses of Medieval Britain.* New Haven, CT: Yale University Press, 2003.

Raguin, Virginia Chieffo, and Sarah Stanbury, eds. *Women's Space: Patronage, Place, and Gender in the Medieval Church.* Albany: State University of New York Press, 2005.

Reynolds, Susan. *Fiefs and Vassals: The Medieval Evidence Reinterpreted.* New York: Oxford University Press, 1994.

Richardson, Catherine, ed. *Clothing Culture, 1350–1650.* Burlington, VT: Ashgate, 2004.

Riches, Samantha J. E., and Sarah Salih, eds. *Gender and Holiness: Men, Women, and Saints in Late Medieval Europe.* New York: Routledge, 2002.

Rickert, Edith. *Chaucer's World.* Edited by Claire C. Olson and Martin M. Crow. New York: Columbia University Press, 1948; reprinted 1968.

Rigby, S. H. *Chaucer in Context: Society, Allegory, and Gender.* New York : Manchester University Press, 1996.

Rossignol, Rosalyn. *Chaucer A to Z.* New York: Facts On File, 1999.

Rowland, Beryl. *Blind Beasts: Chaucer's Animal World.* Kent, OH: Kent State University Press, 1971.

Salisbury, Joyce E., ed. *The Medieval World of Nature: A Book of Essays.* New York: Garland, 1993.

Saunders, Corinne, ed. *A Concise Companion to Chaucer.* Malden, MA: Blackwell, 2006.

Saunders, Corrinne, Françoise Le Saux, and Neil Thomas. *Writing War: Medieval Literary Responses to Warfare.* Rochester, NY: D. S. Brewer, 2004.

Schildgen, Brenda Deen. *Pagans, Tartars, Moslems, and Jews in Chaucer's "Canterbury Tales."* Gainesville: University Press of Florida, 2001.

Schofield, John. *Medieval London Houses.* New Haven, CT: Yale University Press, 1994.

Scott, Margaret. *Medieval Clothing and Costumes: Displaying Wealth and Class in Medieval Times.* New York: Rosen, 2004.

Scully, Terence. *The Art of Cookery in the Middle Ages.* Woodbridge, Suffolk, England: Boydell Press, 1995.

Sedgwick, Henry Dwight. *The Black Prince.* New York: Barnes & Noble, 1993.

Simson, Otto Georg von. *The Gothic Cathedral: Origins of Gothic Architecture and the Medieval Concept of Order.* 3rd ed. Princeton, NJ: Princeton University Press, 1988.

Singman, Jeffrey L., and Will McLean. *Daily Life in Chaucer's England.* Westport, CT: Greenwood Press, 1995.

Skinner, Patricia, ed. *The Jews in Medieval Britain: Historical, Literary, and Archaeological Perspectives.* Rochester, NY: Boydell & Brewer, 2003.

Slater, T. R., and Gervase Rosser, eds. *The Church in the Medieval Town.* Brookfield, VT: Ashgate, 1998.

Slavitt, David R. *Lives of the Saints.* New York: Atheneum, 1989.

Smith, Warren S., ed. *Satiric Advice on Women and Marriage: From Plautus to Chaucer.* Ann Arbor: University of Michigan Press, 2005.

Smoldon, William L. *The Music of the Medieval Church Dramas.* Edited by Cynthia Bourgeault. New York: Oxford University Press, 1980.

Snyder, James. *Medieval Art: Painting-Sculpture-Architecture, 4th–14th Century.* New York: H. N. Abrams, 1989.

St. John, Michael. *Chaucer's Dream Visions: Courtliness and Individual Identity.* Burlington, VT: Ashgate, 2000.

Staley, Lynn. *Languages of Power in the Age of Richard II.* University Park: Pennsylvania State University Press, 2005.

Stannard, Jerry. *Herbs and Herbalism in the Middle Ages and Renaissance.* Edited by Katherine E. Stannard and Richard Kay. Aldershot, England: Ashgate, 1999.

Stein, Robert M., and Sandra Pierson Prior. *Reading Medieval Culture: Essays in Honor of Robert W. Hanning.* Notre Dame, IN: University of Notre Dame Press, 2005.

Strickland, Debra Higgs. *Medieval Bestiaries: Text, Image, Ideology.* New York: Cambridge University Press, 1995.

Strohm, Paul. *Social Chaucer.* Cambridge, MA: Harvard University Press, 1989.

Swabey, Ffiona. *Medieval Gentlewoman: Life in a Gentry Household in the Later Middle Ages.* New York: Routledge, 1999.

Swatos, Jr., William H., and Luigi Tomasi, eds. *From Medieval Pilgrimage to Religious Tourism: The Social and Cultural Economics of Piety.* Westport, CT: Praeger, 2002.

Sweeney, Michelle. *Magic in Medieval Romance from Chrétien de Troyes to Geoffrey Chaucer.* Portland, OR: Four Courts Press, 2000.

Telesko, Werner. *The Wisdom of Nature: The Healing Powers and Symbolism of Plants and Animals in the Middle Ages.* New York: Prestel, 2001.

Thirsk, Joan. *Alternative Agriculture: A History. From the Black Death to the Present Day.* Oxford, England: Oxford University Press, 1997.

Thomson, John A. F. *Popes and Princes, 1417–1517: Politics and Polity in the Late Medieval Church.* Boston: Allen & Unwin, 1980.

Thordeman, Bengt. *Armour from the Battle of Wisby, 1361.* In collaboration with Poul Nörlund and Bo E. Ingelmark. New ed. Union City, CA: Chivalry Bookshelf, 2002.

Trim, D.J.B., ed. *The Chivalric Ethos and the Development of Military Professionalism.* Boston: Brill, 2003.

Tyerman, Christopher. *England and the Crusades, 1095–1588.* Chicago: University of Chicago Press, 1988.

Ullmann, Walter. *Jurisprudence in the Middle Ages.* London: Variorum Reprints, 1980.

———. *Medieval Foundations of Renaissance Humanism.* Ithaca, NY: Cornell University Press, 1977.

Unger, Richard W. *Beer in the Middle Ages and the Renaissance.* Philadelphia: University of Pennsylvania Press, 2004.

Usilton, Larry W. *The Kings of Medieval England, c. 560–1485: A Survey and Research Guide.* Lanham, MD: Scarecrow Press, 1996.

Vale, M.G.A. *The Princely Court: Medieval Courts and Culture in North-West Europe, 1270–1380.* New York: Oxford University Press, 2001.

Valente, Claire. *The Theory and Practice of Revolt in Medieval England.* Burlington, VT: Ashgate, 2003.

Van Arsdale, Anne. *Medieval Herbal Remedies.* London: Routledge, 2002.

Verdon, Jean. *Travel in the Middle Ages.* Notre Dame, IN: University of Notre Dame Press, 2003.

Vernier, Richard. *The Flower of Chivalry: Bertrand Du Guesclin and the Hundred Years War.* Rochester, NY: D. S. Brewer, 2003.

Waldman, John. *Hafted Weapons in Medieval and Renaissance Europe: The Evolution of European Staff Weapons Between 1200 and 1650.* Boston: Brill, 2005.

Webb, Diana. *Medieval European Pilgrimage, c. 700–c. 1500.* New York: Palgrave, 2002.

———. *Pilgrimage in Medieval England.* New York: Hambledon and London, 2000.

———. *Pilgrims and Pilgrimage in the Medieval West.* New York: I. B. Tauris, 2001.

Weber, Elka. *Traveling Through Text: Message and Method in Late Medieval Pilgrimage Accounts.* New York: Routledge, 2005.

West, Richard. *Chaucer 1340–1400: The Life and Times of the First English Poet.* New York: Carroll and Graf, 2000.

Whatley, E. Gordon, Anne B. Thompson, and Robert K. Upchurch, eds. *Saints' Lives in Middle English Collections.* Kalamazoo: Medieval Institute Publications, Western Michigan University, 2004.

Wilkins, Nigel E. *Music in the Age of Chaucer.* Totowa, NJ: Rowman and Littlefield, 1979.

Wilkins, Sally E. D. *Sports and Games of Medieval Cultures.* Westport, CT: Greenwood Press, 2002.

Wilson, Katharina M., and Elizabeth M. Makowski. *Wykked Wyves and the Woes of Marriage: Misogamous Literature from Juvenal to Chaucer.* Albany: State University of New York Press, 1990.

Wood, Diana, ed. *Women and Religion in Medieval England*. Oakville, CT: David Brown, 2003.

Wood, Margaret. *The English Mediaeval House*. London: Bracken Books, 1983; reprinted 1985.

Wright, Nicholas. *Knights and Peasants: The Hundred Years War in the French Countryside*. Rochester, NY: Boydell Press, 1998.

Ziegler, Philip. *The Black Death*. Gloucestershire, England: Sutton, 1998.

Index

Bold face denotes main listing for an entry.

Abelard, Peter, 341
Abigail, **3–4**, 28, 150
Abortifacient, 304
Abraham, **4**, 28, 383–84
Absolom, "The Miller's Tale," 144, 321
Absolute. *See* Alchemy
Achates, **5**, 29, 443
Achelous, 122
Achilles, **6–7**, 29, 441–43
Acid, 19, 273; hydrochloric,19; nitric, 19; sulphuric, 19
Actaeon, 7, 29, 233, 235
Adam, **8–9**, 28, 151–52, 326, 338
Adonis, **10–11**, 29
Aeëtes, King of Colchis, 293
Aeneas, 5, **11**, 29, 443
Aeneid, 5, 11, 25–26
Aeolus, 20
Aesop, 31
Æthelbert, 88, 398
Agamemnon, 91, 442–43
Agincourt. *See* Hundred Years War
Agriculture, **12–15**, 224, 365; climate, 13, 14, 459; crops, 13, 14, 83, 84, 149; irrigation, 13; three-field system, 14
Agrimony, 17
Ahasuerus, King of Persia, 150

Alan. *See* Reeve's Tale
Albigensians, 222
Alchemy, **16–20**, 56, 229, 304, 381, 466; Absolute, 18, 19; Elixir of Life, 20; Emerald Table, 19; Ferrarius, 18; Four Elements, 18, 187; Hermes Trismegistus, 19; *Ignis Innaturalis* (secret fire), 19, 20; *Materia Prima*, 19, 20; Philosopher's Stone, 19, 20; puffers, 19; Philosophic Egg, 20
Alcohol, 19, 173, 174, 409
Alcyone, **20–21**, 29
Aldergate. *See* London
Aldgate. *See* London
Ale. *See* Food
Alexander V, Pope, 211
Alexander the Great, 22, 247, 286
Alexandria, **22**, 24, 286, 431
Alfonso XI, King of Castile and León, 23
Alfred the Great, 416, 417
Algeciras, **23–24**, 213, 315
Alison, 326; "The Miller's Tale," 5, 108, 144, 321; Wife of Bath, 4, 61, 78, 123, 150, 209, 225, 248, 253, 269, 306, 384
Allegory, **24–28**, 31, 62, 129, 145
Allusions, **28**, **29**, 30, 117, 129, 220, 235, 458

Althea of Calydon, 122
Ambler. *See* Horse
Amphion, **29–30**
Anchises, 11
Anelida and Arcite, 269, 270
Anglo-Saxons, 21, 174, 176, 220, 263,
   277, 289, 326, 392, 398, 409, 457
Animals, **30–32**, 62, 111, 112, 127, 134,
   156, 173, 190, 210, 221, 373, 383,
   407, 440, 457; boar, 10, 11, 32,
   70–71, 91, 127, 168, 171, 233, 426;
   dog, 31, 32, 69, **129–30**, 178, 211,
   233, 352; fox, 31–32, **189–91**, 256,
   308, 337, 373; hare, 31–32, 125, 156,
   170, 171–72, 177, 212, 213, **217**,
   233, 454; horse, 31, 32, 41, 43, 46,
   68, 69, 76, 100, 105, 136, 148, 161,
   162, 166, 170, 177, 202, 204, 205,
   224–25, 263, 305, 306, 312, 313,
   318, 319, 326, 338, 339, 345, 362,
   396, 438, 440, 442, 448, 449, 460;
   lamb, 118, 126, 388; ram 54, 84, 308,
   389; rat, 65, 68; sheep 3, 14, 31, 32,
   67, 84, 117, 118, 148, 170, 361, 362,
   388–89, 405, 455, 459; sow, 118,
   190, 237, 308; wolf, 32, 134, 233,
   388, 389, **454–55**
Anne of Bohemia, 27, 370
Annulment, 290
Annunciation Day, 9, 83, 84
Antiope, 29
Anti-Semitism, 251, 403
Apollo, 29, 30, **32–34**, 53, 90, 110, 116,
   121–22, 403, 442
Apothecary, 228, 297, 299
April, 54, 73, 84, 84, 336
Aquarius, 55, 56
Aquitaine, 107, 141, 174, 231, 401, 434
Arabs/Arabic, 4, 13, 23, 250, 341, 379
Aragon, 94
Archery, 45, 102, 202, 204, 466
Archimedes, 378
Architecture, **34–39**, 95, 98, 104, 220,
   298; buttresses, 36, 37, 38; Byzantine,
   36; Early Christian, 34; Gothic, 37, 38;
   High Gothic, 37; Rayonant, 37; Ro-
   manesque, 35, 37
Arcite, "The Knight's Tale," 30, 40, 41,
   188, 208, 209, 269, 270, 303
Ares, 10
Argonauts, 237, 431
Ariadne, 29, **39**
Aries, 19, 53, 54, 56, 84, 85

Aristocracy, 67, 78, 125, 136, 147, 148,
   233, 251, 367, 371, 439
Aristotle, 105, 136, 164–65, 227, 296,
   297, 301, 339, 340, 378, 379, 380
Arithmetic, 137, 227, 316
Armor, 5, **40–46**, 47, 50, 143, 166, 195,
   219, 220, 221, 232, 263, 265, 273,
   274, 437, 442, 447–48, 450, 451;
   bascinet, 43–44; bracer, 45, 456, 465,
   46; breastplate, 40, 42, 44, 447; *chapel
   de fer*, 44; chausses, 46; coif, 42, 44;
   courboille 42, 45; cuirass, 44;
   gambeson, 45; gauntlet, 45; greaves,
   46; harness, 41, 42, 45, 46, 204, 219;
   hauberk, 40, 41, 42, 45, 203, 204; helmet, 41, 43, 44, 198, 173, 203, 204,
   220; lames, 42, 45; mail, 6, 40, 41, 42,
   43–46, 204, 441, 447, 448; spurs, 42
Ars Amatoria. See *Art of Love*
Artemis, 7, 30, 328
Artillery, 21, 450, 451; cannon, 41, 448,
   451; mangonel, 450; trebuchet, 92, 450
Art of Love, 107
Ascension Day, 224
Asia, 252
Asterius the Minotaur, 39, 116
Astrolabe, **46–49**, 49, 53, 55, 56, 229
Astrology, 18, 20, **49–56**, 69, 84, 85,
   224, 227, 297, 302, 381, 468
Astronomy, 48, **49–56**, 69, 85, 137, 224,
   227, 229, 342, 378, 381, 411, 468
Athens, 39, 55, 124, 293, 412
August, 84, 118, 172
Aurelias, "The Franklin's Tale," 32
Autumn. *See* Calendar
Avignon Papacy. *See* Great Schism
Ax. *See* Weapons

Bacchus, 29, 34, 39, **59–60**, 348
Backgammon. *See* Games
Bacon, Roger, 379
Bagpipes. *See* Music
Bailly, Harry (*The Canterbury Tales*), 19,
   70, 217, 276, 418
Baker. *See* Food
Ball, John. *See* Peasant Revolt of 1381
Balliol College, 139, 276
Banking, 104, 147, 251
Banquet. *See* Food
Banu Marin. *See* Morocco
Baptism, **60–61**, 126, 336, 366, 370
Barber, 295, 296, 297, 298, 299, 300,
   301, 343, 380

Barley, 14, 84

Bascinet. *See* Armor

Basilica, 34, 243, 410

Bastard Feudalism. *See* Feudalism

Bath, 4, **61–62**, 78, 123, 150, 209, 225, 248, 253, 269, 289, 290, 306, 384, 385, 413, 414, 432, 433, 467, 468

Bathing, 7, 63, 64, 236, 301, 403

Baton, 203, 206

Bayeux Tapestry, 426

Beard. *See* Fashion

Beaufort. *See* John of Gaunt

Bed. *See* Furniture

Beer. *See* Food

Beggary, 178, 194, 213

Bells, 119, 159

Benedict XIII, Pope, 211

Benedictines, 88, 352, 400, 407, 419, 452

Benefice. *See* Feudalism

Betrayal, 11, 124, 237, 293

Bible, 4, 28, 29, 31, 128, 143, 151, 236, 252, 269, 276, 370; Book of Revelation, 25

Bile, 172, 188, 296, 380

Birds, 21, 31, 32, **62–63**, 69, 111, 112, 127, 134, 156, 173, 189, 191, 210, 373, 418; crow, 62, **109–11;** cuckoo, 62, **111–12;** dove, 62, 107, 108, 110, **126–27;** eagle, 26, 27, 62, 64, 125, **133–34**, 210, 303; falcon, 62, **155–56**, 233, 234, 396; goose, 31, 62, 107, **209–10;** hawk, 62, 210, 233; hen, 62, **372–73;** rooster, 55, 62, 84, 190, 227, **372–73**

Birth, 4, 10, 11, 50, 56, 60, **63–64**, 99, 116, 148, 192, 208, 209, 221, 301, 303, 305, 310, 354, 366, 368, 402, 404, 409

Black, 21, 27, 32, 64, 65, 91, 105, 110, 118, 124, 135, 136, 143, 160, 165, 172, 188, 219, 220, 235, 237, 304, 308, 339, 373, 460

Black Death, **64–69**, 71, 103, 104, 147, 149, 189, 210, 213, 221, 231, 232, 250, 280, 296, 299, 301, 305, 314, 343, 380, 381, 422

Black Prince, Edward the, 90, 140, **141–43**, 231, 253, 254, 255, 326, 370

Blacksmith, 119, 411, 417

Blanche, Duchess of Lancaster, 27, **70**, 254, 255

Blancmangere. *See* Food

Blind Man's Bluff. *See* Games

Bloodletting, 55, 56, 66, 187, 298, 299, 302, 343

Boar, 10, 11, 32, **70–71**, 91, 127, 168, 171, 233, 426

Boccaccio, Giovanni, 65, **71–72**, 183; *Decameron,* 71; *Filostrato,* 72

Boethius, Anicius Manlius Severinus, 48, **72–74**, 160, 168, 182, 340, 341

Boniface IX, Pope, 211

Book of Hours, 13, 15, 84

Book of the Duchess, 6, 11, 21, 25, 26, 27, 28, 70, 91, 124, 128, 135, 151, 180, 182, 188, 189, 255, 256, 280, 281, 293, 294, 295, 296, 301, 327, 357, 380

Books, 19, 25, 49, 90, 105, 106, 123, 128, 136, 139, 143, 165, 171, 228, 271–73, 297, 339, 379, 413

Bow. *See* Weapons

Bowls. *See* Games

Bracer. *See* Armor

Brain, 188, 302

Bread. *See* Food

Breakfast. *See* Food

Breastplate. *See* Armor

Breeches. *See* Fashion

Bribes, 194, 195, 421

Bride. *See* Marriage

Bridgegate. *See* London

Bristol, 280

Bruges, **74–75**, 467, 468

Bubonic Plague, 65, 66, 68

Burghers, 103, 197

Burgundy, **75–76**, 169

Business and Commerce, 42, 50, 53, 74, **76-79**, 104, 165, 243, 307, 309, 312, 343, 363, 364, 391, 439, 460

Buttons. *See* Fashion

Buttresses. *See* Architecture

Byzantine, 13, 36, 271, 286, 374, 431

Calais, 140, 142, 229, 230, 231, 232

Calendar, **83–85**, 118, 120, 224, 336, 365, 368, 370, 399, 417; fall, 14, 118; Friday, 54, 119; spring, 14, 33, 83, 84, 173; summer, 84, 118, 387; winter, 6, 21, 83, 84, 118, 119, 163, 171, 235, 354, 368

Caliope, 29, **85–86**

Calkas (*Troilus and Criseyde*), 53

Cambok. *See* Games

Cambridge, **86–87**, 138, 139

Camden, William, 453

Camp ball. *See* Games

Candles, 96, 119, 355, 409

Cannon. *See* Artillery

Canon, 196, 256, 271, 272

Canon's Yeoman (*Canterbury Tales*), 20, 256, 466

Canon's Yeoman's Tale. See *Canterbury Tales*

Canterbury, **88–90**, 93, 96, 143, 169, 225, 279, 337, 348, 353, 392, 393, 398–99, 405, 427, 434, 435, 438; Canterbury Cathedral, 35, 36, 38, 88, 143, 432, 433

Canterbury Tales: Canon's Yeoman's Tale, 17, 19, 20, 256, 257, 378, 381; Clerk's Tale 135, 146, 149, 180, 208, 253, 292; Doctour of Phisik's Tale, 418; General Prologue, 12, 22, 23, 45, 54, 56, 61, 76, 85, 100, 102, 105, 106, 125, 126, 136, 158, 164, 165, 168, 172, 176, 177, 178, 179, 187, 190, 192, 194, 212, 213, 214, 217, 224, 225, 236, 237, 242, 243, 248, 251, 265, 271, 274, 275, 287, 303, 306, 307, 308, 309, 313, 315, 320, 321, 334, 336, 339, 342, 343, 344, 345, 347, 351, 357, 362, 363, 365, 374, 389, 391, 393, 396, 397, 399, 400, 401, 403, 404, 411, 415, 419, 420, 421, 427, 429, 432, 438, 455, 456, 458, 459, 466, 467; Knight's Tale, 7, 8, 10, 30, 41, 42, 44, 54, 72, 122, 180, 185, 187, 203, 204, 208, 209, 219, 221, 232, 233, 235, 263, 265, 293, 294, 303, 322, 447; Manciple's Tale, 30, 32, 62, 110, 321, 454, 455; Man of Law's Tale, 6, 39, 52, 53, 121, 123, 151, 152, 253, 275, 276, 280, 281, 422; Merchant's Tale, 3, 30, 53, 55, 59, 108, 150, 151, 152, 181, 218, 291, 314, 349, 385, 387; Miller's Tale, 5, 49, 50, 51, 106, 108, 109, 139, 144, 145, 170, 291, 321, 401, 411, 412, 417, 432, 433; Monk's Tale, 121, 123, 180, 183, 185, 286, 410, 431; Nun's Priest's Tale, 6, 26, 31, 54, 55, 62, 84, 85, 118, 120, 128, 185, 188, 190, 191, 227, 228, 256, 321, 337, 338, 354, 373; Pardoner's Tale, 201, 206, 207, 316, 321, 322, 429; Parson's Tale, 5, 8, 10, 55, 85, 121, 151, 162, 248, 249, 414;

Prioress's Tale, 250, 252; Reeve's Tale, 87, 106, 139, 404; Second Nun's Tale, 402, 403; Shipman's Tale, 74, 75, 306, 399, 406, 407; Squire's Tale, 54, 85, 156, 188, 269; Summoner's Tale, 71, 392, 440; Tale of Melibee, 4, 300, 414; Wife of Bath's Tale, 4, 123, 209, 253, 269, 289, 290, 384, 385, 413, 414, 432, 433

Capet, Hugh, 75

Capetian Dynasty, 75

Cardamom, 170

Cards. *See* Games

Carolingians, 35, 36, 101, 166, 250, 310, 457; Carolingian Empire, 75, 310, 457; Charles Martel, 75

Carpenter, 50, 165, 362, 401, 411, 412, 432

Cassandra, 29, **90–91**, 127, 128, 441, 443

Castile, 23, 142, 143, 183, 254, 255

Castles, 38, **91–94**, 95, 103, 116, 172, 198, 254, 319, 354, 355, 357, 372, 373, 413, 425, 426, 450, 451; drawbridge, 93; moat, 93; motte and bailey, 92; portcullis, 21, 93

Catalonia, **94**

Cathars, 222

Cathedrals, 35, 36, 37, 38, 61, 88, 89, 90, 94, **95–98**, 103, 143, 270, 279, 310, 365, 366, 369, 370, 394, 401, 405, 407, 408, 432, 434; Chartres, 36, 37, 38, 95, 365, 366; narthex, 35; nave, 35; transept, 35, 452; vault, 36, 37, 38

Catholicism. *See* Religion

Cato, 25, 128, 228

Cephisus, 327

Ceres, 34

Cetura, 4

Ceyx, 20, 21

Chair. *See* Furniture

Chapel de fer. See Armor

Charlemagne, 35, 36, 75, 77

Charles V, King of France, 231

Charles VI, King of France, 231, 232, 370

Charles VII, King of France, 232

Charter, 87, 167, 279, 382

Chartres. *See* Cathedrals

Chaucer, Agnes, mother of Chaucer. *See* Chaucer, Geoffrey

Chaucer, Elizabeth, daughter of Chaucer. *See* Chaucer, Geoffrey

Chaucer, Geoffrey: death, 452; employ-
     ment, Clerk of the King's Works, 452
Chaucer, John, father of Chaucer. *See*
     Chaucer, Geoffrey
Chaucer, Lewis, son of Chaucer. *See*
     Chaucer, Geoffrey
Chaucer, Philippa, wife of Chaucer. *See*
     Chaucer, Geoffrey
Chaucer, Thomas, son of Chaucer. *See*
     Chaucer, Geoffrey
Chauntecleer, "The Nun's Priest's Tale,"
     25, 55, 84, 128, 227, 321, 373
Chausses. *See* Armor
Cheapside. *See* London
Chemistry, 19, 304
Chess. *See* Games
Chests. *See* Furniture
Childhood/Children, 60, 63, 64, 67, 70,
     98-99, 112, 136, 137, 139, 141, 174,
     205, 235, 237, 249, 250, 251, 254,
     255, 289, 290, 301, 303, 305, 310,
     325, 329, 366, 368, 369, 404, 459
China, 65
Chivalric Code. *See* Knight
Chivalry, 22, **99-103**, 109, 144, 220,
     261, 264, 265, 371, 396, 437
Christianity, 4, 50, 251, 274, 313, 357,
     374, 379, 398
Christmas, 118, 224, 368, 405
Chronicles, 196, 254
Cicero, 26, 180, 226, 227
Cinnamon, 170, 173, 174
Cities, 12, 61, 65, 74, 77, 78, **103-5**,
     176, 202, 213, 275, 355, 404
Citole. *See* Music
Clairvaux, 313, 401
Clavichord. *See* Music
Clement VII, Pope, 211
Cleopatra, 286
Clergy, 35, 60, 67, 147, 318, 367, 416
Clerk, **105-7**, 110, 123, 136, 139, 164,
     227, 229, 292, 341, 336, 338, 364,
     413
Clerk of the King's Works. *See* Chaucer,
     Geoffrey
"Clerk's Tale." *See* *Canterbury Tales*
Climate. *See* Agriculture
Cloth, 44, 61, 67, 74, 78, 159, 163, 355,
     459, 460, 467, 468
Clytemnestra, 91, 443
Cnut of Denmark, 409
Coat of Arms, 41, 219-21, 265, 381, 382
Coathardie. *See* Fashion

Cochineal, 426
Coif. *See* Armor
Communion, 367
Compendium medicinae, 298
"Complaint of Mars," 47, 48
Conception, 301
Confessions, 340
Consolation of Philosophy, 74, 160, 168,
     182, 340
Constantine, 247, 431
Constanza of Castile. *See* John of Gaunt
Controller of Petty Customs. *See* Chaucer,
     Geoffrey
Controller of the Customs of Wools, Skins,
     and Hides. *See* Chaucer, Geoffrey
Cook (*Canterbury Tales*), 179, 192
Cornwall, 142, 347, 382, 416
Coronation, 232, 255, 279, 310, 311,
     437, 452
Coronis, 32
Corruption. *See* Religion
Cottage, 61, 74, 78, 118, 120, 146, 353,
     354, 355, 416, 459
Counsel of Clermont, 436
Courboille. *See* Armor
Courtly Love, 101, 102, **107-9**, 144,
     289, 290, 293, 396, 435, 437
Cranmer, Thomas, 90
Cream of Tartar, 19
Crécy. *See* Hundred Years War
Crete, 39, 116
Criseyde, 11, 53, 108, 122, 182, 183,
     184, 219
Crops. *See* Agriculture
Crow. *See* Birds
Crusades, 77, 92, 102, 159, 247, 263,
     265, 319, 347, 401
Cuckold, 50, 71, 74, 110, 111, 307, 314,
     385, 407
Cuckoo. *See* Birds
Cuirass. *See* Armor
Cupid, 34, 210
Cupping. *See* Medicine
Currency, 77, 146
Custace, "The Man of Law's Tale," 53

Daedalus, 62, **115-16**, 296, 380
Daily Life, 50, 85, 104, **117-21**, 144,
     179, 197, 198, 223, 224, 237, 273,
     322, 256, 367, 457, 458
Damask. *See* Fashion
Dame Fortune, 74, 340, 341. *See also*
     Fortune

Daniel, 28, **121**, 326

Dante, 72

Daphne, 29, **121–22**

Decameron. See Giovanni Boccaccio

Degree: Bachelor's, 106, 137; Master's, 137; Professional, 137

Deianira, 29, **122–24**

Deiphebus, 90

Delphi, 32

Demophon, 29, **124–25**

Dentistry. *See* Medicine

DeRoet, Philippa. *See* Philippa Chaucer

Devil, 9, 110, 190, 191, 201, 253, 316, 322, 403, 409, 429. *See also* Satan

Dialectic, 137

Diana, 7, 121, 122, 234, 235, 458

Dice. *See* Games

Dido, 5, 11

Dijon, 75, 401

Dill, 305

Dinner. *See* Food

Dionysos. *See* Bacchus

Disease. *See* Medicine

Divorce. *See* Marriage

Doctor. *See* Physician

Doctour of Phisik. *See* Physician

"Doctour of Phisik's Tale." *See Canterbury Tales*

Dog, 31, 32, 69, **125–26**, 178, 211, 233, 352; greyhound, 125, 212; hound, 7, 126, 350, 351; lapdog, 125

Dominicans, 195, 221

Dorigen, "The Franklin's Tale," 55, 108, 280, 291

Doublet. *See* Fashion

Dove. *See* Birds

Drawbridge. *See* Castles

"Dream of Scipio," 25, 26

Dreams, 21, 25, 28, 121, **127–29**, 188, 227, 228, 256, 413

Dream visions, **24–27**, 129, 145

Drink. *See* Food

Drums. *See* Music

Dubbing. *See* Knight

Durham, 404, 405

Dyer (*Canterbury Tales*), 165

Eagle. *See* Birds

East End. *See* London

Easter, 83, 118, 224, 336, 368, 399, 405, 417

Echo, 29, **135–36**, 292, 327

Economy, 64, 74, 77, 149, 242, 263, 369

Eden, 8, 151

Education, 99, 106, **136–40**, 226, 227, 273, 301, 306, 341, 342, 368, 380, 381, 426, 433

Edward II, 297, 318, 371

Edward III, 70, 139, **140–43**, 143, 196, 230, 231, 253, 255, 276, 310, 311, 370, 471

Edward, the Black Prince. *See* Black Prince, Edward the

Edward the Confessor, 279, **409–10**, 452

Eggs. *See* Food

Eglantyne, Madame, the Prioress, 211, **351–53**

Egypt, 22, 247, 256, 286, 425

Eleanor Cross, 368

Eleanor of Aquitaine, 107, 174, 401, 434

Elixir of Life. *See* Alchemy

Embroidery, 41, 99, 164, 204, 329, 396

Emerald Table. *See* Alchemy

Emily, "The Knight's Tale," 7, 122, 180, 235, 327

Emma of Normandy, 409

Enarete, 20

England, 13, 61, 63, 67, 69, 75, 78, 87, 88, 92, 104, 141, 142, 141, 147, 148, 196, 220, 222, 229, 230, 250, 251, 254, 255, 272, 276, 277, 279, 297, 311, 319, 357, 371, 382, 394, 398, 399, 405, 409, 427, 432, 433, 434, 449, 452, 457, 459, 460, 467

Entertainment, **143–46**, 202, 207, 316, 318, 322, 347, 355, 369–70, 430, 436, 437

Estates, **146–50**, 167, 193, 209, 213, 265, 288, 309, 311, 314, 338, 353, 356, 364, 451, 466

Esther, 28, **150–51**

Etruscans, 280

Euclid, 378

Eve, 8, 9, 28, **151–52**, 338

Extreme Unction, 368

Ezekiel, 25

Fair Maid of Kent, 142

Fairs, 78, 143, 439

Falcon. *See* Birds

Fall. *See* Calendar

Fame, 27, 28, 85, 94, 116, 117, 134, 142, **156–58**, 180, 186, 400, 453

Fashion, 40, 41, 43, 75, 76, 78, **158–65**, 218, 274, 306, 325, 392, 396, 426, 434, 447, 460, 468; beard, 76, 109, 164, 176, 190, 192, 235, 306, 308,

362, 386, 391, 406, 415; breeches, 162; buttons, 161, 163; coathardie, 159, 163; damask, 159; doublet, 163; hat, 159, 163; headdress, 159; hood, 42, 44, 139, 160, 163, 362, 363, 368, 456, 465; hose, 75, 76, 161, 162; houppelande, 163; kirtle, 159, 162, 163; leggings, 162; mantle, 163; mustache, 164; shoes, 76, 78, 159, 162, 163–64, 273; silk, 158, 159, 160, 163, 164, 250, 263, 426, 439; sumptuary laws, 159, 263; surcoat, 45, 161, 220; wimple, 163, 351, 352

February, 84, 171, 372, 418

Fencing. *See* Games

Ferrarius. *See* Alchemy

Feudalism, 15, 149, **165–67**, 288, 369; bastard feudalism, 167; Benefice, 105, 136, 164, 166; freehold, 148, 466; homage, 166; servile holding, 148; vassal, 166

Fiddle. *See* Music

Figs. *See* Food

Filostrato. See Boccaccio

Fines, 458

First Estate. *See* Estates

Flail. *See* Weapons

Flanders, 43, 61, 74, 76, 100, 164, 196, 201, 230, 306, 322, 395, 429, 459, 467

Flea, 65, 68

Florence, Italy, 71

Food, 12, 13, 15, 62, 66, 78, 84, 118, 148, **167–79**, 192, 193, 197, 198, 224, 233, 234, 287, 296, 314, 319, 347, 380, 400, 428, 429, 430, 457; baker, 176, 177, 178; banquet, 93, 145, 168, 170, 173, 175, 224, 254, 316, 355; beer, 174, 325, 428, 429; blancmangere, 172; bread, 27, 70, 118, 119, 126, 170, 171, 173, 175, 176, 177, 178, 192, 304, 312, 351, 367, 415, 417; breakfast, 119, 175; dinner, 119, 172, 175, 197, 219, 236; eggs, 62, 111, 112, 170, 171, 172; figs, 173; fork, 175; hanap, 175; mazer, 175; pastry, 173; ravioli, 169; reresoper, 175; spoon, 172, 173, 175; table dormant, 176, 192; trencher, 175; vegetables, 13, 14, 169, 171, 273

Football. *See* Games

Fork. *See* Food

Fortress, 36, 96, 103

Fortune, 50, 53, 56, 74, 157, **179–86**, 205, 285, 286, 340, 341

Fortune Telling. *See* Games

"Four Elements." *See* Alchemy

Four Humors, 20, 55, 56, 66, 69, 171, **186–89**, 296, 297, 298, 302, 305, 343, 380, 381

Fox, 31–32, **189–91**, 256, 308, 337, 373

France, 43, 75, 140, 142, 165, 196, 210, 229, 230, 231, 232, 250, 265, 310, 357, 401, 406, 407, 435, 451, 459

Franciscans, 195, 221

Franklin (*Canterbury Tales*), 61, 158, 165, 178, 179, **191–93**, 415, 416

"Franklin's Tale." See *Canterbury Tales*

Freehold. *See* Feudalism

Friar, 71, 178, **193–95**, 212, 213, 221, 248, 320, 336, 379, 382, 409, 421, 439

Friday. *See* Calendar

Froissart, Jean, **195–96**, 254, 265

Fulling, 460

Furniture, **197–98**, 354, 356, 457; bed, 105, 136, 164, 165, 188, 197, 288, 289, 339, 354, 356, 385, 386, 387, 415, 416, 425, 428; chair, 197, 356; chests, 197, 356

Gaddesden, John. *See* Medicine

Galen. *See* Medicine

Galileo Galilei, 49, 380

Gambeson. *See* Armor

Gambling, 201, 202, 205, 206, 207, 318, 322, 429

Games, 180, **201–7**, 235, 437; backgammon, 205; blind man's bluff, 205; bowls, 205; cambok, 204; camp ball, 205; cards, 206; chess, 26, 180, 202, 203, 205; dice, 206, 207, 285; fencing, 202; football, 204, 205; fortune telling, 205; handball, 204; hazard, 206, 207; kailes, 205; quits, 205; sports, 202, 204, 435, 437; shuttlecock, 205; stickball, 204; stoolball, 205; tug-of-war, 205

Ganelon, 191

Garbage, 104, 177, 178

Garter, 142, 162

Gascony, 142, 231, 254

Gauntlet. *See* Armor

Gemini, 19, 47, 56

General Prologue. See *Canterbury Tales*

Genoa, 94
Gentile da Foligno, 66, 296, 299
Gentilesse, 100, 102, 149, **207–9**, 363
Geometry, 137, 227
Germans, 73, 277, 310, 457
Gibralter, 23
Gilbertus Anglicus. *See* Medicine
Ginger, 170, 174
Gittern. *See* Music
Glastonbury, 409, 416
Glaucus, 293
Glyndwr, Owain, 382
Godparent, 60–61
Gold, 16, 17, 18, 19, 20, 70, 77, 96, 105,
    134, 159, 172, 177, 190, 208, 209,
    219, 220, 263, 308, 309, 311, 312,
    339, 343, 350, 351, 377, 378, 382,
    410, 426, 434, 435, 442
Golden Fleece, 237, 293, 431
Golden Thumb. *See* Miller
Goldfinch Diagnosis. *See* Medicine
Good Works, 221, 242
Goose. *See* Birds
Gossip, 60, 145, 210
Grain of Paradise, 170, 174
Grammar, 137, 227
Great Hall, 93, 192, 355
Great Schism, **210–13**, 276, 365, 370;
    Avignon Papacy, 210
Greaves. *See* Armor
Greece, 32, 59, 124, 226, 286, 425, 431, 442
Greenwich, 22
Gregory XI, Pope, 210
Gregory XII, Pope, 211
Gregory the Great, 88, 317, 398
Grenada, 23, **213–14**, 315
Greyhound. *See* Dog
Grisilde, "The Clerk's Tale," 149, 208,
    253, 292
Groom. *See* Marriage
Guilds, 103, 104, 165, 306, 319
Gunpowder, 69, 102, 148, 167, 450, 451

Haberdasher (*Canterbury Tales*), 165
Hackney. *See* Horse
Hagar, 4
Halberd. *See* Weapons
Halcyon Days, 21
Haman, 150
Hanap. *See* Food
Handball. *See* Games
Hare, 31–32, 125, 156, 170, 212, 213,
    217–18, 233, 454

Harness. *See* Armor
Harðacnut, 409
Harp. *See* Music
Harvey, William. *See* Medicine
Hastings, Battle of, 410
Hat. *See* Fashion
Hauberk. *See* Armor
Hawk. *See* Birds
Hazard. *See* Games
Headdress. *See* Fashion
Heart. *See* Medicine
Heaven, 48, 49, 50, 51, 52, 53, 157, 185,
    208, 242, 314, 342, 368, 397, 405
Hector, 6, 11, 69, 440, 442
Hecuba, 90
Helen of Troy, 29, **218–19**
Hell, 190, 384, 387
Helmet. *See* Armor
Henry I, 220, 279
Henry II, 138, 433
Henry IV (Henry Bolingbroke), 70, 90,
    254, 255, 310, 342, 371–72
Henry V, 231
Henry VI, 231
Henry VII, 37, 255
Henry VIII, 88, 90, 435
Hera, 135
Heraldry, **219–21**, 383, 437
Herbal Medicine, 304–5
Herbs, 17, 66, 176, 295, 299, 304, 356
Hercules, 6, 122, 123
Heresy, 73, **221–23**, 232, 276, 309, 370
Heretics, 18, 147, 255, 276, 308, 365
Hermes Trismegistus. *See* Alchemy
Herod, 144
Hippocrates, 187, 296, 378, 380
Holidays, 83, 85, 87, 106, 118, 143,
    223–24, 336, 368
Holofernes, 183
Holy Land, 35, 102, 247, 248, 345, 401
Homer, 442
Honey, 64, 171, 174, 303, 355
Honor, 30, 59, 100, 101, 116, 122, 181,
    182, 185, 207, 256, 264, 349, 396, 449
Hood. *See* Fashion
Horse, 31, 32, 41, 43, 46, 68, 69, 76,
    100, 105, 136, 148, 161, 162, 166,
    170, 177, 202, 204, 205, **224–25**,
    263, 305, 306, 312, 313, 318, 319,
    326, 338, 339, 345, 362, 396, 438,
    440, 442, 448, 449, 460; ambler, 225;
    hackney, 225; jade, 225; palfrey, 225;
    rouncey, 225

Hose. *See* Fashion

Hound. *See* Dog

Houppelande. *See* Fashion

House of Fame, 5, 6, 11, 26, 27, 33, 53, 62, 85, 94, 116, 124, 128, 134, 157, 182, 237, 256, 293, 322, 413, 432, 433

Hugh of Lincoln, 249–50

Humanism, **225–29**, 316, 378

Hundred Years War, 44, 46, 75, 76, 140, 143, 195, 196, 210, **229–33**, 254, 265, 299, 371, 451, 466; Agincourt, 102, 231; Crécy, 142, 196, 231

Hunting, 10, 125, 155, 178, 213, 225, **233-35**, 412, 415, 426, 457, 458

Hurdy-Gurdy. *See* Music

Hussites, 22, 222

Hydrochloric Acid. *See* Acid

Hygiene, 63, 169, 175, **235–37**

Hypsipyle, 29, **237–38**

Hyssop, 305

Icarus, 62, 115, 116, 157

Ignis Innaturalis (secret fire). *See* Alchemy

The Iliad, 442

Indigo, 159, 426, 460

Indulgences, **241–43**, 334, 335, 370

Infant Mortality, 60, 63, 366

Innocent III, 430

Inns of Court. *See* Law

Inquisition, 221, 222, 251

Iron, 17, 21, 42, 44, 45, 155, 354, 378, 395, 448

Irrigation. *See* Agriculture

Isaac, 4

Isabella of France, 140

Isabella of Valois, 370

Ishmael, 4

Islam, 4, 205, 213, 341

Italy, 65, 73, 77, 250, 271, 293, 296, 341, 406, 418, 459

Jacob, 255, 383, 384

Jadwiga of Poland, 274

January, 83, 224

January, "The Merchant's Tale," 30, 59, 150, 152, 218, 349, 385, 386, 387

Jason and the Argonauts, 237, 293, 431

Jerusalem, 150, **247–49**, 252, 344, 422

Jesus, 4, 143, 194, 195, 242, 247, 256, 276, 288, 289, 344, 347, 383, 401, 403

Jews, 4, 121, 150, 159, 247, **249–52**, 317

Joab, 5

Joan of Arc, 229, 232

Joan of Kent. *See* Fair Maid of Kent

Joan of Navarre, 90

Job, 28, 31, **252–53**, 417

Jogailo, King of Lithuania, 274

John, "The Reeve's Tale," 87, 404

John, the Carpenter, "The Miller's Tale," 50, 51, 108, 144

John of Gaunt, 23, 27, 28, 70, 142, 143, 171, 196, 214, **253–55**, 276, 279, 311, 319, 337, 338, 370, 372, 382, 396; Beaufort, 255; Constanza of Castile, 23, 254

John II, The Good, 75, 142, 231

John XXII, Pope, 87

John XXIII, Pope, 211

Jongleurs, 145, 318

Joseph, 25, 28, **255–56**, 326

Joust, 202, 203, 206, 435, 437

Jove, 34, 52

Judaism, 4, 247

Judas Iscariot, 28, 191, **256–57**

Judge, 272, 326, 458

Jugglers, 143

Julian Calendar, 83

Julius Caesar, 6, 83, 431

July, 84

June, 66, 71, 84, 141, 337

Juno, 20, 135

Jupiter, 10, 17, 21, 29, 32, 50, 51, 135, 378

Justice of the Peace. *See* Geoffrey Chaucer

Justin, 73

Kailes. *See* Games

Kempe, Margery, 429

Kent, 88, 142, 337, 392, 398, 432, 433

King Arthur, 144, 382

King David, 3, 4, 5, 247

Kiss, 102, 108, 109, 166, 188, 386, 387

Kitchen, 93, 168, 169, 174, 175, 176, 179, 354, 355

Knight, 5, 6, 22, 23, 41, 42, 43, 44, 45, 46, 54, 59, 91, 93, 99, 100, 101, 102, 108, 142, 148, 149, 159, 161, 164, 166, 167, 170, 202, 203, 204, 205, 207, 209, 214, 220, 221, 225, 231, 232, 234, 236, **261-66**, 274, 275, 286, 291, 315, 325, 357, 373, 374, 382, 383, 396, 422, 430, 431, 434, 435, 436, 437, 439, 441, 448, 449, 451, 458, 466; chivalric code, 264; dubbing, 102, 236, 264

Knight's Tale. See *Canterbury Tales*
Knights Templar, 222
Knives, 158, 169, 175, 233, 319
Koran. *See* Qur'an

Labyrinth, 39, 116
Lamb, 118, 126, 388
Lamech, 28, **269–70**
Lames. *See* Armor
L'Amour courtois (Courtly Love), 107
Lancaster, 27, 70, 254, 342, 396
Lance. *See* Weapons
Lapdog. *See* Dog
Law, 71, 137, 138, 139, 159, 166, 224, 263, **270–73**, 279, 287, 288, 301, 309, 382, 385, 420, 457, 458; Inns of Court, 272, 287
Lead, 17, 18, 19, 235, 303, 378
Leather, 42, 43, 45, 46, 76, 78, 105, 136, 162, 164, 165, **273–74**, 313, 339
Leda, 218
Legend of Good Women, 5, 11, 26, 39, 54, 55, 70, 85, 123, 124, 151, 182, 237, 255, 280, 293, 418, 419
Leggings. *See* Fashion
Lemnos, 237
"L'Envoy de Chaucer a Scogan," 54
Leo X, Pope, 243
Leprosy, 297, 298, 304
Lewis, C. S., 107
Liberal Arts, 136, 137, 139, 227, 316, 318
Licorice, 170
Lily, 373
Lindisfarne, 404, 405, 417
Linen, 44, 45, 46, 60, 64, 74, 159, 160, 162, 163, 164, 197, 467
Lionel, Duke of Clarence, 196
Liriope, 327
Literacy, 137
Lithuania, **274–75**, 357, 374, 430
Lollards, 222, 223, 255, **275–77**
Lombardy, 171
London, 21, 22, 41, 165, 168, 174, 176, 177, **277–80**, 300, 301, 306, 337, 347, 355, 369, 382, 389, 392, 393, 394, 419, 433, 434, 438, 440, 452, 453, 455, 457; Aldgate, **21–22**, 280, 337, 338; Bridgegate, 21; Cheapside, 437; East End, 21, 419; Ludgate, 21; Southwark, 264, 392, **393–94**, 419, 427, 438; Tower of London, 41, 278, 279; Whitechapel, 21

Lord. *See* Feudalism
Lothair, 75
Louis XVI, 75
Love: courtly, 101, 102, **107–9**, 144, 289, 290, 293, 396, 435, 437; divine, 52, 226, 384; human, 52, 226
Loyalty, 30, 64, 125, 146, 220, 255, 292, 396, 439
Lucifer, the Morning Star, 55
Lucina, moon goddess, 32, 33
Luck, 54, 93, 180, 410
Lucrece, 29, **280–81**
Ludgate. *See* London
Lute. *See* Music
Luther, Martin, 243, 276, 430
Lycus, 29
Lyre. *See* Music

Macedonia, **285–86**, 431
Macrobius, 25
Madder, 159, 426
Mail. *See* Armor
Manciple (*Canterbury Tales*), 30, **287–88**, 362, 421
"Manciple's Tale." See *Canterbury Tales*
Mandrake, 304
Mangonel. *See* Artillery
Manners, 101, 175, 176, 211, 236, 342, 351, 352
Man of Law (*Canterbury Tales*), 39, 276
"Man of Law's Tale." See *Canterbury Tales*
Manor, 14, 15, 93, 146, 148, 197, 254, 309, 37, 354, 355, 356, 362, 363, 364, 425
Mantle. *See* Fashion
March, 83, 84, 171, 404
Markets, 12, 74, 77, 78, 147, 149, 176, 177, 224, 225, 369, 439, 459, 467
Marriage, 23, 50, 59, 63, 109, 122, 148, 149, 151, 152, 193, 231, 254, 269, 274, **288–93**, 307, 329, 352, 367, 370, 384, 385, 387, 398, 402, 410, 411; bride, 290, 293, 307, 373; divorce, 289, 367; groom, 59, 290, 385
Mars, 10, 11, 16, 17, 50, 51, 53, 210, 377, 378
Marsyas, 33
Martin V, Pope, 211
Mary I, 229
Mass, 34, 95, 120, 147, 164, 223, 290, 329, 335, 336, 345, 368, 369, 373
Materia Prima. See Alchemy

May, 59, 67, 100, 123, 224, 232, 395, 396, 398

May, "The Merchant's Tale," 30, 385, 386, 387

May Pole, 205

Mead, 174

Meat, 62, 118, 119, 126, 170, 171, 172, 175, 177, 178, 179, 187, 192, 233, 235, 313, 351, 415, 457, 458

Medea, 29, **293–94**

Medicine, 19, 20, 31, 32, 50, 55, 56, 66, 68, 69, 118, 137, 139, 187, 189, 229, 237, **294–305**, 341, 342, 343, 378, 380, 381; cupping, 302, 303; dentistry, 236, 299; disease, 50, 64, 65, 66, 68, 69, 104, 289, 298, 302, 343, 422; Gaddesden, John, 297; Galen, 296–97, 301, 378, 380; Gilbertus Anglicus, 297, 298, 301, 302; Goldfinch Diagnosis, 302; Harvey, William, 296, 381; heart, 25, 33, 118, 187, 294, 296, 301, 303, 381; Scholastic Medicine, 295–96, 297, 301, 380; sickness, 24, 25, 27, 66; Socratic Method, 295, 380; stomach, 45, 56, 168, 188, 296, 305, 380, 381; surgeons, 295, 296, 297, 298, 299, 300, 301, 342, 343, 380; surgery 63, 299, 300, 304, 342

Melancholy, 126, 187, 188, 189, 228, 326

Melee, 203, 205, 436

Mendicant Orders, 178, 194, 195

Menelaus, King of Sparta, 218, 442

Menstruation, 301

Mercantilism, 147, 345, 427

Mercenary, 23, 73, 214, 264, 265, 315, 389, 430, 448, 455

Merchant (*Canterbury Tales*), 61, 74, 76, 77, 78, 148, 149, 159, 160, 164, 165, 197, 250, 251, 279, 287, 299, **305–7**, 312, 347, 387, 390, 391, 406, 407, 439, 440, 450, 459, 460, 467

"Merchant's Tale." See *Canterbury Tales*

Merciless Parliament, 371

Mercury, 17, 51, 235, 303, 378

Merovingians, 75, 457

Merton College, 139

Metamorphosis, 26

Methusela, 269

Michelmas, 224

Middle Class, 61, 71, 125, 136, 147, 148, 158, 159, 174, 192, 195, 225, 251, 306, 311, 345, 466

Midwife, 63, 64

Milk, 117, 126, 158, 170, 178, 234, 350

Miller (*Canterbury Tales*), 87, 119, 139, 144, 177, 190, 236, **308–9**, 320, 348, 412, 420, 421; golden thumb, 309

"Miller's Tale." See *Canterbury Tales*

Minos, 39, 116

Minotaur, 39, 116

Minstrels, 143, 145, 224, 318, 319

Miracles, 36, 400, 405, 412

Misogyny, 11, 108

Moat. *See* Castles

Monarchy, 140, 251, **309–11**, 315, 457

Monasticism, 195, 313, 314, 329, 365, 399, 400; Cenobitic, 313, 314, 400; Eremitic, 313

Money, 64, 67, 78, 105, 106, 118, 124, 139, 145, 149, 166, 192, 207, 241, 242, 250, 251, 252, 256, 290, 307, 309, **311–12**, 314, 318, 333, 334, 339, 343, 345, 347, 354, 374, 396, 429

Monk, 8, 18, 74, 110, 123, 125, 149, 178, 179, 195, 212, 213, 225, **312–14**, 329, 336, 339, 353, 370, 398, 399, 400, 401, 403, 407, 410, 416, 421

"Monk's Tale." See *Canterbury Tales*

Moon, 17, 33, 50, 51, 53, 55, 161, 162, 378, 390, 391

Moors, 23, 213

Morocco, 23, 213, 273, **315,** 413; Banu Marin, 214, 315

Morpheus, 20

Mortimer, Roger, 140

Motley, 76, 306

Motte and bailey. *See* Castles

Muse, 72, 73, 85, 453

Music, 30, 32, 52, 99, 137, 143, 144, 145, 223, 227, 229, **315–22**, 385, 396, 402, 430; bagpipes, 145, 317, 319; citole, 320; clavichord, 320; drums, 145, 319; fiddle, 105, 136, 145, 165, 319, 320, 339; gittern, 319, 320, 321, 322; harp, 133, 134, 201, 315, 316, 319, 320, 321, 322, 429; hurdy-hurdy, 320; lute, 201, 318, 319, 320, 322, 429; lyre, 30, 319; organ, 319, 320, 373; psaltery, 135, 136, 319, 321, 339; shawm, 319; tabor, 319; trumpet, 94, 157, 319

"Music of the Spheres," 52, 317

Muslims, 22, 247, 317, 422

Mustache. *See* Fashion

Mutilation, 458
Mystery Play, 143, 144, 145

Nabal, 3, 4
Narcissus, 29, 135, **327–28**
Narthex. *See* Cathedrals
Natural History, 305
Nature, 22, 31, 34, 53, 55, 74, 84, 134,
    156, 188, 191, 250, 303, 304, 341,
    379, 434
Nave. *See* Cathedrals
Naxos, 39
Nebuchadnezzar, 121
Nemesis, 327
Nessus the Centaur, 122, 123
New Testament, 25, 28, 256
Nicholas, "The Miller's Tale," 50, 51,
    106, 108, 144, 321, 412, 432, 433
Niobe, 30
Nitric Acid. *See* Acid
Noah, 51, 126, 144
Nobility, 27, 41, 100, 119, 125, 145, 147,
    148, 149, 156, 158, 159, 160, 208,
    220, 224, 233, 236, 285, 290, 291,
    302, 318, 338, 355, 363, 401, 448,
    457, 460
Norman Conquest, 61, 230, 263, 457
Normandy, 78, 231, 409, 410
November, 73, 84
Nun (*Canterbury Tales*), 149, 211, 213,
    328–29, 336, 351, 352, 353, 370, 419
Nuncheon, 175
"Nun's Priest's Tale." See *Canterbury
    Tales*
Nycteus, 29
Nymph, 7, 135, 327, 349

Oats, 14, 84
October, 22, 84, 382, 406, 410, 453
Odoacer, 73
Odysseus, 442
Oeneus of Calydon, 122
Old Testament, 3, 4, 5, 8, 25, 28, 121,
    150, 151, 252, 255, 269, 310, 385,
    414
Olympus, 32
Oracle of Delphi, 32
Order of the Knights of the Garter, 140
Orders. *See* Estates
Organ. *See* Music
Orpheus, 30
Orpiment, 17, 378
Ostrogoths, 73

Ovid, 21, 26, 107
Oxford, 87, 105, 106, 136, 138, 139,
    276, 339, 343, 366, 380, 411, 412

Paganism, 48, 50, 62, 95, 100, 226, 319,
    339, 340, 368, 379, 398, 399, 402,
    403, 407, 410
Palamon ("The Knight's Tale") 10, 30,
    42, 221
Palfrey. *See* Horse
Palisade, 92
Pandarus (*Troilus and Criseyde*), 10, 53
Paracelsus, 19, 381
Pardoner (*Canterbury Tales*), 217, 241,
    242, 243, **333–35**, 336, 418, 421,
    429
"Pardoner's Tale." See *Canterbury Tales*
Park House. *See* Chaucer, Geoffrey
Paris, France, 35, 37, 138, 298, 351, 379,
    380, 398, 406, 410, 413, 419, 426,
    450
Paris, Prince of Troy, 90, 218, 386, 442,
    443
Parish, 147, 242, 243, 313, 334, 336,
    364, 366, 368
Parliament, 140, 141, 311, 371, 394, 452
Parliament of Fowls, 26, 27, 52, 62, 74,
    107, 108, 111, 126, 127, 128, 134,
    155, 156, 209, 210, 218, 341, 349,
    418
Parson (*Canterbury Tales*), 162, 242, 275,
    276, 314, **335–37**, 364, 370, 389,
    390, 455
"Parson's Tale." See *Canterbury Tales*
Pasiphae, 39, 116
Pastry. *See* Food
Peasant Revolt of 1381, 15, 22, 149, 280,
    309, 311, **337–38**, 371, 372; Ball,
    John, 338; Straw, Jack, 337; Tyler, Wat,
    311, 337, 338, 371, 392
Peasants, 13, 15, 67, 99, 119, 145, 146,
    147, 148, 149, 164, 166, 170, 197,
    224, 225, 234, 236, 309, 318, 325,
    337, 345, 354, 355, 362, 363, 371,
    392, 439, 440, 457
Pedro the Cruel, King of Castile, 142,
    183, 255
Penance, 119, 186, 194, 213, 242, 243,
    334, 344, 366, 368, 416
Peneus, 121
Pentecost, 118, 224, 368
Perrers, Alice, 141
Persephone, 10

Pertelote, "The Nun's Priest's Tale," 25, 128, 227, 372, 373

Peter I of Cyprus, 22

Petrarch, 72, 196, 226–27

Phaedra of Athens, 124

Pharaoh, 256

Philip II of Macedonia, 286, 431

Philippa of Hainault, 70, 141, 253

Philip the Bold, 75

Philosopher's Stone. *See* Alchemy

Philosophic Egg. *See* Alchemy

Philosophy, 18, 73, 74, 105, 106, 107, 134, 136, 165, 227, 251, 295, **338–42**, 378, 380

Phlegmatic, 188

Phoebus, 33, 47, 110, 122, 321

Phyllis of Rhodope, 124

Physician, 55, 56, 63, 66, 69, 187, 189, 229, 295, 296, 297, 298, 299, 301, 302, 305, 337, **342–44**, 380

Pikeman, 449

Pilgrim, 36, 54, 71, 84, 88, 164, 217, 225, 236, 248, 335, 344, 345, 347, 392, 393, 416, 427, 429, 432, 438, 440

Pilgrimage, 45, 90, 96, 248, 249, 276, 336, **344–48**, 353, 393, 416, 422, 427, 429, 430, 434, 435, 438, 439, 440; Santiago de Compostela, 345

Pipe. *See* Music

Plague. *See* Black Death

Planets, 47, 48, 49, 52, 54, 55, 157, 317

Plato, 25, 73, 107, 108, 340, 378

Plays, 143, 145, 316, 370

Pliny, 296, 305, 380

Plowman (*Canterbury Tales*), 12, 15

Poetry, 22, 32, 48, 71, 85, 143, 144, 180, 229, 316, 320

Poet's Corner. *See* Westminster Abbey

Poitiers, 142, 231

Poitou, 142

Poland, 274, 275, 357, 430

Poliphete (*Troilus and Criseyde*), 11, 219

Poll tax, 337

Polyphony, 317

Pompey, 6, 431

Pontefract Castle, 372

Population, 12, 15, 64, 65, 68, 69, 77, 103, 104, 147, 148, 279, 280, 306, 407, 459, 467

Portcullis. *See* Castles

Potiphar, 256

Priam, 90, 442, 443

Priapus, 29, 210, **348–49**, 386, 387

Priest, 60, 67, 102, 147, 161, 194, 195, 221, 242, 257, 276, 335, 336, 344, 362, 365, 368, 369, 388, 389, 407, 414, 418, 434, 439, 455

Primogeniture, 309, 310

Primum Mobile, 51

Prioress (*Canterbury Tales*), 125, 149, 175, 178, 211, 213, 251, 252, 314, 329, 336, **350–53**, 370, 411, 419

"Prioress's Tale." See *Canterbury Tales*

Private Houses, 38, 94, 120, 179, 198, **353–57**, 426

Prophecy, 32, 90, 373, 404, 415, 416

Prostitutes, 159, 429

Protestant Reformation, 210, 222, 243, 276, 344, 365

Prussia, 40, 265, 343, **357–58**, 430, 447

Psaltery. *See* Music

Ptolemy, 49, 51, 378

Puffers. *See* Alchemy

Puppeteers, 143

Purgatory, 60, 242, 334

Purim, 150

Quadrivium, 137, 227, 316

Quicksilver, 17, 378

Quince, 305

Quits. *See* Games

Qur'an, 4

Rabbit. *See* Hare

Rachel, 255

Ram, 54, 84, 308, 389

Ransom, 42, 142, 203, 231, 436

Rape, 280

Raptu. See Rape

Rat, 65, 68

Red, 20, 27, 70, 76, 100, 105, 107, 118, 127, 136, 159, 162, 164, 165, 172, 174, 178, 190, 191, 204, 220, 235, 237, 254, 308, 339, 343, 351, 372, 373, 395, 426, 460

Reeve (*Canterbury Tales*), 224, 348, **361–64**

"Reeve's Tale." See *Canterbury Tales*

Relics, 36, 96, 242, 334, 335, 344, 347, 439

Religion, 4, 61, 64, 95, 144, 213, 247, 252, 256, 276, 314, 318, 322, 329, 335, 336, 348, 353, **364–70**, 381, 387, 398, 399, 401, 403, 404, 405,

407, 409, 410, 411, 412, 413, 414,
416, 417, 418, 419, 421, 422, 438;
Catholicism, 31, 34, 52, 60, 73, 95,
101, 147, 210, 221, 226, 242, 247,
317, 334, 336, 344, 365, 367, 403,
418; corruption, 276, 336, 365, 421
Reresoper. *See* Food
Revolts, 15, 22, 67, 231, 309, 311, 337,
338, 371
Reynard the Fox, 31, 190
Rheims, 232
Rhetoric, 137, 227
Rhodope, 124
Richard II, 18, 22, 27, 28, 70, 141, 171,
196, 255, 276, 311, 337, 338, **370–
72**, 382, 393
Richard III, 70
Robin Hood, 144
Romance, 48, 71, 110, 418
Roman de la Rose, 327, 386
Romans, 21, 256, 310, 393, 450
Rome, 73, 90, 210, 211, 226, 241, 243,
276, 280, 286, 333, 334, 344, 345,
398, 400, 413, 414, 416, 417
Rooster. *See* Birds
Rosa medicinae anglicae, 297
Rose, 10, 64, 174, 236, 254, 303, 327,
402
Rose window, 96
Rouen, 232
Rouncey. *See* Horse
Round Table, 140, 325, 437
Royalty, 318, 325, 460
Rue, 305
Rural, 61, 63, 65, 77, 78, 88, 103, 104,
147, 221, 299, 354, 355, 368, 439,
466
Russia, 78, 265, 274, 357, **374**

Sacraments, 137, 147, 276, 289, 290,
336, 366, 367
Saffron, 170, 172, 304
Saladin, 247
Salt, 16, 17, 19, 60, 64, 78, 171, 173,
176, 235, 378, 416
Salvation, 83, 96, 243, 334, 335, 344,
365, 366, 368, 389
Sampson, 6
Sanguine, 187, 192, 415
Sanitation, 104
Santiago de Compostela. *See* Pilgrimage
Sarah, 4, 327
Satan, 8, 9, 151, 252, 253, 409

Saturn, 10, 11, 16, 17, 51, 377, 378
Scandinavia, 65, 74, 75, 78
Scholar, 50, 71, 87, 105, 136, 137, 139,
226, 271, 276, 339, 379
Scholastic Medicine. *See* Medicine
Science, 18, 20, 50, 105, 171, 227, 270,
301, 341, **377–81**
Scipio, 25
Scotland, 196, 277, 371
Scrope-Grosvenor Trial, 221, **381–83**
Second Estate. *See* Estates
Second Nun's Tale. See *Canterbury Tales*
Secret Fire (*Ignis Innaturalis*). *See*
Alchemy
Semele, 59
September, 70, 84, 118, 171
Serf, 148, 149, 166, 318, 337, 338
Sergeant at Law, 270, 272
Servile Holding. *See* Feudalism
Seven Deadly Sins, 137, 195, 437
Sex, 59, 145, 217, 292, 293, 305, 314,
318, 349, 367, 370, **383–88**, 389,
400, 454
Shawm. *See* Music
Sheep, 3, 14, 31, 32, 67, 84, 117, 118,
148, 170, 361, 362, **388–89**, 405,
455, 459
Shepherd, 29, 204, 369, 388, 389, 390,
404, 455
Shield. *See* Weapons
Shipbuilding, 77
Shipman, 179, **390–92**
Shipman's Tale. See *Canterbury Tales*
Shoes. *See* Fashion
Shuttlecock. *See* Games
Sickness. *See* Medicine
Silk. *See* Fashion
Silver, 16, 17, 77, 78, 158, 159, 204, 256,
311, 312, 377, 378, 404, 456, 465,
466
Sin, 8, 9, 10, 37, 52, 60, 137, 156, 161,
190, 195, 202, 236, 242, 249, 250,
257, 275, 344, 368, 379, 437, 439
Sir Thopas, 70
Sittingbourne, **392**, 394, 440
Sleep, 24, 25, 26, 27, 107, 157, 187, 188,
189, 304, 354, 355, 390, 415
Socrates, 6
Socratic Method. *See* Medicine
Soldier, 42, 43, 69, 92, 101, 102, 166,
167, 205, 231, 264, 299, 405, 433,
449
Sorbonne, Robert de, 138

Soul, 35, 37, 105, 147, 228, 236, 242, 249, 263, 334, 335, 340, 348, 365, 366, 368, 379, 380, 388, 389, 443, 455

Southwark. *See* London

Sovereignty, 288, 291

Sow, 118, 190, 237, 308

Spain, 23, 120, 196, 213, 315, 345, 379, 459

Sparrow. *See* Birds

Spices, 78, 170, 174, 250, 299, 343, 439

Spinning, 61, 329, 460

Spoon. *See* Food

Sports. *See* Games

Spring. *See* Calendar

Spurs. *See* Armor

Squire, 100, 102, 156, 159, 164, 204, 209, 320, 373, 387, **395–97**

Squire's Tale. See *Canterbury Tales*

Stars, 6, 47, 49, 50, 51, 53, 54, 321

St. Augustine: of Canterbury, 88, 90, **397–99**, 405, 418; of Hippo, 340

St. Benedict, 88, 90, 194, 195, 212, 313, 339, 352, 398, **399–401**, 407, 412, 419, 452

St. Bernard, 313, 314, **401–02**

St. Cecilia, **402–3**

St. Christopher, **403–4**, 456, 466

St. Cuthbert, **404–5**, 418

St. Denis, **405–8;** Abbey, 37; Cathedral, 96, 407, 408; Saint, **405–8,** 410; town, 405, 406, 407

St. Dunstan, **408–9**, 452

Steadfastness, 74, 181, 341

St. Edward the Confessor. *See* Edward the Confessor

Steel, 40, 41, 42, 44, 203, 204, 447, 448, 449

St. Elegius, **410–11**

St. Frideswide, **411–12**

St. Giles, **412–13**

Stickball. *See* Games

St. Jerome, **413–14**

St. John's Wort, 305

St. Julian, 191, 192, **414–16**

St. Neot, **416–17**

Stomach. *See* Medicine

Stoolball. *See* Games

St. Pachomius, 313, 328

Stratford-at-Bow, 350, 351, **419–20**

Straw, Jack. *See* Peasant Revolt of 1381

St. Ronan, **417–18**

Student, 48, 87, 106, 137, 138, 139, 202, 272, 341, 412, 428

St. Valentine, 134, **418–19**

Sugar, 64, 78, 171, 174, 303, 312

Suicide, 11, 21, 30, 122, 280

Sulphuric Acid. *See* Acid

Summer. *See* Calendar

Summoner, 217, 235, 237, 253, 336, 384, **420–21**

"Summoner's Tale." See *Canterbury Tales*

Sumptuary Laws. *See* Fashion

Sun, 11, 17, 47, 51, 52, 53, 54, 55, 83, 84, 85, 116, 118, 119, 134, 161, 373, 378, 435

Sunday, 76, 120, 224, 290, 368, 406

Surcoat. *See* Fashion

Surgeons. *See* Medicine

Surgery. *See* Medicine

Sword. *See* Weapons

Swynford, Katherine, 255

Sybil, 91, 127, 441

Symbolism, 18, 31, 62, 134, 158, 310, 388

Synod of Whitby, 399, 405, 417

Syria, 171, 247, **422**

Tabard Inn, 393, 427, 429, 438

Table dormant. *See* Food

Tabor. *See* Music

Tale of Melibee. See *Canterbury Tales*

Tapestry, 99, 165, 198, 234, 262, **425–27,** 460

Tarot, 52, 206

Tarquinus Collatinus, 280

Taurus, 19, 55, 56

Taverns, 174, 178, 193, 194, 201, 212, 213, 322, 347, **427–30,** 440

Taxes, 67, 140, 148, 231, 251, 279, 337, 338, 459

Technology, 36, 68

Tesieda della nozze de Emilia, 72

Thames Street. *See* London

Thebes, 30

Theobald, Archbishop of Canterbury, 433

Theodoric, 73

Theseus of Athens, 39, 124, 293

Thessaly, **431–32**

Third Estate, 69, 148, 149

Thomas à Becket, 90, 225, 348, **432–35,** 438

Three-field system. *See* Agriculture

Tithes, 336, 364, 368, 369

Toas, King of Lemnos, 237

Tournament, 41, 44, 102, 122, 142, 202, 203, 220, 221, **435–37**

Tower of London. *See* London

Towns, 53, 55, 61, 77, 78, 84, 92, **103–5**, 139, 145, 149, 177, 194, 203, 220, 224, 228, 273, 308, 336, 337, 354, 355, 364, 369, 392, 394, 407, 428, 457

Trade, 61, 65, 68, 74, 76, 77, 78, 87, 103, 104, 119, 143, 149, 159, 177, 178, 242, 250, 277, 279, 298, 299, 306, 311, 334, 343, 345, 347, 362, 379, 438, 439, 460, 467

Transept. *See* Cathedrals

Transportation, 224, 440

Travel, 11, 36, 45, 50, 65, 66, 78, 90, 94, 119, 164, 194, 196, 205, 224, 225, 319, 336, 345, 347, 348, 353, 357, 368, 392, 415, 422, 425, 427, 428, **438–41**, 466

Treason, 235, 337, 371

Treatise on the Astrolabe, 48, 53, 229

Treaty of Brétigny, 231

Trebuchet. *See* Artillery

Trencher. *See* Food

Trivium, 137, 227

Troilus, 6, 7, 10, 33, 43, 86, 90, 91, 108, 122, 128, 182, 183, 184, 219

Troilus and Criseyde, 6, 7, 10, 11, 26, 34, 52, 53, 54, 55, 72, 85, 86, 91, 108, 122, 127, 128, 144, 180, 182, 183, 184, 185, 323, 321, 441, 442

Trojan War, 6, 11, 183, 218, **441–43**

Troubadours, 145, 373

Trumpet. *See* Music

Truth, 6, 31, 64, 100, 182, 227, 264, 300, 313, 326, 340

Tug-of-war. *See* Games

Tyler, Wat. *See* Peasant Revolt of 1381

Unicorn Tapestry, 234, 426

Universities, 138, 220, 297, 299, 341, 379; University of Bologne, 138; University of Paris (Sorbonne), 138

Urban VI, Pope, 211

Urbanization, 12, 69

Uroscopy, 297, 302

Uterus, 301, 302

Valarian root, 16, 17

Valois-Bourgogne, 75, 370

Vashti, 150

Vassal. *See* Feudalism

Vault. *See* Cathedrals

Vegetables. *See* Food

Veil, 159, 163, 164, 242, 334, 347

Velvet, 159, 160

Venice, 94

Venus, 10, 11, 16, 17, 34, 46, 47, 51, 52, 53, 54, 59, 85, 86, 182, 210, 218, 235, 237, 293, 348, 377, 378, 417

Via Dolorosa, 248

Vikings, 61, 74, 220, 279, 450

Villages, 14, 61, 67, 77, **103–5**, 118, 120, 143, 147, 148, 166, 205, 221, 314, 316, 345, 347, 354, 362, 363, 369, 440, 457

Virgil, 11, 25, 26

Virginity, 7, 384, 402, 412

Virgin Mary, 37, 96, 401, 403

Virgo, 55, 56

Wages, 67, 146, 149, 312, 363

Waldensians, 222

Wales, 142, 196, 224, 277, 372, 427

Walter, "The Clerk's Tale," 146, 147, 149

War of the Roses, 254

Water, 13, 20, 21, 61, 63, 64, 92, 104, 134, 159, 168, 174, 176, 188, 189, 236, 273, 276, 304, 354, 390, 391, 440, 460

Watling Street, 392

Wattle and daub, 120, 354, 355

Wat Tyler's Rebellion. *See* Peasant Revolt of 1381

Weapons, 41, 92, 166, 203, 232, 263, 265, 396, 405, 436, 437, **447–52**, 466; ax, 40, 447, 449; bow, 40, 41, 319, 448, 449, 450, 446, 465, 466; halberd, 449; lance, 44, 166, 173, 202, 436, 448, 449; shield, 40, 41, 42, 70, 204, 219, 220, 382, 447; sword, 42, 44, 166, 202, 204, 206, 229, 233, 273, 403, 448, 449, 456, 466

Weaver, 61, 165, 468

Weaving, 61, 99, 329, 425, 426, 459, 460, 468

Weights and Measures, 177

Westminster Abbey, 37, 279, 371, **452–54;** Poet's Corner, 452, 453

Wheat, 14, 84, 194, 382, 400

White, 20, 27, 32, 40, 41, 43, 60, 68, 70, 100, 110, 116, 118, 119, 126, 151, 158, 162, 163, 164, 171, 172, 173, 177, 178, 192, 210, 220, 235, 236, 254, 255, 302, 303, 304, 351, 373, 395, 415, 430

Whitechapel. *See* London

Wife of Bath, 4, 61, 62, 78, 123, 150, 209, 225, 248, 253, 269, 306, 384, 468

"Wife of Bath's Tale." See *Canterbury Tales*

Wimple. *See* Fashion

Wine, 59, 75, 78, 118, 171, 173, 174, 175, 178, 179, 192, 193, 280, 306, 367, 390, 391, 400, 415, 420, 428

Winter. *See* Calendar

Woad, 159, 426

Wolf, 32, 134, 233, 388, 389, **454–56**

Wood, 17, 50, 92, 104, 120, 170, 173, 197, 204, 205, 274, 303, 355, 362, 378, 449, **456–59**, 466

Woodstock, 90, 141, 143

Wool, 22, 61, 62, 67, 74, 78, 148, 159, 160, 162, 280, 356, 390, 426, **459–61**, 467

Wycliffe, John, 139, 255, 276

Yeoman, 19, 20, 256, 404, 456, 458, **465–67**

Yersinia Pestis, 65, 69

Ypres, 61, 75, **467–68**

Zeno, 73

Zeus, 29, 59, 135, 218

Zodiac, 33, 47, 51, 52, 53, 54, 55, 84, 85, 299

About the Author

SHANNON L. ROGERS is presently an independent scholar and was Assistant Professor of History at Juniata College. She has also taught at Penn State, Abington College, and Saint Joseph's University. She has previously published on medieval Wales and medievalism in the works of Thomas Hardy and Benjamin Disraeli.